Translations and essay collections by Quintus Curtius:

On Moral Ends

On Duties

Sallust: The Conspiracy of Catiline and The War of Jugurtha

Stoic Paradoxes

Thirty-Seven

Pantheon

Pathways

ABOUT THE TRANSLATOR

Quintus Curtius is the pen name of writer and translator George Thomas. He graduated from MIT in 1990 and served on active duty for a number of years as a US Marine Corps officer, with deployed service worldwide. After leaving active duty, he enrolled in law school and began to practice law after graduating in 1998. He resides in Kansas City and travels frequently. He can be found at www.qcurtius.com.

ON MORAL ENDS

By

Marcus Tullius Cicero

A New Translation Of

De Finibus Bonorum Et Malorum

With Notes, Commentary, Illustrations, And Index

By
QUINTUS CURTIUS

On Moral Ends

Cover design by James Seehafer

Printed in Charleston, South Carolina, USA

Published by Fortress of the Mind Publications
www.qcurtius.com

ISBN: 978-0-578-40967-2

Remains of the Dipylon (Δίπυλον) Gate at Kerameikos in Athens, mentioned by Cicero in the text at V.1. It covered 1800 sq. meters and was one of the largest gateways in antiquity. Constructed around 478 B.C., it had four towers and a sizeable courtyard.

If a man was to compare the effect of a single stroke of the pickaxe, or of one impression of the spade, with the general design and last result, he would be overwhelmed by the sense of their disproportion; yet these petty operations, incessantly continued, in time surmount the greatest difficulties, and mountains are levelled and oceans bounded by the slender force of human beings.

—Dr. Samuel Johnson

TABLE OF CONTENTS

FOREWORD

This book is a translation of Cicero's philosophical work *On Moral Ends*. Its full Latin title is *De Finibus Bonorum et Malorum*, but this is often shortened to *De Finibus*. The meaning of the title will be discussed in the introduction. The work is a series of dialogues in which the speakers debate the competing views of three influential philosophical schools of Cicero's day: Epicureanism, Stoicism, and the Academic (Platonist) philosophy of Antiochus of Ascalon. The unifying theme of the dialogues is the search for answers to the following questions:

1. What is our "end" (i.e., the final objective or ultimate goal of human life) that provides us with a rational plan for living happily and doing good works?

2. What is the most desirable principle sought after by nature?

3. What is the greatest evil that nature avoids?[1]

On Moral Ends is thus a work of moral or ethical philosophy. In three separate dialogues, Cicero's speakers guide us through the intricacies of each of these competing schools of thought. We thereby hear proposed answers to the questions noted above. The beauty and value of the work lies not so much in its conclusions— for these are open to differing interpretations—but rather in how each speaker argues his corner and makes his case. It is a rigorous treatise, and perhaps Cicero's most intensely focused. But the

---

[1] *See* I.11 and the final paragraph of I.29.

16

rewards it offers are beyond valuation. If the reader can complete the journey to the end of the fifth book, he or she will have gained a deep and nuanced appreciation of some of life's most fundamental questions. Cicero's passion for the subject matter shine through on every page, and help make the reader's sojourn a memorable and moving experience.

This foreword will explain the special features included in this book. The introduction that follows it will provide background information essential for an understanding of the text of *On Moral Ends*. My goal was to produce an English rendition of the Latin text that would be as modern, clear, and faithful to the original as possible. *On Moral Ends* is a detailed and sometimes technical work, yet also frequently conversational and argumentative. It rises to soaring and inspiring eloquence, especially in Book V. The translator must be able to articulate these divergent literary qualities in modern, lucid English. It is his responsibility to convey the flavor of Cicero's elegant Latin through the use of appropriate English idiom, phrasing, sentence structure, rhythm, and overall tone. If an original author is eloquent, passionate, and disputatious, then his translator must try to convey these qualities using the tools his own language gives him.

Translators love to talk about translating, and I am no exception. We are fond of pronouncing our theories of translation, and reminding readers of the difficulties we have overcome. Every sculptor is proud of his chisel, and every painter defensive of his brush. Translation is an interpretative art: one is conveying words, ideas, idioms, and rhetorical flavors from one verbal universe to another. The translator must not only know his text well, but he must know his author well; he must be attuned to his likes, dislikes, peccadilloes, personality, and idiosyncrasies. I believe an original text should be preserved in form and spirit by a careful attention to its rhetorical style, grammatical constructions, and idiomatic peculiarities. When a literary work in Latin (or any other language) is translated into English, all of English's flexible tools must be deployed with these purposes in mind. The act of translation must challenge and—I am not afraid to say it—torment the translator, so that he or she is forced to invent novel structures, phrases, and stylistic devices to evoke a different world. Brute labor must be enlightened by bursts of innovative creativity.

But this is not all. In a serious and detailed philosophical work, it is important to present the text in a way that enhances understanding. Too often, translators of classical literature have failed to appreciate just how much a text's appearance, formatting, and presentation can contribute to—or detract from—a reader's comprehension. As I explain below, I have opted to use modern conventions in the formatting of the dialogues. It is often forgotten that *On Moral Ends* is, after all, *a series of dialogues*. It was written as a set of dialogues, and we should read it as such. Its interpretation should begin from this reference point.

Some editors of classical texts choose to format dialogues such that the successive statements and responses of speakers are placed alongside each other, one after the other, in single, cumbersome paragraphs. This may be due to a desire to save printing space or costs; or it may be due to a lack of concern for the needs of readers. In any case, the final result resembles a hodgepodge of quotation marks, commas, and verbiage that is frustratingly difficult for the eyes to follow. The reader begins to lose track of who is saying what to whom, and inevitably loses interest. The reader of a philosophical text deserves better. He has enough challenges on his plate without having to suffer through bad formatting and presentation.

Clearly, the old printing conventions were unacceptable. A new approach was needed in presenting the dialogues. I have opted to use modern dialogue formatting, *where each speaker's statement gets its own separate indented paragraph*. Statements and responses follow in succession down the page, and the reader can easily see who is saying what to whom. Legibility is enhanced, and comprehension is strengthened.

Footnotes explain every name, concept, or point that requires explanation. Preceding this Foreword, I have created a topical "table of contents" as an aid in perusing the text and locating subjects easily. The reader can see at a glance what topics are in each book and chapter, and will know on what page that subject can be found. This method is more efficient and useful than embedding marginal notes within the text. Commentaries are included at the end of each book. In the Introduction, I have also included something that was sorely needed: a table that cross-references each dialogue by speaker, topic, date, and location.

I strongly believe that, before plunging into the waters of *On Moral Ends*, the reader should have a basic understanding of Epicureanism, Stoicism, and the moral philosophy of the later Academy. I have provided this information in the introduction. My goal is to equip the reader with no prior experience in the subject matter with every tool needed to understand and appreciate *On Moral Ends*, and to do this in one self-contained volume. This was the approach taken in my translations of *On Duties* and Sallust, and it was well-received by readers. For this reason I believe this book is ideal for classroom use as well as for the motivated self-learner.

I have included original photographs of the three locations of the dialogues: Tusculum and Cumae in Italy, and Athens in Greece. All of the photographs in this book were taken by me in the spring and summer of 2018. There are two reasons why I believe the inclusion of photographs is important. Firstly, the fatigued mind needs visual refreshment when working its way through a serious text. The presence of photographic images can provide a psychological break, a cheerful distraction, and will contribute to preserving the reader's endurance. To this same purpose, I have included additional illustrations on the opening page of each of the five books.

Secondly, I thought that if the reader could actually see what Tusculum, Cumae, and the Platonic Academy in Athens looked like, he or she would gain a more intimate appreciation of the settings of the dialogues. I have included photographs of other locations in Athens and Italy where their presence would contribute to an appreciation of the text. Thus the reader will find images of Italy's Amalfi Coast, the Dipylon Gate in Athens (mentioned in V.1), Aristotle's Lyceum (the home of the Peripatetics), Kerameikos, the Temple of the Olympian Zeus, and the Roman Agora in Athens. The charm of a place becomes indelibly linked to the understanding of an idea. As Cicero himself says (V.4), "The intangible spirit that resides in the former haunts of great men evokes their memories with more clarity and resonance." We very much agree with him. If we can see what a place looks like, if we can get a sense of the terrain, then we will add something special and intangible to our comprehension.

Perhaps the reader will bear with me as I explain these pilgrimages. I visited the secluded ruins of Tusculum in May 2018. It is located in the beautiful Alban Hills outside Rome. To get there, I took a train from Rome to Frascati in the early morning, then walked along winding roads for about an hour to reach the site. The conditions for such a visit could not have been more ideal. The weather was pristine; the spot was almost deserted; and an archaeological dig happened to be in progress. As I walked about Tusculum, I happened to see an exposed skull lying in view in one of the pits, which to me was a startling reminder of the Stoic admonition to remember our own mortality.

As the reader will see from the photographs in the text, Tusculum is a tranquil and secluded place, an ideal setting for a gathering of friends to talk philosophy. Cicero's villa there must have been a restful escape from the fury of Roman politics. Several days later I drove with a friend to Naples, seeing the Amalfi Coast along the way. We explored the impressive ruins of Cumae, with its strange mixture of seaside charm and prophetic gravity; after all these centuries, one feels that the Cave of the Sibyl still jealously guards its secrets.

Athens I visited in August 2018. The dialogue in Book V takes place at the site of the Platonic Academy, and it was this hallowed ground that I needed to visit. It turned out to be a very short walk: first along Elefsinion Street, then Lenorman, then Alexandrias, and then finally the ground of the Academy itself. The ruins are located in a public park in a residential area; in early morning it is serene and quiet, with dog-walkers, joggers, and elderly people starting their days. We are told that the site was only discovered in the 20th century; before that, scholars had a general idea of its location, but not a precise one. In classical times it was located in the midst of groves away from the city; now, of course, it is within the city, since Athens has expanded to absorb it.

The only site that was marked was that of the old gymnasium; the palaestra dates from a later period, probably the 1st century A.D. There was even a cistern for the students' bathing. Book learning and physical fitness went hand-in-hand, a lesson that should not be lost on us today. The site is still largely unmarked. It deserves restoration, but this is likely to have to wait future generations. It appeared to me that the Academy originally had different clusters of buildings, possibly lecture-halls, classrooms, or libraries. As I walked the grounds, I indulged my romantic impulses with some fanciful musings:

O stones, ye have here rested three and twenty centuries! Ye sturdily kept a continent's foundation when Europe was young; ye heard the laughter of youth, the pleas of truth's seekers, and the disputations of the great; ye have witnessed the Master speak of the Divine Forms, and of the secrets of their emanations; ye knew Aristotle in his noble prime, and felt the learned perambulations of Speusippus, Xenocrates, Polemo, and a hundred other names now lost in time's swirling mists; and ye laughed at the follies of empires and kings. Speak, ye stones, and say what secret lieth within ye!

There was no response, of course. Yet as I walked through the place, the bees still hummed about the ruins, and the birds, engrossed in their domestic tasks, still tweeted and chirped; and the groves still rioted with tangled foliage and brambles. Life has inherited the Academy. Its stones speak not, but the living world surrounds and envelops them, and speaks for them in its own reverential tones. And so we may say that the Academy is, in its own way, still alive: it lives in accordance with nature. As I left the place, I reflected much on these things.

Every era needs instruction on how to live. We desire counsel on what is important, and what is not; we wish to know what our ultimate goals and purposes should be in this life, and how such goals may be attained. Modern science, as we know, continues to advance so rapidly that we feel imprisoned in a perpetual state of bewilderment; we have come to expect dislocating surprises around nearly every corner. Science has achieved undoubted glories in the advancement of health, the banishment of disease, and the understanding of the natural world; and yet, despite all this, we feel keenly the fraying of the social fabric, the marginalization of ancient institutions, and the steady replacement of the solace provided by community and neighbor with the frightening atomization of the individual. These are not insignificant problems. What is needed, perhaps, is rigorous instruction on the science of living life and the importance of virtue. As Leo Tolstoy once noted:

> People must live. But in order to live they must know how to live. And men have always obtained this knowledge—well or ill—and in conformity with it have lived and progressed. And this knowledge of how men should live has—from the days of Moses, Solon, and Confucius—always been considered a science, the very essence of science.[2]

---

[2] Leo Tolstoy, *Recollections and Essays*, London: Oxford Univ. Press (1961), p. 178.

On Moral Ends rises to this challenge, and gives us this crucial instruction. We may not agree with some of its conclusions, but what matters is how it arrives at those conclusions; our exposure to its methods stimulates the engine of character development.

I owe a debt of gratitude to many for assistance in the preparation of this book. Once again, James Seehafer has lent his creative skills in the inspired cover design, just as he did for *On Duties* and *Sallust*. Special gratitude is owed to Zeljko Ivić, who took the time to drive through Italy and show me many fascinating locations in that beautiful land. He spent many hours on unfamiliar country roads in Italy without a whisper of complaint. I would also like to thank Dr. Michael Fontaine of Cornell University, whose personal encouragement was very much appreciated. His enthusiasm, courtesy, and hearty sense of humor embody the best of the humanist tradition.

Beatum cui etiam in suis laboribus contigerit ut benevolentiam liberalitatemque aliorum invenire possit: happy is he who, even in his labors, can discover the generosity and kindness of others.

Quintus Curtius
Kansas City
August 2018

INTRODUCTION

CICERO'S LIFE

Marcus Tullius Cicero was born at Arpinum (modern Arpino) on January 3, 106 B.C. His family was not patrician, but his father was able to provide a good education for his sons. Plutarch reports that the young Cicero showed a great aptitude for learning in every branch of literature and philosophy, with a particular fondness for poetry.[3] As a young man he was exposed to the doctrines of Epicureanism, Stoicism, and Platonism, and developed a passionate interest in philosophy. According to Plutarch, he attended the lectures of Philo the Academic[4] in Rome, a man who was admired by the Romans for his eloquence and character. In his late twenties (79 B.C.) he visited Athens and attended the lectures of Antiochus of Ascalon, and later moved on to Rhodes to study rhetoric. Cicero was a motivated and serious student; he rose so quickly in Roman politics simply because he had more natural ability, and a greater capacity for work, than any of his competitors.

---

[3] *Life of Cicero* 2.
[4] The word "Academic" refers to the doctrines of Plato's Academy, or to the doctrines of the school's successors.

24

We need not sketch Cicero's entire political career here.[5] It is enough for us to say that Cicero was elevated to the consulship in 63 B.C., and achieved lasting fame for his key role in exposing the coup attempt of the renegade senator Lucius Catiline. Cicero was living in a turbulent and dangerous era; the Roman republic was being torn apart by a combination of civil strife, factionalism, and the ambitions of ruthless men like Pompey, Caesar, and Antony. Cicero tried to navigate these waters as best he could; but despite his oratorical brilliance, he was no match for the sharks that infested Roman political waters. Cicero was a patriot, and a passionate believer in the need to preserve the Roman republic. Yet he found it difficult to accept the fact that political and social changes had made that goal unattainable even before Caesar invaded Italy in 49 B.C. He took Pompey's side in the civil war that erupted between Pompey and Caesar; and when Caesar emerged the winner, Cicero could do little except watch in despair from the sidelines.

He would, however, eventually reconcile with Caesar. The death of his beloved daughter Tullia in 45 B.C., combined with his realization that the republic was gone forever, dealt him crippling blows. He was out of power, unable to practice law, and crippled by grief; he must have known by this time that his days were numbered. His brilliant but reckless oratorical attacks on Mark Antony (the so-called *Philippics*) in the period after Caesar's assassination led directly to Cicero's tragic murder on December 7, 43 B.C. as he was attempting to flee Italy.

---

[5] This topic was covered in the introduction to my translation of Cicero's *On Duties*.

HIS PHILOSOPHICAL WORKS

As stated above, philosophy was one of Cicero's consuming interests. This is not surprising: his mind was restless, probing, and disputative, capable of testing and savoring all the nuances of philosophic concepts. He had learned Greek in his youth and could absorb the best that the Greek sages had to offer; he read and discussed philosophy with friends while he was in politics; and he even had a Stoic thinker named Diodotus live with him in his house for a time. As Cicero's personal and professional life unraveled, he turned to philosophy for solace. It had captivated him as a youth, and would comfort him as an older man. At some point he embarked on a project that would ensure his lasting influence: he resolved to write, in the Latin language, a number of books that would introduce Greek philosophy to his fellow Romans. In the two years from 46 to 44 B.C., he was writing constantly, and produced an impressive number of philosophical and rhetorical works. He made no claims to originality in ideas. This fact has unfortunately caused some historians of philosophy to undervalue the importance of his writings.

Originality can come in many forms. It need not be found solely in the assertion of new ideas. In Cicero's case, the originality is found in (1) the creative arrangement and presentation of Greek philosophy to an audience unfamiliar with Greek, and (2) the invention of a new corpus of philosophical terms in Latin. This importance of this last point cannot be overstated. In Cicero's day, the conventional wisdom among Romans (and Greeks, of course) was that the only language suitable for science and philosophy was Greek. Cicero, patriot and literary visionary that he was, turned this conventional wisdom on its head. He audaciously declared that not only was there nothing inadequate about Latin as a vehicle for philosophical expression, but that Latin was in fact *superior* to Greek!

In truth I am constantly amazed at the scornful contempt directed against our native literary output. This may not exactly be the right place for this discussion, but I believe and have often tried to show that the Latin language is not only *not* deficient (as some uninformed people believe) but is actually *more* well-endowed in expressive attributes than Greek. When have we—here I mean our great poets or orators—ever seen our expressive power deficient in the arenas of either ornate or fastidious eloquence?[6]

For a Roman in Cicero's day to make such a claim was astonishing, and he knew it. He does not stop there; in Book III, he repeats his claims on the superiority of the Latin language:

We have often said—and we have directed this complaint not only against the Greeks themselves but also against those who would like to be considered Greek—that we Latin speakers are not only *not bested* by the Greeks when it comes to richness of vocabulary, but are in fact *their superiors*. We must strive relentlessly to demonstrate our true worth, not only in our own arts, but also in those fields considered the exclusive domain of the Greeks.[7]

One senses the iron determination in these lines. He accomplished what he set out to do, and his achievement was gratefully acknowledged by his fellow countrymen in the generations after his death. The historian Velleius Paterculus, writing around 30 A.D., reminds his readers that "[Cicero's] life was as brilliant as his genius was surpassing," and that he "rescued us [Romans]

---

[6] I.10.
[7] III.5.

from being conquered in the field of learning by those whom we had conquered militarily [i.e., the Greeks]."[8] With the advent of Cicero's philosophical writings, old traditions and longstanding psychological prejudices against Latin came crashing down. For the first time, Romans were exposed to abstract philosophical terms and concepts in their own language. Cicero was so successful, and his influence was so pervasive, that Latin prevailed as the language of philosophy in Western Europe for nearly another sixteen centuries. Very few other writers in the Western tradition can match this achievement.

We will now briefly summarize the three philosophical systems discussed in *On Moral Ends*. Our purpose here is not to provide a comprehensive analysis of each school, for this would take an entire volume. But we can highlight each school's major points, so that the reader will have some frame of reference when reading Cicero's text.

EPICUREANISM

Epicurus (341 B.C.—270 B.C.) was an unapologetic materialist. Born in Samos, he studied philosophy in Athens at Plato's Academy. He found much to admire in Plato, and much that he disagreed with. In 306 B.C. he took up permanent residence in Athens, and began to teach students himself. His personal integrity was beyond reproach. It is unfortunate that his name has become an adjective to describe carefree hedonism, for Epicurus himself lived an ascetic and austere life. He accepted students from all backgrounds, including women, commoners, and slaves. He disliked politics and organized religion, preferring to keep to himself and live quietly. He is said to have written three

---

[8] *Historiae Romanae* II.34.

hundred books, but time has obliterated them all save a few fragments. Epicurus's writings, with their materialist and pleasure-seeking patina, would not have pleased the medieval church; it is not surprising that there was little motivation for monastic copyists to preserve his literary legacy. Our chief ancient sources for his views are Lucretius's brilliant didactic poem *On the Nature of Things* (*De Rerum Natura*), and book ten of Diogenes Laertius's *Lives of the Philosophers*.[9] The latter work preserves several of Epicurus's short letters, as well as his so-called "Sovran Maxims,"[10] a collection of forty basic principles that Epicurean initiates would probably have had to memorize.

One of his primary goals was to free men from what he believed were religion's oppressive terrors. It is pointless to worry about the gods, and harmful to obsess over theology; religion, he believed, depended on fear and ignorance that shackled the minds of its adherents. The gods exist, but they are indifferent to human affairs, and it is useless to try to understand their motivations. He adopted the atomist views of Democritus and refined them to a high degree. The world, he taught, was composed of nothing but atoms and the void; the movement of atoms (their "swerving" or "declination") accounted for the physical phenomena observed in nature. The universe is essentially boundless; it had no beginning, and will have no end. Epicurus rejected Plato's theory of Forms, believing that man could attain knowledge through the senses and personal experience. Both soul and body exist, but soul can only act with the body. Death terminates them both; there is no mystical soul that persists after our death.

---

[9] The serious student of Epicureanism is advised to consult both of these works. Many editions of Lucretius exist. As for Diogenes Laertius, the only readily obtainable English translation is that by R.D. Hicks (Cambridge: Harvard University Press, 2005). The Hicks translation dates back to 1925, but is still very accessible. It is a work of great value, and belongs on the bookshelf of every student of classical philosophy.

[10] Diog. Laert. X.138 *et. seq.*

But it was Epicurus's ethical doctrine that primarily concerns Cicero. Epicurus accepted that the purpose of philosophy was to teach us the road to happiness; but his advice on how to obtain happiness was distinctly his own. There was nothing wrong with physical pleasures, provided they were taken in moderation; virtue was a means to an end, rather than an end in itself. Pain is an evil. Wisdom is the ultimate good, because it frees man from his enslavement to his desires and fears. But Epicurus defined pleasure not as voluptuary indulgence but as "freedom from pain," a curiously passive view that perhaps overemphasized the avoidance of life's unpleasantness. The following are two of his "Sovran Maxims":

3. The magnitude of pleasure reaches its limit in the removal of all pain. When pleasure is present, so long as it is uninterrupted, there is no pain either of body or of mind or of both together...

34. Injustice is not in itself an evil, but only in its consequence, namely the terror which is excited by apprehension that those appointed to punish such offenses will discover the injustice.[11]

Epicureanism as propounded by its founder was an honest attempt to liberate man from the sorrows and fears of life. To counteract the terrors of theology, it deployed the materialism of atomic theory and a moral ethic based on reason's control of the senses. To alleviate the fear of death, it taught that death brings all to an end. To soften the hardships of living, it advised a sensible enjoyment of pleasure tempered by a wisdom that could check excessive desire. Epicurean communities persisted for a long time after the master's death in 270 B.C., and there is no doubt that many found comfort in their founder's doctrines.

---

[11] Diog. Laert. X.139, 153 (Trans. by R.D. Hicks).

Yet there is something unsatisfying in this philosophy. It does not inspire us to great deeds; it lacks the soaring imaginative power and mystical allure of Platonism. It sees no beauty or redemptive artistry in religion, and it fails to appreciate its central importance in providing a moral code for society. It failed to grasp that religious myth and ritual provided a necessary consolation for the old, the sick, and the bereaved that outweighed any alleged "terrors" that a believer might face. And even if the belief in an afterlife is illogical, is Epicureanism really offering anything better? Are we supposed take comfort in being told that we are nothing but a collection of atoms, and that death represents our permanent annihilation?

There are other problems as well. Epicurus should have known human nature well enough to foresee that his ethical theories would be susceptible to misunderstanding and abuse. Talking too much about pleasure to students is always perilous; and to preach pain avoidance as a major goal of life is to open the door to weakness, moral cowardice, and hedonism. Epicurus probably placed too much faith on reason's ability to moderate our taste for sensory delights. Epicureanism was not a philosophy for the masses; it was appropriate only for a select few who had the integrity to implement it correctly. It demanded disciplined, ascetic personalities who would not be tempted to abuse its doctrines. We may say that this was not Epicurus's fault; but the fact remains that it is a philosopher's responsibility to imagine the foreseeable consequences of his teachings.

Cicero was right when he noted that Epicureanism was not a philosophy for statesmen, soldiers, or men of affairs. No great man has ever made pain avoidance his primary focus. Suffering, Cicero knew, was an unavoidable part of life for those who wished to accomplish anything productive. The only way to inspire men to greatness was to prepare them sternly for this fact. Cicero understood that it was better for individuals and society alike to teach men that virtue *was an end in itself*, and that moral goodness *should* be sought for its own sake.

STOICISM

The founder of the Stoic school was Zeno of Citium (c. 334 B.C.—c. 262 B.C.). He was apparently of mixed Phoenician and Greek ancestry, and as a young man accumulated substantial wealth from commercial activities. He lost it all, Diogenes Laertius tells us, during a voyage to Greece when his ship was wrecked. From this point he turned his attentions to philosophy, and studied for a time with Crates the Cynic. The Cynics were mendicant ascetics, but Zeno found much of value in their beliefs; other major influences on him were Heracleitus and, of course, Plato. He opened his own school around 301 B.C., and was known for his exemplary personal conduct. He taught in Athens for many decades, delivering his lectures in the so-called "Painted Porch," a place located on the north side of the Agora. In ancient Greek "Painted Porch" is *Stoa Poecile*;[12] it is from this phrase that the Stoics took the name of their school. When he died around 262 B.C., he was succeeded by Cleanthes of Assus and then by Chrysippus of Soli. These two thinkers built on what Zeno had begun, and constructed a sophisticated philosophy that proved to be one of antiquity's most influential schools.

The universe, according to the Stoics, is created, destroyed, and created again in an endless cycle of rebirth. Matter is infused with its own potential energy, and is in constant motion. The Stoics did not share the Epicureans' negative view of religion; they recognized the need for a supreme being, and had a vague, pantheistic conception of a universe infused with a divine will. The human soul does exist, and upon our death it is reabsorbed into the universal soul that permeates all creation.

Since all nature was a divine creation, it seemed only reasonable that man should follow the will of nature. This principle—

---

[12] ἡ ποικίλη στοά.

following nature's rule or living "in accordance with nature"—
was the keystone of Stoic ethics. Pleasure was not the aim of human life. Evil might befall a man, but he could overcome it if he
understood that it was part of nature's design. Physical pleasure
and luxuries are a distraction; they upset our tranquility, and often
leave their seekers worse off after they have been attained. The
way to peace of mind is to accept the will of nature; a man should
focus his energies on achieving virtue and shunning vice.

With regard to virtue, the traditional Stoics took an offensively
severe line. They held that there were no "degrees" of virtue; a
person was either virtuous or he was not. If a man had achieved a
state of virtue, he was wise and happy, and could not be adversely
affected by any harm that came to him; but if he had not yet
achieved virtue, he was still miserable, regardless of any progress
he might have made. Virtue was its own reward, and something
that should be sought for its own sake. Taking one's own life was
permissible if the Stoic adherent believed that continuing it would
be harmful to himself or others. The Stoics did not develop a
sophisticated theory of politics; they believed that it was more
important to change the individual than to shape societies.

Stoicism is an admirably masculine ethic. It did not counsel a
timid retreat into solitude, as Epicureanism arguably did; it had
the honesty to acknowledge pain as an unavoidable feature of life,
and taught that tolerating it was one of our primary duties. It
acknowledged the presence of an omnipotent deity and
appreciated the central importance of religious faith. In practice
Stoicism's harsher edges were probably softened by human
realities; we can imagine that there were many kindly Stoic
instructors who made due allowances for the youth and
inexperience of their pupils. And even if the Stoic rule was harsh,
was it not better to have this as an ideal instead of the Epicurean
rule, which perhaps lent itself to irresolute backsliding?
Stoicism's contempt for pleasure-seeking contrasts sharply with
the Epicurean fixation on avoiding pain, and it understood that

good character is developed through struggle, sacrifice, and hardship. Cicero admired its logical consistency and its usefulness as a tool for personal discipline. Soldiers and statesmen found in it a reservoir of strength that could sustain them through difficult periods. When the chips were down, one would much rather have a Stoic at one's side than an Epicurean.

On the other hand, Stoicism arguably inclined its adherents to a passive resignation to fate. Its overall tone was melancholy. Its obsession with living "in accord with nature" sounded fine in theory, but could be dangerously variable in interpretation. By refusing to admit to degrees of virtue, it unnecessarily discouraged potential seekers who sought to improve themselves. And how can we know what is, and what is not, in "accordance" with nature's laws? Could our assessment of nature's will in fact be only our own disguised desires?

THE ACADEMIC PHILOSOPHY OF ANTIOCHUS

The third point of view discussed in *On Moral Ends* is the Academic philosophy of Antiochus of Ascalon. Like any institution, Plato's Academy evolved over time. Even in antiquity, it was recognized that it had passed through three distinct phases; these doctrinal evolutions were assigned the names Old, Middle, and New Academy. The period of the Old Academy covered the immediate successors of Plato who served as scholarch (i.e., the head of the school). These names were Speusippus, Xenocrates, Polemo, and Crates; the period covered was roughly from 340 B.C. to 266 B.C. The Middle Academy period began with the appointment of Arcesilaus as scholarch around 266 B.C., and ended about 160 B.C. Arcesilaus steered the Academy to a cautious skepticism that emphasized the human inability to know absolute truth with certainty.

The New Academy phase began around 155 B.C. with the elevation of Carneades as scholarch. This was the school to which Cicero himself belonged, if we assume his eclectic tendencies allow him to be linked to a specific school. As previously noted, Cicero had studied under Philo of Larissa as a young man when the latter resided in Rome; and Philo was a skeptic who had served as the Academy's scholarch. Carneades continued the Academy's skeptical leanings, and it is to this period that Antiochus of Ascalon belongs.

Antiochus (c. 125 B.C.—c. 68 B.C.) is an interesting figure who attempted to reconcile the views of the Stoics and Peripatetics (Aristotelians) with traditional Platonism. History categorizes him nominally as an Academic philosopher, but he represents something more than this. He studied under Philo of Larissa in Athens, but Philo's skepticism was not to his liking; truth could indeed be known, he believed, under the right conditions. He saw himself as returning to Platonic traditionalism, but in practice he sought to infuse Platonism with Stoic and Peripatetic ideas. In this sense he was an original thinker and a true eclectic; when Cicero studied in Athens as a young man in 79 B.C., he received instruction directly from Antiochus. It is regrettable that his writings have not survived, for he was held in high regard in his time. He even seems to have given instruction in Egypt (Alexandria) and Syria, where he died.[13] There is no doubt that Cicero absorbed a great deal from him.[14] As we see in the fifth book of *On Moral Ends*, Antiochus believed that virtue was enough for a happy life, but that bodily goods are also important and should not be ignored.

---

[13] *Academics* II.61.
[14] He summarizes Antiochus's views in *Academics* I.18—25.

The Content and Structure of On Moral Ends

We will now take a close look at the text. The title Cicero gave to this book was *De Finibus Bonorum et Malorum*. A literal rendering of this would be *On the Ends of Goods and Evils*, a phrase that by itself makes little sense in English. The title is sometimes shortened to *De Finibus* (*On Ends* or *On Moral Ends*), but even this does not tell us very much. What does the title mean, and what is the subject matter of the book?

One of the questions of Greek philosophy that predated Cicero was the question of what man's proper "End" was. The capitalization of the word conveys its importance as an ethical goal. The Greek term for this "End" was *telos*, and it basically meant the final objective or ultimate goal that would provide a guide for a happy life. What is mankind's chief end or ultimate good? Of course, a question so basic and fundamental inevitably invited competing theories. Over time, different thinkers and schools arrived at their own views of what man's End was. Philosophers recognized that there was a variety of "goods" in life, including both mental and physical goods. It was also clear that there was a variety of "evils" that could burden one's life. According to this reasoning, there must be some Ultimate Good that represented the best of all the possible "Goods." This is our End, or End of Goods. Conversely, there must be some "evil" that represented the worst possible evil in life.

It is this Ultimate Good that we should direct all our energies toward, and to which everything in life should "refer back." Cicero's term for the Ultimate Good is *summum bonum*; to avoid monotony in the text I have variously translated it as Ultimate Good, Supreme Good, or Chief Good. While the term may vary, the meaning is the same: it is the *End of Goods*, the highest possible Good.

As we noted in the foreword, Cicero is very clear about what he proposes to investigate in *On Moral Ends*. He wants to explore three related questions: (1) What is our "end" (i.e., the final objective or ultimate goal of human life) that gives us a rational plan for living happily? (2) What is the most desirable principle that nature seeks? (3) What is the greatest evil that nature avoids?

On Moral Ends was most likely composed in the summer of 45 B.C. In Cicero's day, the three philosophical schools that offered different views on the End of Goods were the Epicureans, the Stoics, and the Platonists (i.e., Academics) under Antiochus of Ascalon. Debating philosophical questions in dialogue form was an old tradition that dated back to Plato, and Cicero makes good use of it. He was argumentative (and occasionally sarcastic) by nature, and must have enjoyed arranging his personal friends as mouthpieces for opposing philosophical perspectives. But at the same time he takes his task very seriously.

The translator who works his way through the entire text becomes aware that it has been composed with more care than scholars have generally recognized. Through all five books of *On Moral Ends*, he never loses sight of his purpose. Topics are raised, discussed, and then revived when needed to hammer home a particular point. The language is rich, engaging, at times even sarcastic; and in the fifth book, Cicero rises to a level of majestic eloquence that constitutes a pinnacle of Latin prose.

There are three separate dialogues in *On Moral Ends*. Each dialogue takes place at a different location and time. Cicero chooses friends or colleagues as advocates for the different schools; for himself he reserves the role of gadfly and critic. It is important for the reader to understand at the outset who is talking to whom, and who believes what. The following table summarizes each dialogue's speakers, topic, date, and location:

Dialogue	Speakers	Topic	Date	Location
First dialogue (Books I and II)	Lucius Manlius Torquatus; Cicero; Caius Valerius Triarius	Epicurean moral philosophy, and criticisms of it	50 B.C.	Cumae, Italy
Second dialogue (Books III and IV)	Marcus Porcius Cato; Cicero	Stoic moral philosophy, and criticisms of it	52 B.C.	Tusculum, Italy
Third dialogue (Book V)	M. Pupius Piso Calpurnianus; Cicero (Also present are Cicero's brother, his cousin, and his friend Titus Pomponius Atticus)	Moral philosophy of the Academics (Platonists) as interpreted by Antiochus of Ascalon	79 B.C.	Athens, Greece

Torquatus, the exponent of Epicureanism, came from an old patrician family (the Manlii) but was a strong supporter of Cicero during the latter's political career. Marcus Porcius Cato (Cato the Younger) was the great-grandson of Cato the Elder, one of the most distinguished of the old Romans. Both Catos were famous for their incorruptibility and strong sense of moral righteousness. He is the perfect choice as the advocate for the Stoic viewpoint. Marcus Pupius Piso Calpurnianus was a politician who had won a consulship in 61 B.C.; he and Cicero were friends in their younger years but had drifted apart as they grew older. Cicero himself has speaking roles in the second and third dialogues; his role is to challenge the main speakers and compel them to elaborate their points. The remaining speakers or attendees are of minor significance.

Readers will have to decide for themselves whether they believe Cicero gives a fair hearing to each of these philosophical schools. In a general sense, Cicero was strongly influenced by Plato. But Plato's Academy underwent significant changes in the centuries after Plato's death. Its third phase, which began in 155 B.C. with Carneades as scholarch, has been called the "New Academy." The New Academy was tinged with skepticism in the sense that it believed absolute truth could never really be known. In practice, Cicero was an eclectic with strong Stoic leanings. He admired Stoicism's masculine strength and logical structure, but objected to its inflexibility.

Epicureanism he disliked for its supposed inconsistencies and because he considered it unsuitable for those seeking positions of leadership or responsibility. As a lawyer, he liked to examine all sides of a question; and as we have previously noted, Cicero was an Academic skeptic with an eclectic bent. But he did have a strong core of beliefs that he retained his entire life and never deviated from. He was passionately committed to the redemptive power of moral goodness, personal responsibility, and the enduring power of virtue. He believed that men should pursue lives of moral rectitude, seek to accomplish great deeds, and serve their fellow citizens. Despite the anguish of his later life, Cicero always remained an idealist in the marrow of his bones; there is something sublime, something quietly inspiring, about his devotion to these principles and to philosophy under the extremely adverse conditions of his final years. He gifted philosophy to Rome, and a moral vision to posterity.

The text of *On Moral Ends* is well preserved and generally clear. I have consulted several Latin texts in the preparation of this translation, including Madvig, J.N. (ed.), *M. Tulii Ciceronis De Finibus Bonorum et Malorum Libri Quinque*, Copenhagen: Libraria Gyldendaliana, 1876; Charles, Emile (ed.) *M. Tulii Ciceronis De Finibus Bonorum et Malorum*, Paris: Libraire Hachette, 1893; and Alanus, Henricus (ed.) *M. Tulii Ciceronis De Finibus Bonorum et Malorum Libri Quinque*, Dublin: Hodges, Smith et. al., 1856.

Each of the five books of *De Finibus* is divided into chapters represented by Roman numerals. Each of these chapters is further divided into subsections represented by Arabic numerals. The citation scheme used in this translation is to refer to *book* and then to *subsection*. Thus, the citation III.20 would indicate book III, subsection 20; the citation V.32 would indicate book V, subsection 32. Note that in the table of contents, however, the paged references are to the *chapters* of each book.

M. TULII CICERONIS DE FINIBUS BONORUM ET MALORUM LIBRI QUINQUE

QUINTUS CURTIUS
DIGESSIT, ORDINAVIT, ET ANGLICE VERTIT.

EDITIO PRIMA

PERPETUIS COMMENTARIIS, PRAEFATIONE INTERPRETIS AD LECTOREM, ET IMAGINIBUS PHOTOGRAPHICIS PROPRIIS ILLUSTRATA. NOTIS DOCTISSIMIS AC UTILISSIMIS LOCUPLETATA. NUMERIS ET CAPITIBUS AD USUM DISCIPULORUM DISTINCTA.

Necnon etiam in hoc volumine additus est rerum, nominum, verborumque memorabilium index copiosus.

CAROLOPOLI:

HOC OPUS EXPLETUM EST ATQUE EMISSUM EX OFFICINA *CASTELLI MENTIS*.

M M X V I I I

41

PRAECEPTORIBUS ET FAUTORIBUS
DE IPSO OPTIME MERITIS

IN
GRATISSIMI ANIMI PIAEQUE OBSERVANTIAE
DOCUMENTUM

HASCE QUALESCUNQUE STUDIORUM PRIMITIAS

D.D.D.
QUINTUS CURTIUS
AUCTOR

Ad rem iudicandam animis mentibusque nostris ducimur.

BOOK I

BOOK I

I. 1. I am not unaware, Brutus, that since we will discuss in the Latin language topics handled in Greek by philosophers of unmatched ability and wide erudition, our efforts will invite criticism from various sources.[15] Some people—even those not quite uneducated—dislike the study of philosophy under any circumstances. Some others, however, do not object to it if done in a free-and-easy way, but they do not think much study or work should be devoted to it. There are also those persons learned in

---

[15] The Brutus referred to is the politician Marcus Junius Brutus (85 B.C.—42 B.C.), a friend of Cicero and a student of philosophy who played a major role in the conspiracy to assassinate Julius Caesar. He was also featured in Cicero's rhetorical work *Brutus*.

Greek letters who look down on us Latins, and prefer to devote themselves to reading the original works in Greek. Finally I suppose there will be others calling me to a different literary activity. They do not believe that this type of writing—even if it may be elegant—is suitable for my public persona or official position.

2. Against all those who say these things I will respond briefly. I have already made an adequate answer to the attacks against philosophy in that book where it was defended and praised by me after being reviled and denigrated by Hortensius.[16] This book was judged a good one by you and by those whom I consider capable of judging such things. So I pressed ahead with my work, fearing I might be seen as a man stirred by a subject yet unable to apply himself completely to it. Those who are favorably disposed to philosophy nevertheless want it studied in moderation; they propose a difficult temperance in this subject that, once begun, cannot be held back or taken in small doses. In fact I consider those who discourage philosophy altogether to be more reasonable than those who advocate for moderation, and try to impose boundaries on a subject that only gets better as one's knowledge of it increases.

3. If wisdom can be attained, we should not only receive it, but also enjoy it; and if this[17] proves to be difficult, there is still no other way of tracking down the truth except by finding it. Fatigue in searching for wisdom is disgraceful when what is sought is beautiful in the extreme. Indeed if we find pleasure in writing, who would be so hateful as to discourage us from it? Even if we find it a chore, who would impose boundaries on the efforts

---

[16] This is the lost work *Hortensius*, which St. Augustine credited with igniting his interest in philosophy. The book is named after the noted orator Quintus Hortensius Hortalus (114 B.C.—49 B.C.).

[17] I.e., finding the truth.

of others? Probably a person similar to Terence's rude character Chremes, who wanted his new neighbor "neither to dig, nor cultivate, nor finally to produce anything at all."[18] He might deter a man from ignoble labor but not from noble work: and only a meddler would be offended by work that does us so little harm.

II. 4. However, it is more difficult to respond satisfactorily to those who say that philosophical writings in Latin are of little value. The first thing that surprises me about this attitude is: why are such people not pleased to discuss serious subjects in their native language when at the same time they happily read Latin plays translated word-for-word from Greek originals? Who has such an aversion to the very name "Roman" that he would spurn or reject Ennius's[19] *Medea* or Pacuvius's[20] *Antiope* simply because he hates books written in Latin, even if he says he enjoys the same plays of Euripides? Such a person says: "Should I read the *Synephebos* of Caecilius[21] or Terence's *Maid of Andros* rather than the same ones written by Menander?"

5. I disagree with these people so much that, even though Sophocles wrote his *Electra* brilliantly, I still believe I should read Atilius's[22] inadequate translation of the work. Licinius[23] referred to him as an "iron writer": but he was still a writer, and should be read. To be altogether ignorant of our own poets demonstrates either an extremely lazy feebleness or a surplus of pampered snobbery. For my own part I consider no one erudite who is unacquainted with our own writers. If we read the line

---

[18] Terence's play *Heautontimorumenos* (*The Self-Tormentor*) I.1.17
[19] Ennius (c. 239 B.C.—c. 169 B.C.), an early Roman poet.
[20] Marcus Pacuvius (c. 220 B.C.—c. 130 B.C.), a Roman tragic poet.
[21] Caecilius Statius (c. 220 B.C.—c. 166 B.C.), a Roman comic poet. His work, like that of Pacuvius and Ennius, survives only in fragments.
[22] The identity of this translator is not known with certainty.
[23] Probably a contemporary of Pacuvius and Caecilius.

If only that in the woods…[24]

as easily as the same line in Greek, will it not please us to see
Plato's dialogues on moral goodness and right living presented for
us in Latin?

6. And suppose we do not limit ourselves to the role of
translator, but, while upholding the doctrines of our selected
authors, add to them our own judgments and our own sequence of
presentation? How could naysayers then rate Greek philosophical
works superior to works in Latin that are both beautifully written
and not just translations of Greek texts? If some people say that
these subjects have already been discussed before, then why
should one even bother to read the many different Greek authors
that are supposed to be read?[25]

In the Stoic school of thought, what has been overlooked by
Chrysippus?[26] Nevertheless we still read Diogenes, Antipater,
Mnesarchus, Panaetius, and many others[27] (the most important of
whom is our companion Posidonius[28]). Don't you agree? Doesn't
Theophrastus provide us adequate value even though he covers

---

[24] The first line of Ennius's *Medea*, adapted from the Euripidean play of the
same name. Plots were considered common property in the ancient world.
Early Roman poets and playwrights adapted Greek literary productions for
Roman audiences.

[25] I.e., if the various Greek authors have already discussed these philosophical
subjects, what reason would a person have for plodding through all these
different Greek volumes? Cicero is trying to demonstrate why his opponents'
arguments are not logical.

[26] Chrysippus of Soli (c. 279 B.C.—c. 206 B.C.), a Greek Stoic philosopher.

[27] The Stoic philosophers named here are Diogenes of Babylon (c. 228
B.C.—c. 140 B.C.); Antipater of Tarsus (c. 200 B.C.—c. 130 B.C.);
Mnesarchus (c. 170 B.C.—88 B.C.); Panaetius of Rhodes (c. 185 B.C.—109
B.C.).

[28] Posidonius of Apamea (c. 135 B.C.—c. 51 B.C), a Stoic philosopher and
astronomer who wrote voluminously on diverse subjects.

ground already trod by Aristotle? Do you see my point? Do the Epicureans—as they see fit—stop writing about the same topics that Epicurus and the ancients wrote about? If Greeks are read by other Greeks when the same subjects are arranged in different ways, why shouldn't our writers be read by us?

III. 7. Even if I unartfully translated Plato and Aristotle (as our poets have done with Greek dramas), I believe I might very much gain the favor of my countrymen by offering these divine intellects for their consideration. I have never yet done this; but still I think I should not be prohibited from doing it. If necessary I will translate certain passages (usually from the philosophers named above) when the occasion calls for it, just as Ennius has done with Homer and Afranius[29] with Menander. Nor indeed will I protest—as our Lucilius[30] has done—if the entire world reads my books. How I wish that Persius were here; I miss Scipio and Rutilius[31] even more. Dreading their criticism, he claims to write for the people of Tarentum, Consentia and Sicily. This is certainly clever, just as his other statements are; but at that time there were not enough educated people for whose favorable judgment he might exert himself. His writings are rather light; they show the highest polish, but a mediocre level of learning.

8. As for me, shall I fear any reader if I dare to write for you, who yields nothing to the Greeks when it comes to philosophy? I was challenged to undertake this task by that most appreciated

---

[29] A Roman comic poet who flourished at the beginning of the first century B.C. He took the Greek dramatist Menander (c. 342 B.C.—c. 290 B.C.) as a literary model.
[30] Caius Lucilius (c. 180 B.C.—c. 101 B.C.), the earliest Roman satirist. He fought alongside Scipio Aemilianus at the siege of Numantia in 134 B.C.
[31] Publius Rutilius Rufus (c. 158 B.C.—c. 78 B.C.), statesman and historian. Interestingly, he made significant reforms to Roman bankruptcy law. *See* Levinthal, L., *The Early History of Bankruptcy Law*, Univ. of Pennsylvania Law Review 223, 235-236 (1918).

book *On Virtue* that you sent me. But I believe that people shrink away from Latin philosophical works because they have come into contact with haphazard and pathetic books scribbled in bad Greek and even worse Latin. I agree with these people on this point, provided they think that Greek writers on the very same subjects also should not be read. But who would not read a good literary production in Latin with well-chosen words and a highly refined style? Unless it be someone who wants to be called a Greek, just as Albucius was greeted by Scaevola when he was praetor at Athens.

9. Lucilius tells this anecdote with great charm and engaging wit when he gives Scaevola these wonderful lines:

> You prefer to be thought of as a Greek, Albucius, instead of a
> Roman or Sabine,
> Or a native of Pontius or Tritannus;
> And you washed your hands of the centurions,
> Of the greatest men and foremost standard-bearers.
> Therefore, praetor of Athens, you preferred a salutation in
> Greek when
> You approached me, and I said:
> *Chaire, Titus!*[32]
> Then the lictors and the entire troop and chorus said,
> *Chaire, Titus!*
> From here Albucius sees me as an enemy,
> From here as someone hostile.

10. This was something rightly said by Mucius. In truth I am constantly amazed at the scornful contempt directed against our native literary output. This may not exactly be the right place for

---

[32] The word *chaire* was a Greek salutation. The point of the verses here is to ridicule those Romans who tried to act like Greeks.

this discussion, but I believe and have often tried to show that the Latin language is not only *not* deficient (as some uninformed people believe) but is actually *more* well-endowed in expressive attributes than Greek. When have we—here I mean our great poets or orators—ever seen our expressive power deficient in the arenas of either ornate or fastidious eloquence?

IV. Because I always shouldered my responsibility for the public services, labors, and dangers that came with the offices the Roman people entrusted me with, so also should I exert myself as much as possible with devotion, energy, and patience to help my fellow citizens become more learned in these matters. Nor will I worry about fighting with those who prefer to read Greek, as long as they actually read it and not pretend to do so. I aim to serve those who prefer books in either language or those who (if they have such books in their own languages) do not very much want Greek ones.

11. Those who prefer me to write about other things ought to be reasonable. I have already written a great deal—no one in fact has produced more—and will continue to write as long as life allows. Still, someone who has carefully examined my philosophical writings will judge none of them more worth reading than this one.[33] For what should be sought in life more diligently than all the important questions of philosophy, especially the major issue examined in this book: *what is the end (i.e., the final objective or the ultimate goal) that provides us with a rational plan for living well and doing good works?* What is the most desirable principle sought after by nature? And what is the greatest evil that nature avoids? On these questions the wisest philosophers disagree profoundly. Who, therefore, would consider searching for the best and truest principles for every

----

[33] This suggests that Cicero considered *On Moral Ends* the most important of his philosophical works.

responsibility of life as a task unworthy of the trust each man might grant me?

12. Or should the important men of state concern themselves with discussing whether the offspring of a servant-girl is the property of her master, with Publius Scaevola and Manius Manilius having one opinion and Marcus Brutus having a dissenting view? (Of course this is an important issue and one useful for the public; we read and will gladly continue to read about these disputes and others of the same type).[34] Should these basic philosophical questions that deal with the essence of life be neglected? While commercial questions may be more marketable, philosophical questions are without doubt more profitable. Readers of such matters will have to judge for themselves. In the chapters that follow I believe I have thoroughly explored the question of the "Ends of Goods and Evils." We will herein examine, as far as possible, not only the ideas with which we ourselves concur but also the doctrines advanced by the various philosophical schools.

V. 13. Let us first begin with something basic: the essential doctrines of Epicurus, which are well-known to many. You will perceive that our summary here will be as accurate as one given by those claiming to belong to the Epicurean school. But our purpose is to discover the truth, not to vanquish some intellectual adversary. Epicurus's theory of pleasure was carefully defended by a certain Lucius Torquatus,[35] a man well-schooled in the various philosophical systems. I responded to him. Present at the

---

[34] The schools of rhetoric used such hypotheticals as ways of teaching argumentation and debate. *See*, e.g., the *Controversiae* of Seneca the Elder, which has many such model legal "cases."

[35] Lucius Manlius Torquatus (?—46 B.C.) was a Roman politician and the son of a famous consul with the same name. He serves as Cicero's mouthpiece to argue on the side of the Epicurean school.

discussion also was Caius Triarius, a highly educated young man with a serious character.

14. Each of these men came to visit me at Cumae.[36] We first spoke a bit about literature, as both of them were keen devotees of the subject.

Then Torquatus said, "Since we've found you at a moment of leisure, I'd definitely like to hear not what you hate about my guide Epicurus (as most people do who disagree with him), but what you find illogical. For I believe him to be the one man who has figured out the truth about human nature and to have freed us from the greatest errors; he has provided us with everything worth knowing about the good life and happiness. But it seems to me that, like our good friend Triarius, you find Epicurus off-putting because he pays no attention to the ornaments of rhetoric that are found in the works of Plato, Aristotle, and Theophrastus.[37] For I find it hard to believe that you really think his doctrines are incorrect."

15. "You are very much wrong about this, Torquatus," I answered. "The prose style of this philosopher[38] does not bother me. He uses his words in the way he wants and I understand the things he says. Of course I don't reject eloquence in a philosopher if he is capable of it; but if he is not, I don't very much insist on it. I find Epicurus's views somewhat unsatisfactory on a variety of issues. But since 'there are as many men as there are ways of thinking,'[39] I may very well be wrong.

"What things do you find unsatisfactory?" he replied. "I see you as a fair judge as long as you know what Epicurus's ideas really are."

---

[36] The dialogue takes place in Cicero's residence at Cumae (modern Cuma in the province of Naples).

[37] Theophrastus (c. 371 B.C.—c. 287 B.C.), Greek philosopher and scientist, considered the successor of Aristotle in the Peripatetic school.

[38] Epicurus.

[39] Cicero uses the proverb *Quot homines, tot sententiae.*

16. "Not unless you think Phaedrus[40] or Zeno[41] were lying to me!" I exclaimed. "I have heard both of them lecture, yet to me they proved nothing except their painstaking adherence to all the standard points of Epicurean doctrine. With our friend Atticus[42] I often listened to those speakers I've just named; Atticus held them both in high regard but especially loved Phaedrus. Every day we used to discuss the things we heard from the lecturers. There never was any argument over what I could understand, but rather what I could agree with."

VI. 17. "So what is it, then?" he rejoined. "I want to hear what it is that you disagree with."

"First," I began, "when we look at his ideas about science (which he is very proud of), it's clear he borrows everything from other people. He repeats Democritus[43] with a few alterations; and when he tries to correct him, it seems to me that he only distorts him. Democritus posits the existence of things called 'atoms' (bodies that are indivisible due to their structure) that he believes are moving in boundless empty space: this void has neither top, bottom, middle, limit[44] nor end. The resulting collisions and fusions of these atoms generate the physical objects that exist and that we perceive with our senses. The movement of atoms in space has no temporal beginning; it is meant to be understood as having been going on forever.

---

[40] Phaedrus the Epicurean (c. 138 B.C.—c. 69 B.C.), the head of an Epicurean school in Athens and a contemporary of Cicero.

[41] Zeno of Sidon (c. 150 B.C.—c. 75 B.C.), an Epicurean philosopher from the Phoenician city of Sidon.

[42] Titus Pomponius Atticus (c. 110 B.C.—32 B.C.), a close friend of Cicero and the recipient of much of his surviving correspondence.

[43] Democritus of Abdera (c. 460 B.C.—c. 370 B.C.), influential Greek philosopher considered the founder of atomic theory. His ideas on atoms were borrowed extensively by the Epicureans.

[44] Instead of *ultimum* (limit), some manuscripts have here *intimum* (middle).

Ruins near the acropolis at Cumae

View from Cumae to the Tyrrhenian Sea. The island of Ischia is just outside the left border of this photo.

18. "Epicurus, however, generally does not stumble when he follows Democritus's lead. Yet I still do not agree with both of them in many things, primarily this: when talking about the nature of things, two questions must be asked. The first is: what is the material from which each thing is made? The second is: by what force is each material thing made? They[45] have discussed the question of material composition; but they have neglected the questions of force and generative cause. This mistake they both have in common. I will now mention the defects particular to Epicurus. He believes that these individual, solid bodies are carried downwards in a straight line by their own weight; and he believes that this is the natural motion of all bodies.

19. "When he realizes that, if all bodies are carried downward from some place and (as I said earlier) in a straight line, then no atom would ever be able to touch another atom, this intelligent man introduced his own little contrivance. He said that the atom 'swerves' a little bit by a degree that is hardly detectable. Thus are produced the combinations, unions, and linkages of the atoms among themselves which create the entire physical world, its component parts, and everything therein that exists.

"Not only is all of this puerile fiction, but it does not even accomplish the purpose that its author desires. This 'swerving'[46] is a product of his imagination: he says that atoms swerve for no reason, and no idea is more objectionable for a scientist than to say that something happens without a cause. He also arbitrarily takes away from atoms that natural motion of all bodies with mass that he himself has mandated (that is, movement downwards to a lower region). Nevertheless, he does not achieve the goal for which this fanciful theory was created.

---

[45] Epicurus and Democritus.
[46] *Declinatio*.

20. "For if all atoms are moving at a declination, none of them will adhere with each other; and if some move at a declination while others move on a straight path by their own accord, then this will essentially be like we are 'assigning areas of responsibility'[47] to atoms, where some travel in straight lines and others move at an oblique. Finally, this turbulent collision of atoms (a theory that Democritus also stubbornly clung to) would not be able to produce the refined beauty of our physical world. Neither is it right for a scientist to believe in one basic, fundamental unit of matter. Epicurus never would have advocated this theory if he had allowed his friend Polyaenus[48] to teach him geometry, rather than allowing Polyaenus himself to throw it away. Democritus—as he was an educated man who knew geometry well—considered the sun to be immense; Epicurus thought it was about a foot in diameter. He thinks the sun is about as large as it seems to the eye, or perhaps a little more or less than this.

21. "Thus, Epicurus corrupts all the doctrines of Democritus that he tampers with: atoms, the void, the theory of images (which are called *eidola*, whose physical contact with us produces not only sight but thought), and the idea of infinity (which they call *apeiria*). All these ideas originally come from Democritus, including the idea that numberless planets are created and destroyed every day. In no way do I endorse any of these doctrines. Nevertheless I wish Epicurus—who followed Democritus slavishly—had not so ill-treated Democritus, who is praised by everyone.

VII. 22. "We now consider the other part of philosophy: the part that concerns how to seek knowledge and how to describe

---

[47] *Primum erit hoc quasi provincias atomis dare.*
[48] Polyaenus of Lampsacus (c. 340 B.C.—c. 285 B.C.), Greek mathematician and friend of Epicurus.

it,[49] which is called *logike*.[50] It is clear to me that your master is helpless and exposed here. He does not bother with definitions; he teaches us nothing about division and partition;[51] he never shows us how the reasoning process takes place and what its boundaries are; and he does not explain how thorny issues are resolved, or how ambiguous things may be distinguished from one another. Our awareness of the world he attributes to sensory inputs; once the senses accept something to be true that really is false, he then immediately thinks that every benchmark for truth and falsity is taken away.[52]

23. "He very much emphasizes the things that (as he says) nature herself ordains and endorses: pleasure and pain. Everything we pursue, and everything we avoid, ultimately relates back to these two states. Although this is Aristippus's[53] idea and is defended more eloquently and stridently by the Cyrenaics, my judgment is that nothing could be more unworthy for a man. For it seems to me that nature has created and shaped us for something greater than this. It could be that I am wrong; but I am firmly of the opinion that the Torquatus[54] who first won that cognomen did

---

[49] *Quaerendi ac disserendi.*

[50] Λογική (logic).

[51] I.e., using the logical technique of dividing or dissecting something into its constituents.

[52] Editors of the Latin text believe there is lacunae of uncertain length after this sentence and before the next one.

[53] Aristippus of Cyrene (c. 435 B.C.—c. 356 B.C.), founder of the Cyrenaic school of philosophy. The Cyrenaics believed that pleasure should be the ultimate goal of the wise man.

[54] Titus Manlius Imperiosus Torquatus, general and political figure who held three consulships and three dictatorships from 348 B.C. to 340 B.C. He was legendary for his harsh discipline and martial ardor. He killed a large Gaul in single combat in 361 B.C. and stripped him of his neck ornament (torque) as a trophy. This was the origin of the name "Torquatus" that his descendants inherited.

View of the Tyrrhenian Sea from Cumae

Ruins of the Temple of Apollo at Cumae

not strip it from his battlefield enemy in order to feel physical pleasure. Neither did he fight with the Latins at Veseris[55] during his third consulship for the sake of pleasure. On the contrary, it seems to me that he deprived himself of many pleasures by having his son beheaded, since he chose to give preference to the sanctity of the law and the responsibility of command rather than to his natural affections as a father.

24. "Consider the Titus Torquatus who was consul with Cnaeus Octavius. He applied harsh measures to his natural son, who had come under the parentage of Decius Silanus by adoption. Macedonian envoys had accused the son of having taken bribes while serving as praetor in that province; Torquatus compelled him to respond to the indictment. Having heard both sides of the case, he judged the son to have behaved in office in a way unbecoming of his ancestors, and forbade him thereafter from being in his presence.[56] Does it seem to you that Torquatus was acting with his own pleasures in mind? I am not even mentioning the dangers, labors, and pains that every good man shoulders for the good of his country and his friends. Not only does he not seek out pleasures, but he actually neglects all kinds of enjoyment. He prefers to endure any kind of sorrow rather than neglect any part of his official responsibility. We should now move on to issues that, while appearing less serious than those already discussed, are equally probative.

25. "Torquatus, how does the knowledge of literature or history, or the unrolling of classic poetry books and the memorization of verses, bring you—or Triarius here—any pleasure? And you should not answer me like this: 'these things

---

[55] The Battle of Veseris (340 B.C.) in which the consul Titus Manlius Imperiosus Torquatus had his son executed for disobedience.
[56] This event is related in Valerius Maximus's *Memorable Deeds and Sayings* (V.8) and took place in 140 B.C.

are pleasurable to me just as those other things you mentioned earlier were pleasurable to the Torquati.' For neither Epicurus nor Metrodorus[57] ever tried to defend this way of reasoning, nor did anyone else if he had a brain or was well-read in these studies. It is often asked why so many men are Epicureans. Although there are other reasons, what most entices the crowd is that they think he says that morally right and honorable things are inherently a source of joy (that is, a source of physical pleasure). Sincere people recognize that, if this proposition were true, it undermines the entire system. For if we concede that moral goodness is pleasurable on its own, or for its own sake (even if unrelated to physical stimulation), then virtue and knowledge must be sought for their own sake. Yet this is not what Epicurus intended.

26. "So I can't agree with these doctrines of Epicurus," I emphasized. "With regard to the rest, I wish he could have been more trained in formal learning (since you must notice that he is not refined enough in those areas of scholarship that allow a person to be considered educated), or that he had not discouraged others from formal learning. Although I see indeed that you have not been deterred at all!"

VIII. Although I had said these things more to challenge Torquatus than to announce my own position, Triarius said gently with a smile, "Well, you have tossed out Epicurus completely from the chorus of philosophers. What have you left, other than the fact that despite how he talks, you understand what he is saying? In physics he repeated the ideas of others, and even these ideas were unacceptable to you. If he wanted to improve on these,

---

[57] Metrodorus of Lampsacus (c. 331 B.C.—c. 278 B.C.), one of the original Greek proponents of Epicureanism. He is not to be confused with a pre-Socratic philosopher of the same name, known as Metrodorus of Lampsacus the Elder.

he only made things worse. He had no talent for critical explanation. When he said that physical pleasure was the greatest good, this view was in the first place flawed, as well as derivative. Aristippus had said this before, and more cogently. And on top of all this, you added that Epicurus was uneducated!"

27. "Triarius," I said, "there can be no real meeting of the minds if you do not tell someone what you find objectionable about his views. If I agree with what he says, what then prevents me from being an Epicurean?[58] Especially when learning his system is equivalent to child's play! You must not berate people for critiquing different philosophical systems. As I see it, insults, verbal abuse, and slander, along with angry discourse and stubborn controversy, are unworthy of philosophy."

28. "By all means I agree," Torquatus shot back. "One cannot debate without finding fault, yet one cannot argue properly under the influence of anger or blind stubbornness. But related to this point, I have something I'd like to say, if it is not out of line."

"Do you think I would have spoken as I did, unless I wanted to hear you?" I pressed him.

He replied, "Would you like me to review Epicurus's entire system, or just discuss the one topic 'pleasure,' which is the main point of contention?"

"That," I smiled, "is something that will have to be your decision."

"Then I will do this," he answered. "I will explain one subject, the one I consider most important. The natural sciences I will leave for another time. I intend to demonstrate for you the 'swerve' of atoms and the size of the sun, as well as the fact that Epicurus pointed out and corrected many of Democritus's mistakes. I will talk a bit about physical pleasure; while I won't

---

[58] I.e., if I concur with all of Epicurus's opinions, I will be seen as just another Epicurean.

present any original ideas, I am confident you will find my arguments convincing."

"Certainly," I replied, "I won't shut my ears to what you have to say; and if you can win me over by your arguments, I will gladly change my opinion."

29. "I will do so, as long as you give what I say a fair hearing. But I actually prefer a continuous dialogue rather than the method of asking questions and then being asked in return."

"As you wish," I shrugged. Then he began to speak.

IX. "I will begin in the same way that the author of the system himself preferred to do. I will lay out the nature and features of what we are looking for, not because I think you are ignorant of these things, but so that our discourse moves in a logical and ordered progression. We are therefore asking: *what is the final and ultimate Good, which all philosophers believe should have the essential quality that everything else relates back to it, and that it serves no other end outside of itself.*[59] Epicurus assigned this role to 'pleasure.' He wanted this to be the highest good, and pain to be the greatest evil. He chose to demonstrate his theory in the following way.

30. "As soon as it is born, every animal seeks out pleasure and cherishes it as the ultimate good thing; it loathes pain as the greatest evil and pushes it away as much as possible. It does this as long as it is normal with an uncorrupted nature, and free of mental shortcomings.

For this reason he does not believe it is necessary to show by logic or discussion that pleasure is something to be sought, and pain is something to be avoided. Epicurus thinks these are things to be *felt*, just as fire is hot, snow is white, and honey sweet—none of which need to be confirmed by convoluted reasoning. It is sufficient simply to take note of them.

---

[59] I.e., the Ultimate Good is that principle which is the final "end" to which all "means" lead. The Ultimate Good itself serves nothing higher than itself.

Remains of the Temple of Apollo at Cumae

A well-preserved Roman road at Cumae

"For there is a difference between (1) evidence and formal conclusions of logic, and (2) the ordinary noticing and acknowledgment of something. The former is way of discovering things hidden or partially obscured, and the latter is for evaluating things that are manifest and obvious. Since nothing remains once you deprive a man of his senses, it is clear that what is (and what is not) in accordance with Nature can only be decided by Nature herself. How else except through pain or pleasure does Nature perceive and judge things, or determine what one should seek or avoid?

31. "Some of us[60] want to polish this doctrine even more. They deny that the judging of what is good or bad can be done by sense perception alone. The fact that pleasure is itself desirable—and that pain is itself loathsome—is something that can be understood by both the mind and by rational argument. That we feel one of these sensations should be sought after, and the other avoided, is something (they claim) that is almost naturally imprinted on our minds. Although a number of philosophers have supplied various reasons to explain why pleasure should not be counted as a good nor pain considered an evil, other men (with whom I agree) judge that we should not be too assured of our position. These men believe that an inquiry into the nature of pleasure and pain must be based on argumentation, meticulous discussion, and diligent reasoning.

X. 32. "But in order to make you see how this pitfall of condemning pleasure and approving of pain originated, I will give a complete description of Epicureanism. I will explain the actual ideas of the discoverer of the truth, that architect of the fulfilling life. No one rejects, dislikes, or flees from pleasure itself simply because it is pleasure, but because great sorrows land on the shoulders of those who do not know how to handle pleasures in a rational way. Neither is there anyone who loves or wants to seek

---

[60] Epicureans.

out pain simply because it is pain, but instead because situations sometimes happen where one makes use of labor and pain to achieve the higher goal of pleasure. To give a small illustration of this: who among us would undertake physical exercise unless something advantageous would result from it? Who can justifiably blame someone who wants to enjoy some pleasure that does no harm, or someone who avoids pain from which no pleasure results?

33. "On the other hand, we reproach and treat with justifiable dislike those who are so bewitched and corrupted by the charms inherent in bodily pleasures that, blinded by lust, they do not anticipate the anguish and suffering that are sure to follow. Similarly culpable are those who abandon their responsibilities through weakness of resolution. I see this as equivalent to fleeing from work and discomfort. These situations are simple and readily identifiable. In our free time, when our power of choice is not restricted and nothing really prevents us from doing what we enjoy, every pleasure should be accepted and all pain rejected. Yet at certain times—due to one's duties or to the inevitable circumstances of life—it may come about that pleasures must be rejected and troubles must be shouldered. Therefore the wise man adheres to this general guideline: *either something better will happen by his repudiating pleasures, or he will prevent something worse from happening by accepting pain.*

34. "Since this is the position that I take, why should I be afraid of not being able to adapt it to the opinions of my ancestors, the Torquati? You mentioned them a little while ago in a way that was factually accurate; and with me you have kept the tone of the dialogue friendly and sincere. Yet your praise of my ancestors has not undermined my resolution, and I have not been weakened in my ability to respond to your arguments. I would ask you this: how do *you* interpret their actions? Do you really think that they attacked an armed foe, or were so cruel to their own children— their own blood relations—without thinking at all about their own

65

advantage or self-interest? Not even wild animals, when destroying things and causing havoc, behave in such a way that we cannot discern the reasons behind their commotions and outbursts of fury. Do you believe that such exceptional men could have done these acts without any reason?

35. "I will soon take a look at what their motive was. Meanwhile I take the position that if there was some reason for those deeds (that were certainly amazing) that they performed, that reason was for them not virtue for its own sake. *He tore off the necklace from his enemy.*[61] He indeed prevented himself from being killed. *But he put himself in great danger.* Even within sight of an army. *What resulted from this action?* Approval and affection, which are the most solid assurances for living one's life without fear. *He had his own son executed.* If there was no reason for this act, then I have no desire that such a monstrous and cruel man be an ancestor of mine. But if, by subjecting himself to personal agony, his goal was to sustain his military authority and enforce proper discipline in the ranks (using the method of fear) during an extremely severe wartime crisis, then he was looking out for the welfare of the citizenry, upon which he realized his own safety depended.

36. "This reasoning can be used in many situations. Those who pursue the study of history—and you yourself especially—are very much in the habit of making use of your eloquence to honor the great and distinguished men of the past and to celebrate their deeds, not for some tangible benefit, but rather to praise an idealized image of moral rectitude. Yet all of this amounts to nothing if the guideline rule[62] I have stated above is put in place; namely, that some pleasures are given up for the sake of getting

---

[61] The following short statements in italics are meant as hypothetical questions, to which proposed answers are then given.

[62] The guideline rule given at the end of I.33.

greater pleasures, and that some sufferings are accepted for the sake of avoiding even greater sufferings.

XI. 37. "But enough has been said here about the celebrated and glorious deeds of great men. The natural movement of all the virtues towards pleasure is a subject that will be discussed in a separate place. I will now explain "pleasure" itself and what its nature is, so that the bad impressions of uninformed people might be corrected, and so that you might understand why the Epicurean school (which is supposedly so hedonistic, self-indulgent, and profligate) is actually rather austere, chaste, and unpretentious. We are not seeking the type of pleasure that excites our bodies with its sweetness and is perceived by the senses as desirable; we are instead aiming at that highest form of pleasure, which we consider to be *the removal of all pain*. When we are freed from pain, the very liberation and absence of discomfort is something we celebrate. Yet everything we celebrate is a pleasure, just as everything that troubles us is some kind of pain. Thus pleasure is correctly identified as the removal of all pain. When hunger and thirst are eliminated by food and drink, this removal of a bodily torment brings pleasure as a consequence. So in every case, the expulsion of pain brings about the advent of pleasure.

38. "Therefore it did not suit Epicurus to have a 'middle condition'[63] between pleasure and pain. For what might be considered a middle condition—a complete absence of pain, as it were—is not only a pleasure, but actually the greatest pleasure. Whoever experiences the inputs received by his senses must necessarily consider them either 'pleasure' or 'pain.' Epicurus believes that the absence of all pain marks the pinnacle of all forms of pleasure. Beyond this point, pleasure may become varied in character or differentiated in form, but it cannot be increased or amplified.

---

[63] A state that was neither pleasure nor pain.

View of the ruins of the lower city at Cumae

Entrance to the Cave of the Sibyl

39. "I used to hear from my father—when he wanted to make fun of the Stoics using humor and wit—that at Athens in the Ceramicus[64] there is a statue of Chrysippus. The figure is seated with an extended hand, and the position of his hand indicates the degree to which he enjoyed posing the following little interrogatory:

Does your hand, whatever its current condition may be, want anything?
No, absolutely nothing.
But if pleasure were a good, the hand would desire it.
Yes, I think so.
Therefore, pleasure is not a good.

"My father said that not even a statue would say this, if it were able to speak. It is sharp enough to be a good rebuttal to the views of the Cyrenaics, but it is ineffective against Epicurus. For if the only kind of pleasure was the kind that more or less titillated the senses and bathed them generously in feelings of satisfaction, neither the hand nor any other part of the body could be satisfied with just an absence of pain *unless* there was also a positive sensation of pleasure to go with it. But if the highest pleasure is (as Epicurus believed) the complete absence of all pain, then the statue of Chrysippus was correct when it 'said' that its hand did not want anything in its current position. But the statue's second statement—when it said that if pleasure was a good, his hand would have wanted it—was *not* correct. The hand did not need pleasure, because the condition of being free from pain *is already* by definition pleasure.

XII. 40. "That pleasure is the highest good is something that can clearly be seen from this example. Suppose we have a man

---

[64] An area (Κεραμεικός) of Athens to the northwest of the Acropolis, where pottery makers and funerary monuments were located. The English word "ceramic" is traced to this word.

who is enjoying pleasures of the mind and body that are intense, plentiful, and long-lasting; suppose also that these pleasures are neither blocked or threatened by any pain. What living condition could be more desirable, or more sought after, than this condition? A person in this situation must be someone constituted with the kind of mental stability that allows him to have no fear either of pain or death. He must know that death is the complete absence of sense perception; and that since pain of long duration is usually light, and pain of short duration usually intense, the quickness of the pain alleviates its intensity, while a low level of pain would compensate for its extendedness.

41. "If we can find such a man, let him neither live in fear of divine will, nor allow the pleasures of the past to be forgotten; let him instead draw enjoyment from regular recollection of them. What situation can be found that is better than this? But consider, on the other hand, someone carrying the greatest sorrows of body and soul that a person can bear, with no hope given him that his load will be lighter; imagine also that he has neither a present nor future expectation of pleasure. Can anyone imagine or describe a more miserable situation? If a life crammed full of agonies is what should be most avoided, it is obvious that the greatest evil is to live in pain. Following reciprocally from this is the idea that the ultimate good is to live in a state of pleasure. The mind, so to speak, has no inherent thing upon which it stands as final. All fears and all anxieties have their origins in pain; and there is nothing else that, by its very nature, can so disturb or trouble us.

42. "The commencement of desire, the avoidance of unpleasant things, and all other actions begin from a starting-point of either physical pleasure or pain. Since this is so, it can clearly be seen that everything morally right and praiseworthy should help a person to live a life of pleasure. What the Greeks call *telos*[65] is the

---

[65] The word *telos* (τέλος) signifies an end, goal, or purpose, and is the root of the word *teleology* (the study of purposiveness).

supreme, the ultimate, and the final Good. *Telos* is not a means to anything higher than itself, but rather is the 'end' to which everything else is a means. One must admit, therefore, that the Highest Good is to live happily.

XIII. "Those who assign the Highest Good to 'virtue'—and who become entranced by the splendor of this word—do not understand what nature ordains for us. If they wish to listen to Epicurus, they will be liberated from a great mistake. Indeed, who would think these extraordinary and noble virtues of yours either praiseworthy or enticing, unless they generated pleasure? We hold medical knowledge in high regard not because of the details of this science, but because it produces good health; the art of maritime navigation is praised not for its abstract artistry, but because it is valuable in steering a ship. In the same way, wisdom—which should be thought of as the 'art of living'— would not be desired if it produced nothing of value. But in fact wisdom *is* sought after. For it is, in a way, the artisan that gathers up and constructs pleasure.

43. "So now you see what it is that I consider 'pleasure,' unless my explanation has been undermined by your negative reaction to some of my words. Since the life of man is very much thrown into confusion by the lack of awareness of what is good and what is evil, Wisdom must be summoned to help us strip away our crippling fears and destructive lusts, and to assist us in tearing down all our false, rashly-considered opinions. Wisdom will serve as our most trustworthy guide to realizing true pleasure. Wisdom is the one thing that can drive out the gloom from our souls, and keep us from shuddering in the presence of anxiety. One can live with peace of mind with her as a teacher, since the flames of all destructive passions will have been extinguished. Our lusts are insatiable; they destabilize not only individual men but entire households, and can even subvert the foundations of society.

Inside the Cave of the Sibyl at Cumae

A group of schoolchildren on a tour of the Sibyl's Cave

44. "Hatred, discord, conflict, sedition, and war all come about as a result of unchecked desires. Not only do they upset order everywhere, and lunge against others in blind attacks, but they even jostle and wrestle with each other when secreted within our own souls. A miserable life is the inescapable result of this dynamic. The wise man—once he has excised and clipped away all vain foolishness and error—can live in peace, without suffering and without fear, within the bounds set by Nature.

45. "Is there anything more helpful or practical for good living than the classification system that Epicurus made regarding the desires? The first category of the desires was composed of those seen as 'natural and necessary'; the second was 'natural but not necessary'; and the third was 'not natural and not necessary.' The underlying rationale of this system is that the necessary desires are satisfied with little effort or cost. The natural desires also do not require much effort, since the riches that Nature herself has—and which are enough to satisfy her—are readily obtainable and limited in quantity. But no boundary or limit can be found with regard to foolish desires.[66]

XIV. 46. "But if we appreciate that all life is thrown into confusion by error and ignorance, and that wisdom is the only thing protecting us from the fury of our lusts and the dread caused by our fears, teaching us to tolerate the injustices of fortune with restraint, and showing all of us the right paths that lead to peace of mind and tranquility, then why should we hesitate to say that wisdom must be our goal because of the pleasures that come with it, and that frivolity should be avoided because of the sufferings that come in its wake?

47. "For the same reason we might say that temperance should not be desired for its own sake, but because it brings peace of

---

[66] The phrase used is *inanium cupiditatum*, meaning empty, hollow, or vain desires. The intention is to draw a contrast with the "natural" desires in the preceding sentence.

mind, soothing and satisfying people with a sense of well-being. Temperance is what advises us to follow the guidance of reason with regard to things we either desire or dislike. It is not enough to decide what must, or what must not, be done: one must stand firm on what has been decided. Many men, however, cannot keep or abide by what they decide. Defeated and impaired, and dominated by their passions, they surrender themselves to the alluring enticements of pleasure, and cannot appreciate the consequences that will follow. And so for the sake of some small and unnecessary pleasure that could be obtained in some other way—or that could have been rejected without discomfort—some people risk serious disease, financial ruin, or disgrace, often even being subjected to punishment by the courts and laws.

48. "However, those who wish to enjoy pleasures in a way such that no negative outcomes result from them, and who maintain their proper judgment to a degree that they are not controlled by lust and do what they know in their hearts should not be done, in fact receive the highest pleasure by not indulging in pleasure. By the same token they will often endure significant pain, if by dodging such pain they will later suffer even more. From this reasoning it is clear that intemperance should not be shunned simply for its own sake; and temperance should be a goal not because it swears off pleasures, but because greater pleasures will come as a result of practicing it.

XV. 49. "The justification for Fortitude will be found in the same way. Neither carrying out one's duties nor shouldering hardships are glamorous in themselves; nor are patience, constant attention, vigilance, nor the oft-praised trait, diligence, nor even courage. But we subscribe to these virtues in order to live without anxiety and fear, and so that we may release our minds and bodies—as much as possible—from perturbation. The tranquility of a peaceful life is upset by the constant fear of death; it is miserable to collapse under the weight of sorrows and bear them with a prostrate and broken spirit. As a result of this feebleness of soul, many men have dragged their parents, friends, and finally their countries to disaster; many have even destroyed themselves.

"Thus a robust and noble soul is altogether free from anxiety and mental distress. This kind of spirit scoffs at death; for those who are in the state of death are only as they were before they were born. Such a spirit[67] is prepared to deal with sorrows by remembering that the greatest sufferings are ended by death, that the small sufferings are separated by many periods of quiet intermission, and that we ourselves can control the sorrows of medium intensity. And if they are tolerable, we can bear them. If they are not, we may depart this life with a contented mind if we find that the theater no longer pleases us. One may conclude from all this that timidity and faintheartedness are not to be condemned, and courage and patience are not to be praised, simply as abstractions in themselves; the former are scorned because they produce pain, and the latter are sought after because they generate pleasure.[68]

XVI. 50. "In order for us to cover all the virtues, we must still speak of Justice. Regarding this virtue, we may state similar arguments that have already been advanced. I have demonstrated that wisdom, temperance, and courage to be so associated with pleasure that in no way can they be alienated or divorced from it: and the same conclusion must be reached with regard to Justice. Not only does it not harm anyone, but in fact it always contributes something with its own special power and quality that calms the human spirit; it also provides us hope that none of the elements needed for a properly-functioning Nature will be deficient.[69]

---

[67] I.e., the robust and noble spirit mentioned in the preceding two sentences.
[68] The balance and elegance of Cicero's periods is illustrated by this sentence, which reads: *Quibus rebus intellegitur nec timiditatem ignaviamque vituperari nec fortitudinem patientiamque laudari suo nomine, sed illas reici quia dolorem pariant, has optari quia voluptatem.*
[69] I.e., justice gives us hope that it will supply the special qualities needed for Nature to function properly and harmoniously.

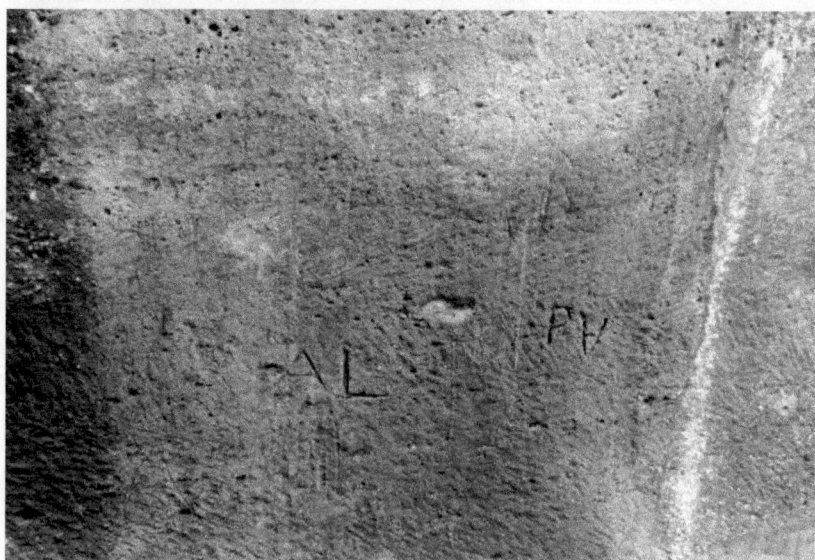

Ancient markings on the walls of the Sibyl's Cave

"In the same way that timidity, lust, and cowardice always torment the mind and provoke violent storms, so wickedness,[70] if it embeds itself in the mind, is a cause of instability by its very presence there. And if a man carries out some evil deed—however covertly it may have been done—he can never be entirely certain that the act will remain hidden. In most cases the first thing that follows evil deeds is suspicion; next come rumors and whisperings; then an accuser, and finally a judge. Many men even betray themselves, just as happened when you were consul.

51. "And even if men consider themselves adequately insulated and protected from public scrutiny, they still live in fear of the watchful eyes of the gods. They believe that these same anxieties—which eat away at their souls day and night—have been sent to them by the immortal gods as a form of retribution. But how much actual help can we expect to get from evil deeds in reducing the amount of problems in our lives, once we really consider (taking into account the psychological burden of a guilty conscience, the legal punishment incurred, and the scorn of our peers) just how much wicked deeds *actually increase* our problems? Nevertheless, for some men there is no restraint in their pursuit of money, glory, power, sexual pleasure, food, or other desires. Immorally acquired gains do not diminish the appetite for such things, but rather stoke the appetite's fires even more, until finally they are more in need of physical confinement than reeducation.

52. "Quite rightly, therefore, true reason draws healthy men to righteousness, equity, and honesty. Unjust behavior is not profitable for a man who is inarticulate or lacking in resources; he cannot easily accomplish what he aspires to do, nor realize his ambitions even if he does complete his plans. Yet a generous disposition is more appropriate for those who are wealthy or

---

[70] *Improbitas.*

fortunate. Those who practice benevolence win a reserve of goodwill (which is the very best thing for living a peaceful life), especially since there is no reason for committing a moral offense.[71]

53. "Those desires that originate from nature are easily satisfied without injury to any other person. One should not, however, yield to the vain desires, as these lead to nothing that is worth pining after. There is more harm in injustice itself than there is any benefit coming from the products of injustice. Therefore one cannot truly say that justice should be desired for its own sake: it is desirable *because it brings about the greatest amount of happiness*. To be held in high regard and to be loved is deeply satisfying, because these conditions create a life that is safer and more filled with pleasure. Thus we believe that dishonesty should be avoided not only because of the inconveniences that come from being dishonest, but far more because unscrupulousness, when it entwines itself around a man's soul, never allows him any relaxation or mental peace.

54. "But even if the praise of these same virtues—which the eloquence of other philosophers harps on so often—cannot find any ultimate purpose unless it is based on pleasure, the fact remains that pleasure is the only thing that calls out to us directly and attracts us by its own nature. It cannot be denied that pleasure is the highest and ultimate of all Goods; to live happily is nothing else but to live with pleasure.

XVII. 55. "I will briefly elaborate on the reliable and well-established ideas that have been related just now. There is no inherent pitfall to be found in the 'ends of goods and evils'

---

[71] Meaning that the wealthy can win the affection of others by being benevolent and generous with their resources. And because they have money and can satisfy all of life's necessities, they have no excuse for committing moral offenses.

themselves (i.e., in pleasure or in pain): rather, people commit moral offenses here when they are unaware how each of these conditions[72] is produced. In addition, we submit that pleasures and pains of the mind arise from the pleasures and pains of the body. I agree with your statement that anyone from our school[73] who argues otherwise discredits himself. I know that many do, but they are not respected thinkers. Yet although mental pleasure brings us satisfaction and mental pain brings us troubles, both of these conditions arise from—and refer back to—the physical body. For this reason it is possible for the pleasures and pains experienced by the mind to be more profound than those of the body.

"Our bodies can perceive only what is learned through the senses and exists at that time; the mind, however, perceives both past and future. Since we can suffer mentally to the same extent that we suffer bodily, a great increase in suffering can come about if we imagine some perpetual and limitless evil to be hanging over our heads. One may transpose the same reasoning when talking about pleasure: our pleasure will be all the greater if we are not gripped by fear of some impending evil.

56. "It clearly follows from this that great *mental* pleasure or pain has more influence in determining whether a life is happy or miserable, than an equally intense amount of *bodily* pleasure or pain. But it does not follow that when pleasure is taken away, anxiety at once returns (unless suffering comes in to replace the pleasure). On the other hand, we rejoice in the cessation of pain, even though no sense-stimulating pleasure comes in to replace the pain. One can understand from this just how much pleasure it is simply to be without pain.

57. "Just as we are excited by the good things that we

---

[72] Pleasure and pain.
[73] I.e., an Epicurean.

anticipate, so we also derive satisfaction in recalling them from memory. Stupid people are tormented by dwelling on the wrongs of the past; wise men take pleasure in past goods revived in a grateful memory. Yet we have it within us to expunge to near permanent oblivion the memories of bad experiences, and to remember sweetly and poignantly our good fortunes.[74] But if we examine the events of the past with a sharp and attentive eye, we see that melancholy accompanies those events that are bad, and happiness comes with those that are good.

XVIII. "What a noble and brilliant way of living—open, uncomplicated, and direct! For without doubt nothing can be better for a man than to be liberated from all anguish and trouble, and to enjoy to the fullest extent the pleasures of the mind and body. Can't you see how this system overlooks nothing that helps to create a good life, in that it more readily assists us in reaching our goal, namely, the Highest Good? Epicurus—the man whom you claim was too fixated on chasing physical pleasure—proudly declares that life cannot be lived agreeably unless it is lived wisely, decently, and justly, and that it cannot be lived wisely, decently, and justly unless it is lived agreeably.[75]

58. "Indeed a nation plagued by internal strife cannot be successful, and neither can a house whose masters are in conflict: much less can a mind at variance with itself and pulled in different directions enjoy any bit of pure and unadulterated pleasure. He who is preoccupied with disputes, contradictory plans, and desires can know neither rest nor tranquility.

59. "And if the enjoyment of life is hindered by serious

---

[74] A sentence with artful alliteration: *Est autem situm in nobis ut et adversa quasi perpetua oblivione obruamus et secunda iucunde ac suaviter meminerimus.*

[75] Another brilliant sentence that loses some elegance in translation: *Clamat Epicurus, is quem vos nimis voluptatibus esse deditum dicitis, non posse iucunde vivi nisi sapienter, honeste iusteque vivatur, nec sapienter, honeste, iuste nisi iucunde.*

afflictions of the body, how much more must it be affected by sicknesses of the mind! Yet unrestrained and vain cravings for riches, glory, power, and sensual pleasures are infections of the mind. On top of this are sorrows, agonies, and feelings of loss, all of which drain the human spirit and contribute to the anxiety of those who do not realize that the only things that should trouble the mind are those things linked to current or future bodily pain. Every fool is stricken with one of these diseases; therefore, every fool is unhappy.[76]

60. "Death is also present; it hovers over us like the Stone of Tantalus.[77] Then there is religious superstition, which never permits anyone imbued with it to enjoy emotional calm. In addition, they do not remember their past good fortunes or find any pleasure in the present moment: they cast their eyes forward to the future, and because what the future holds is uncertain, they are harried by stress and fear. They especially come to grief when—too late—they realize that they have chased in vain after money, power, wealth, or glory. They never live to see any of these pleasures, the anticipation of which had motivated them to take up their great labors in the first place.

---

[76] Literally, "There is no fool who is not stricken with one of these diseases; therefore there is no fool who is not unhappy." *Nec vero quisquam stultus non horum morborum aliquot laborat; nemo igitur stultus non miser.* Since the Latin double negative can be awkward in English, I opted for a more positive rendering of this sentence. Paradox IV of Cicero's *Stoic Paradoxes* repeats the important idea of the fool being of "unsound mind." See my *Stoic Paradoxes*, Charleston: Fortress of the Mind Publications (2015), p. 60.

[77] The myth of Tantalus describes the cruel fate that he was forced to endure in Tartarus. *See* Odyssey, XI.582—592 and Plato's *Cratylus* 395e. Tantalus was made to stand in a pool of water while never being able to grasp the fruit that was suspended just beyond his reach. A variation of the myth has a stone suspended threateningly over his head. For an interesting discussion of the allegorical meanings of this legend, see Scodel, R., "Tantalus and Anaxagoras," *Harvard Studies in Classical Philology,* Vol. 88 (1984), pp. 13-24.

Scenes along the Amalfi Coast

61. "Take a look at all the mean and narrow-minded, or all the congenitally negative and disaffected, the hateful, the troublesome, the secretive, the slanderous, or those dogged by bad luck. Consider also those caught up in the frivolities of sexual adventure. Consider still others who are insolent, reckless, violent, or those lacking self-control or who are cowardly, or those unable to hold a coherent line of thought. The consequence of these personal flaws is that such people never enjoy any break from their troubles. Therefore no fool can be happy, and no wise man can be unhappy. We arrive at this conclusion in a much more logical way than do the Stoics. For the Stoics deny that there is anything good except for that ambiguous illusion they call 'moral goodness,'[78] a concept that is not as solid as it is luminous in name. They say that virtue based on 'moral goodness' does not require pleasure; and that to live a happy life, virtue *alone* should be practiced.[79]

XIX. 62. "Yet these Stoic ideas can be phrased in a way that is not incompatible with our own Epicurean doctrine: that is, in a way that we endorse. In this way does Epicurus describe his ideal 'wise man' who is always happy: his desires have fixed limits; he does not worry about death; he fearlessly perceives the truth about the immortal gods;[80] and he does not doubt that he has the right to leave this mortal life if such a decision were logical. Outfitted in this way, the wise man is always in a state of pleasure. There is no time in which he is not experiencing more pleasure than pain.

"He recalls the past with grateful memories, and experiences the present in a way that is fully aware of the amount of delight he derives from it. He does not pin his hopes on the future, but

----

[78] *Honestum.*

[79] I.e., the wise man can live happily with virtue alone, and does not need any "pleasure."

[80] *De dis immortalibus sine ullo metu vera sentit.* Since the Epicureans were atomist materialists, the speaker is implying that the wise man should be unafraid to admit that the gods do not exist.

calmly awaits it while enjoying the present moment. He is entirely free of all the personal vices which were listed a bit earlier; and when he compares his life with the lives of fools, he feels a certain satisfaction. And if he does happen to encounter personal sufferings, they will never gain such power over him that he thinks more about what vexes him than about what gives him reasons for rejoicing.

63. "Indeed Epicurus spoke well when he stated that 'Fortune does not decisively affect the life of the wise man; life's most serious and important issues are decided by his own deliberation and prudence. No greater pleasure can be gained from a life of infinite length than the satisfaction gained from this life that we know will have an end.' Epicurus did not believe there was anything in your system of logic that was either relevant to the pursuit of a better life, or that could act as a guide in philosophical exposition. He placed great importance on natural philosophy.[81] This natural science can reveal for us the definitions of words, the nature of logical speech, and the laws of deduction and contradiction.[82]

"We are lifted out of superstition by an awareness of the natural world's operative principles. We are liberated from the fear of death. We are not disturbed by our ignorance, from which can arise terrible feelings of dread. Finally, we become endowed with a better character once we learn what Nature truly desires. If we take hold of reliable scientific knowledge—protecting this inheritance as if it were something almost sent down to us from heaven as a basic principle of human cognition, and something on which all our judgments are based—we will outlast the eloquence of any man, and never abandon our inner convictions.

64. "However, unless the inner workings of nature have been closely studied, we will not be able to trust the judgments of our

----

[81] Meaning the natural sciences, or "physics."
[82] This sentence is referring to the study of dialectic.

senses. For everything that we perceive with our minds first begins with sense-perception. So if all the sensations are true—as Epicurus's reasoning tells us—then knowledge will ultimately be able to be perceived and known.[83] Those who discard the actions of the senses (and say that nothing can be perceived) are unable—after taking sense-perception out of the analysis—to offer a coherent doctrine of their own. In addition, once rational thought and knowledge are taken away, every conception of productive human life and achievement is thereby removed. Thus from natural science we draw *courage* to face the fear of death, *steadfastness* to deal with the intimidating aspects of religion, *peace of mind* for removing our ignorance of the hidden mysteries of the world, and *moderation* for revealing the nature of our desires and explaining their differing types. And as I have just explained, the basic principle of the cognitive process (as well as the framework Epicurus set up to evaluate it) provides a way of distinguishing what is true from what is not true.

XX. 65. "We must still address a remaining subject that is very much relevant to our discussion: the topic of friendship. If pleasure truly is the highest good, you suggest that friendship will become entirely irrelevant. But in fact on this issue Epicurus tells us that of all the things that wisdom provides us for good living, nothing is greater, more productive, or more agreeable than friendship. He preached this doctrine not just with words alone, but through the example set by his life, his deeds, and his behavior. The legendary stories of ancient times remind us how great friendship truly is.

"As numerous and diverse as these stories are, if you survey them from the earliest recorded periods, you will hardly run across

---

[83] I.e., we cannot know something for certain unless the bodily sense-perceptions are working properly (i.e., "true").

three pairs of friends as you go from Theseus[84] to Orestes.[85] Yet Epicurus alone in his house (which was certainly a very simple one) had an entire circle of friends, bound together in common purpose by a great deal of shared feeling! This kind of thing still happens among the followers of Epicurus. But let us return to the matter at hand; it is not necessary to use examples drawn from specific people.

66. "I believe that the subject of friendship has been analyzed by us[86] in three ways. Some do not believe that the pleasures experienced by our friends should be desired by us as much as we seek our own pleasures.[87] This idea is seen by some as 'weakening' the stability of friendship. But others uphold this doctrine, and (as I see it) argue their case persuasively. Just as the virtues (which we discussed earlier) cannot be separated from pleasure, friendship cannot be separated from it either. Now since a life without friends, or a life of solitude, is filled with fear and potential disaster, reason itself advises us to cultivate friendship. The soul is elevated by the gaining of friends: and it is not possible to separate this from the hope of *gaining pleasure*.

67. "And just as hatred, envy, and contempt block pleasure, so are friendships the most loyal patrons—and even creators—of pleasure for our friends and for ourselves. Friendships provide delight not only in the present, but also stimulate our hopes for the immediate and distant future. For this reason we cannot realize a solid and continuous joy in life without friendship; neither can this same friendship be sustained unless we value our friends to the same degree as we value ourselves. This situation, therefore, occurs in friendship; and thus are friendship and pleasure connected.

---

[84] Semi-mythical founder of Athens.

[85] A member of the doomed house of Atreus, who is a character in the *Electra* plays of Sophocles and Euripides.

[86] I.e., Epicureans.

[87] This is the first of the "three ways" of analyzing friendship.

We take pleasure in our friends' happiness as much as we celebrate our own; and we grieve equally at their distress.

68. "For this reason the wise man will feel as emotionally committed to his friend as he is to himself. And just as he undertakes efforts for his own pleasure, he will be willing to do the same for the sake of his friend's pleasure. What was said earlier about the virtues (i.e., how they are always linked to pleasures) must also be said about friendship. Epicurus stated it well with words along these lines: 'This same doctrine—that we should not be afraid of eternal evils or long-lasting evils—is what reminds us that friendship is our most reliable protection in this mortal life.'

69. "However, there are some Epicureans who, despite being sufficiently articulate, are a bit more timid in the face of your carping disapproval.[88] They worry that if we think friendship should be pursued only for the sake of *our own* pleasure, then friendship will appear to be completely defective. They say the first encounters and associations—and the normal goodwill of established custom—happen because of our desire for pleasure. But when the progress of the relationship promotes familiarity, then a certain amount of affection is kindled, so that these same friends are loved for their own sake even if nothing advantageous to us results from the friendship. Indeed, if we are in the habit of falling in love—through familiarity—with locations, temples, cities, gymnasia, sporting grounds, dogs, horses, staged bouts and animal fights,[89] then think how much more easily and naturally this same thing can happen in our regular dealings with other men!

70. "Finally, there are those who say there exists a personal covenant among wise men that they should love their friends just

---

[88] This is the second of the "three ways" of analyzing friendship (see section 66, above).

[89] *Ludicra exercendi aut venandi* describes gladiatorial combats and publicly-staged animal fights, common amusements in Rome.

as much as they love themselves.[90] We understand that this can happen, and we see it take place often. Clearly nothing can be found that is more conducive to a pleasant life than this kind of mutual affection.

"From all the foregoing arguments, one can conclude not only that the 'rule of friendship' *is not* undermined if we treat pleasure as the highest good, but also that without this arrangement the institution of friendship *cannot exist at all*.

XXI. 71. "So if these things I've discussed are more bright and lucid than sunlight itself, if everything has been imbibed from the bubbling spring of Nature, if our entire discussion reinforces our full faith in the senses (which are sound and reliable witnesses), and if even inarticulate children or mute animals— instructed and guided by Nature—practically tell us that nothing promotes well-being except pleasure and nothing generates trouble except pain (and they evaluate these things neither wrongly nor corruptly), then should we not feel the utmost gratitude to the man[91] who heard this voice of Nature and comprehended it so thoroughly and so deeply that he was able to guide all healthy men on the path to a life of peace, repose, calmness, and tranquility? You consider him to be a man of meager education. The reason for this is that he believed nothing could be called 'education' unless it actually helped in teaching us how to live a happy life.

72. "Should he have frittered away his time (as you encourage Triarius and I to do) with the verses of poets, in which there is nothing of any practical use, and everything is immature entertainment? Or should he (like Plato) have played around with music, geometry, numerology, and planetary science, which cannot be true since they begin with false premises? And even if these things were true, they would add nothing to make life more congenial (that is, better). Should he, then, have pursued these arts

---

[90] This is the third of the three ways of seeing friendship (see section 66).
[91] Referring to Epicurus.

and neglected the all-important art of living, which is so difficult and at the same time so useful? So Epicurus was not uneducated: the real uneducated people are those who think a man should study, until his senility, those subjects that he should be ashamed not to have learned as a youth."

"In this discussion," he stated in closing, "I have laid out my opinions in order to hear your own views in response. Before this time I have never been given the chance to evaluate them for myself."

COMMENTARY ON BOOK I

The first book of *De Finibus* sets the tone of the whole. The beginning sections of Book I are extremely important from a literary perspective. As we have already noted in the Introduction, Cicero took the revolutionary position that Latin was, or could be, a perfectly adequate language of philosophy. He believed that it was a worthy goal for him to make Greek philosophy accessible to the average Roman. Always the patriot, he makes sure we do not mistake him for the contemptible Roman "Greekling" (I.9) who was too ready to adopt foreign ways. In I.11 and I.12, Cicero announces his purpose of examining the "End of Goods" through differing philosophical perspectives. I.14 places the location of the dialogue at Cumae; it is unfortunate that he does not spend much time describing the locale with the same charm and vividness as he does Athens in Book V.

With these preliminaries addressed, Cicero launches into his criticisms of Epicurean philosophy starting at I.17. He has a dismissive attitude of the atomic theories that Epicurus adopted from Democritus; but it is clear that Cicero lacks the scientific sensitivity that would enable him to appreciate these theories. Whatever one may say about Epicureanism's ethics, it cannot be denied that its physics was a triumph of scientific deduction from intense natural observation. One cannot read Lucretius without marveling at the sophistication of his scientific ideas, with his atoms swerving through the void at various degrees of *inclinatio* and *declinatio*. All this is lost on Cicero; he gives Epicurus no credit for this achievement whatsoever. His criticisms here are carping and uninformed, and do not show him at his best. In I.23 through I.26 he attacks Epicurus's hedonism and contempt for scholarship.

Beginning at I.28, Torquatus, having been forced to listen to Cicero savage the ideas and reputation of his master, finally gets his chance to respond. He decides to limit himself to ethics, and bluntly states that pleasure is indeed the Ultimate Good. As evidence, he cites the fact that all living beings seek to maximize pleasure and minimize pain. But pleasure should not be interpreted to mean voluptuary bliss: Epicurus thought of it as the removal of pain (I.37). In I.40 and I.41, Torquatus gives several examples in an attempt to prove that pleasure is the Supreme Good. We should not think of the virtues as ends in themselves, he says, but instead as a way to achieve pleasure (i.e., avoid pain). Where people go wrong is that they are unable to tell what things generate pleasure, and what things cause pain (I.55). The best way for the wise man to conduct himself is to keep his passions in check; in this way he can stay out of pain's way (I.62).

In I.65, Torquatus takes an unexpected detour into the topic of friendship. This is a welcome diversion from the increasingly negative flavor of Epicurus's ideas. We are relieved to learn of Epicurus's positive views of friendship, and of the central importance he gave to it. These warm passages on friendship are perhaps the best arguments in favor of Epicurus's philosophy that Torquatus makes in Book I. In I.71, Torquatus brings his discourse to an end with a passionate plea in his master's favor, emphasizing Epicurus's focus on the things that truly mattered to humanity, rather than the things that did not matter. It is not that Epicurus was uneducated, he chides Cicero; it is just that he refused to waste his time in idle pursuits.

BOOK II

Book II

I. 1. At this point they both looked at me and showed they were prepared to listen. "First," I said, "I ask you not to regard me as some kind of trained philosopher who is about to deliver a prepared talk on some approved subject, because I never really liked that sort of thing even with the professionals. When did Socrates—who can rightly be called the father of philosophy— ever do such a thing? Rather, this was the practice of those who were called 'Sophists.' Gorgias of Leontini[92] was the first of the

---

[92] Gorgias of Leontini (483 B.C.—375 B.C.), considered one of the founders of Sophism. The Sophists were itinerant teachers who taught rhetoric and argumentation as tools for philosophical inquiry.

Sophists who dared to 'pose a question' in an assembly; that is, to ask anyone to state what he wished to hear debated. It is an audacious tactic, to be sure. Had this technique not been taken up by the philosophers of our own school, I might even call it impudent.

2. "But we know that Socrates laughed at the Sophist named above[93] and others of his school, as one can learn from Plato's dialogues. By using inquiries and pointed questions, Socrates was in the habit of coaxing out his students' opinions, so that he—capitalizing on their responses—might then reveal what he himself believed. This pedagogic method was discontinued by the instructors who came after him. Arcesilaus[94] brought it back; he established a rule that those who wanted to hear his views should not ask him questions, but should state what they themselves believed. Once they had first offered their opinions, he would then try to refute them. Arcesilaus's listeners defended their viewpoints as best they could; with other philosophers, however, someone who poses a question is then silent. Indeed, this is the way things are done now in the Platonic Academy. A student might say, 'I believe that pleasure is the Highest Good,' and then the opposite idea is argued in a structured rebuttal. With this technique, one can easily see that those who say they 'believe' something do not actually believe it, but simply wish to hear the contrary viewpoint.

3. "We will do things more reasonably here. Torquatus has not only said what he believes, but he has also explained why. But although I appreciated his detailed exposition very much, I still think it is more suitable to stop at individual points, in order to

---

[93] Gorgias.

[94] Arcesilaus (c. 316 B.C.—c. 241 B.C.), a head of the Platonic Academy in Athens and traditionally considered the founder of Academic skepticism. The central tenet of skepticism was that nothing could be known with certainty; the limits of human knowledge were represented by probabilities.

understand what each person concedes or denies; from such admissions, one may make the necessary deductions, and finally arrive at an appropriate conclusion. When the discourse gushes forth like a torrent, many subtle points are washed away. You hold on to nothing, and you grasp nothing; nowhere can you curb the speed of the onrushing rhetoric. All philosophical inquiry that has a method and a reason first ought to command that the analysis begin with this formula: *'the topic is as follows.'*[95] This is so that the persons involved in the discussion may know what they are supposed to be discussing.

II. 4. "Plato set up this rule in his dialogue *Phaedrus*.[96] Epicurus endorsed it and believed it ought to be the rule in every debate. But he did not anticipate what the consequence of this would be. He says he does not want to define the topic under consideration, yet without doing this it is often impossible for the participants to concur on what the subject of the debate is—just as is happening in the subject we are now debating. We are searching for the Ultimate Good. But unless we confer among ourselves about the precise meanings of the terms 'Ultimate' and 'Good,' can we really know what we are trying to say when we use the phrase 'Ultimate Good'?

"This practice of exposing something nearly concealed— where we discover what something really is—is what we call 'definition.' Here and there you made use of this principle without realizing it. For you defined the concept of Ultimate Good (or final or ultimate end) to be (1) that transcendent thing to which all good deeds ultimately 'lead,' and (2) the thing that does not 'lead'

---

[95] The phrase used is *ea res agetur*. The verb *disserere* is artfully employed in the clause that follows: *ut inter quos disseritur conveniat quid sit id de quo disseratur*.

[96] This is found in *Phaedrus* 237B.

to anything higher than itself.[97] This certainly makes sense. If needed, you might perhaps have defined 'Good' itself as 'that which we seek by nature' or 'that which is advantageous' or 'that which gratifies us' or 'that which we find agreeable.' Since you do not really have a problem with defining concepts—and in fact you do it when you want—I would like you to define 'pleasure,' the topic that is central to our discourse here, unless this presents a problem for you."

6. "Who, I would like to know, does not understand what pleasure is?" he retorted. "And who needs some formal definition so that he appreciates it more?"

"I can say," I answered, "that I was just such a man, unless I consider myself to have a firm grasp of what pleasure is, and a solid enough comprehension and perception of it. I say that Epicurus himself does not know the definition of pleasure, but instead vacillates about it. He says constantly that we must be scrupulous about disclosing the meanings of the terms we use. But sometimes he does not appreciate the true significance of the term 'pleasure'; that is, the true condition that is represented by this word.

III. At this Torquatus laughed, saying, "Isn't that amazing! Who would have guessed that the very man who told the world that pleasure was the goal of all things worth striving for (the final and Ultimate Good) did not himself even know what pleasure was!"

"Either Epicurus does not know what pleasure is," I shot back, "or every human being—wherever he may be—does not know."

"How can you say that?" he demanded.

---

[97] I.e., the Ultimate Good (or the "End of Goods") is the transcendent thing that all goods "refer back" or "lead" to. The Ultimate Good is the "final end" in the sense that all goods are *a means to arrive at it*. At the same time, it is not a means to achieve anything higher than itself, because by definition nothing can be higher than it.

97

"Because everyone thinks that pleasure, when it is kindled, activates the body's sensory system; our senses are then permeated with a certain agreeable feeling."

7. "So what are you trying to say?" he responded. "Is Epicurus not familiar with the kind of pleasure you're talking about?"

"Not always," I told him. "Sometimes he is very aware of it, of course. He seriously asserts that he doesn't know if any 'good' exists—or where it might be found—outside of the 'good' found in food and drink, the pleasure gained from the sense of hearing, or the primitive kinds of bodily satisfactions.[98] Or were these not the words he used?"

"As if such a statement might shame me, or as if I could not show the context in which these words of Epicurus were used!" he scolded.

"Of course I have no doubt you could easily do this," I answered. "You should not be ashamed of agreeing with a 'wise man' who is the only person—as far as I know—to have dared call himself a wise man. I don't think Metrodorus professed to be a wise man; but when he was called one by Epicurus, he was unwilling to repudiate the label. The Seven Wise Men[99] were not so named by themselves, but had this honor bestowed on them by the grateful judgment of the people.

---

[98] *Obscena voluptate*, meaning sexual pleasures.

[99] The Seven Wise Men (or Seven Sages) was a name given in antiquity to a group of acclaimed philosophers and statesmen before Plato. *See* Plato's *Protagoras* 343A. There was wide dispute in antiquity about the size of the list and what names should be included on it, with different writers all advancing their own preferences. *See* Diogenes Laertius I.40. *Protagoras* (342E) gives the "seven" as Thales of Miletus, Pittacus of Mytilene, Bias of Priene, Solon, Cleobulus of Lindus, Myson of Chenae, and Chilon of Sparta.

8. "At this point I definitely take it that Epicurus, when using these words,[100] believed in the same significance of 'pleasure' that other people did. Everyone uses the Latin word *voluptas*, and the Greek word ἡδονή,[101] to mean a pleasant emotional arousal in which the senses are brightened."

"Then what more do you need beyond this?" he asked.

"I will tell you," I said, "but I will do it more for the sake of acquiring knowledge than because I want to put you or Epicurus in a bad light."

"I also would much more like to learn what you have to say, than disparage your ideas," he responded.

"Then do you recall," I asked, "what Hieronymus of Rhodes[102] said was the Ultimate Good, the thing he believed everything else should relate back to?"

He answered, "I recall that he viewed the Ultimate End as the absence of pain."

"And what did this philosopher think about pleasure?" I queried.

9. "He does not believe pleasure should be sought for its own sake," he replied.

"So then he thinks that experiencing pleasure is different from not experiencing pain?"

"Absolutely," he affirmed. "Yet here he seriously erred. As I have just explained, the outer limit of the increase of pleasure is the removal of all pain."

"I will take a look very shortly at the meaning of the phrase 'not to suffer.' But unless you are extremely stubborn, it is

---

[100] Referring to the preceding section (7), in which Epicurus is alleged to be unsure if "good" exists outside of eating, drinking, pleasant sounds, and sensual pleasures.

[101] This word is transliterated in English as *hedone*.

[102] Hieronymus of Rhodes (fl. 240 B.C.), a Peripatetic philosopher mentioned in Diogenes Laertius IV.41 and V.68.

important you concede that the terms 'pleasure' and 'absence of suffering' have two different meanings."

"You will find out that I am indeed stubborn on this issue," he insisted. "For nothing more true could be said."

"Let me ask you this: is there any pleasure in drinking for someone who is thirsty?"

"Who could deny that?" he countered.

"And is this pleasure the same pleasure as having a quenched thirst?"

"No, it is of a different type. A thirst that is already quenched is a 'static pleasure,' but the pleasure of actually doing the quenching is a 'dynamic pleasure.'"[103]

"Then why," I asked, "do you call two different things by the same name?"

10. "Do you remember what I said just a little while ago? That when all pain has been taken away, pleasure may change according to circumstance,[104] but cannot be augmented?"

"Of course I remember that," I replied. "You said the words in grammatically correct Latin, but your meaning was not very clear. 'Variation'[105] is of course a Latin word. Strictly speaking, the word is used to describe different colors, but in practice it may often be found in a wide range of contexts: for example, a varied

---

[103] The difference is subtle. The speaker is drawing a distinction between two pleasures: (1) the kind of pleasure that a person would have from not having any thirst; that is, a pleasure that comes from an absence of thirst; and (2) the kind of pleasure that a person would get during the physical act of drinking. The first kind of pleasure is a "stable" or "static" (*voluptas in stabilitate*) pleasure; the second is a "kinetic" or "dynamic" (*voluptas in motu*) pleasure derived from some active movement.

[104] The phrase "change according to circumstance" is how I have translated *variare*. This will be relevant in the lines that follow when the meaning of the word *varietas* is discussed.

[105] *Varietas*.

poem, a varied speech, varied habits, and variable fortune. Pleasure may also be said to be 'varied,' when it is received from many different sources all producing different pleasurable sensations. If you are talking about this type of 'variation,' then I understand it, just as I understand it without your explaining the word. But I don't really understand the 'variation' you are talking about when you say 'we are in the highest state of pleasure when we are completely devoid of pain.' I don't understand your point that when we are enjoying things that cause a delightful arousal of the senses, then we are experiencing 'dynamic pleasure' that produces a 'variation' of pleasurable stimuli *but no rise in the level of the other pleasure* that comes about from a lack of pain. I simply don't know why you call this 'pleasure.'"

IV. 11. "But is it possible," he asked me, "to experience anything more gratifying than an absence of pain?"

"Certainly there may be nothing better—although I don't want to probe into this issue yet. Yet is this an adequate basis to conclude that what I might call 'freedom from pain'[106] is equivalent to pleasure?"

"They are obviously the same," he replied with assurance. "Freedom from pain is certainly the greatest of pleasures: it is exceeded by no other."

"Given that your conception of the Highest Good," I interjected, "is based completely on 'not suffering,' why do you hesitate to stick with this idea? Why don't you protect and defend it? 12. Why is it necessary to bring Pleasure into a formal gathering of the Virtues, as if you were bringing a prostitute into a group of respectable women? Her name is odious, disreputable, and suspect. You Epicureans commonly say that we don't understand what Epicurus means when he uses the word 'pleasure.' Although I am an easygoing man when debating, whenever this kind of

---

[106] *Indolentia.*

statement reaches my ears (and I do hear it frequently), I usually get annoyed. Do I not understand what the word *hedone* means in Greek, and *voluptas* means in Latin?[107] Which of these two languages do I not know? How is it that I myself do *not know* what pleasure is, yet everyone who calls himself an Epicurean *does know*? Your school makes the case—very convincingly—that someone who wants to be a philosopher does not need to be educated in formal learning. Thus, just as our ancestors persuaded Cincinnatus[108] to abandon the plow and become dictator, so your sect scours every community in its hunt for recruits who may be decent men, but certainly are not learned.

13. "These other people understand what Epicurus is saying, but I don't? To demonstrate that I do know, I will tell you that the word 'pleasure' means the same as his word *hedone*. Often we need to hunt for a Latin word that has the same meaning as a Greek one; but in this case we do not have to search for anything. Except for the word *voluptas*, no word can be found that gives the exact same meaning in Latin as a word might mean in Greek. Every person who knows Latin—no matter where they are— appreciates that this word has two contexts: (1) happiness of the mind, and (2) the arousal of delightful sensations in the body. For example, a character in one of Trabea's plays[109] talks about happiness as being 'enormous pleasure of the mind,' the same

---

[107] The Greek and Latin words for "pleasure," respectively.

[108] Lucius Quinctius Cincinnatus (c. 519 B.C.—430 B.C.), Roman statesman and military commander whose devotion to masculine virtue and public duty became legendary to later generations. He is supposed to have left his farm on request to serve as dictator in a time of crisis, and then to have returned to this modest life once he had done his duty. *See* Livy III.26.

[109] Quintus Trabea (fl. c.120 B.C.), an early Roman playwright about whom almost nothing is known. Only two short fragments of his works survive, both of them preserved in Cicero's *Tusculan Disputations* (IV.15.35 and IV.31.67).

thing that one of Caecilius's[110] characters means when he says he is 'happy with every kind of happiness.' But there is a difference here. 'Pleasure' is said to exist in the mind as well as in the body. According to the Stoics (who define mental pleasure as 'the ecstasy of a mind that unreasonably believes itself to be enjoying a great good'), mental pleasure is a pernicious thing. But 'joy' and 'pleasure' are apparently not used in connection with the body.

14. "However, for everyone who speaks Latin, the meaning assigned to the word pleasure is a condition where enjoyment is felt by something that arouses the senses. If you want, you can apply the term 'enjoy' to the mind. 'To enjoy' is used in connection with both the body and the mind; and from this root we get the word 'enjoyable.' You should know that someone might say, 'I am so full of happiness that nothing makes any sense,'[111] and another person might say, 'At long last, my soul is now on fire.'[112] Between these two examples—where one speaker is expressing happiness and the other is plagued by agonizing sadness—there is an intermediate condition. The speaker of the line

Although our acquaintance with each other is still recent,[113]

is neither overjoyed nor tormented. In the same way, between the person who acquires for his body the most desirable pleasures, and the person who is tortured by the greatest sorrows, there is the person who is free of both extremes.

V. 15. "So do I appear to have an adequate understanding of the meaning of these words, or should I be taught to speak better

---

[110] The playwright Caecilius Statius, mentioned in book one (I.2.4).

[111] The author of this quote is not known.

[112] A line by Caecilius Statius quoted by Cicero in his oration *Pro Caelio* 37.

[113] Terence, *The Self-Tormentor* I.1. This line is supposed to illustrate the speaker's neutral emotional state.

Greek or Latin? And even if it looks as if I do not understand what Epicurus is saying, I still believe I have a very good command of Greek, so that it is in many ways his fault if his statements are not correctly comprehended. This[114] can happen in two ways without blame. One way is if you do it purposefully, like Heraclitus,

> He for whom the surname The Obscure is affixed,
> Because he spoke too obscurely on nature.[115]

Obscurity may also arise from the nature of the subject discussed, rather than from the words themselves; Plato's dialogue *Timaeus*, for example, has an ambiguous aspect to it. As I see it, however, Epicurus is not trying to avoid speaking openly and plainly if he can, nor is he dealing with a complex subject like physics, nor a technical topic like mathematics. He is instead talking about something clear, simple, and already well-publicized. Although you *don't deny* that we know what pleasure is, you do say we *don't understand* what Epicurus is talking about. We can conclude from this, then, that the issue is *not* that we don't understand the definition of the word, *but that Epicurus is using the word in his own special way*. He pays no attention to our definition.

16. "If Epicurus is saying the same thing as Hieronymus (who believes that the Highest Good is to live without troubles), why does he prefer to use the term 'pleasure' instead of 'absence of pain' like Hieronymus does, who certainly knows what he wants

---

[114] I.e., ambiguity or obscurity.

[115] The source of this quote is not known, but it illustrates Heraclitus's reputation. Heraclitus (fl. 504 B.C.), nicknamed "The Dark" or "The Obscure" (ὁ Σκοτεινός) was famous for his ambiguous and apparently contradictory statements. Despite—or perhaps because of—his obscurity, he remains one of the most influential of the pre-Socratic philosophers.

to say? But if Epicurus believes that this Highest Good must be linked to 'dynamic pleasure' (for this delightful kind of pleasure he calls 'dynamic,' and the kind of pleasure that comes from an absence of pain he calls 'static'[116]), what is he trying to tell us? Epicurus cannot persuade someone who truly knows himself— that is, someone who is aware of his own nature and senses—that 'pleasure' and 'freedom from pain' are the same thing. To tear out from our minds our acquired knowledge of deeply-implanted words: this, my friend Torquatus, would be inflicting violence on our senses.

"Who does not understand that the following three sensory states are found in the natural world: (1) being in a state of pleasure; (2) being in a state of pain; and (3) being in the state that I am in now, and I think you are also in, when there is neither pleasure nor pain? Thus he who dines sumptuously is in a state of pleasure, while he who endures torture is in pain. Don't you see that between these two poles is a very large number of people who are neither joyful nor miserable?[117]

17. "Absolutely not," he answered. "I am saying that everyone who is free from pain is in a state of pleasure, in fact the highest form of pleasure."

"Do you think that when a man—who is not himself thirsty— prepares some honeyed wine for someone else, he experiences the same pleasure as the thirsty man who drinks it?"

VI. Here he exclaimed, "Let us bring this questioning to an end, if possible. Anticipating this sort of dialectical sophistry, I had said at the beginning that I preferred a different method of discourse."

---

[116] See II.9 above for the explanation of the difference between "static pleasure" (*voluptas in stabilitate*) and "dynamic pleasure" (*voluptas in motu*).
[117] These last two sentences are from one beautiful period that I cannot resist quoting: *Ut in voluptate sit qui epuletur, in dolore qui torqueatur: tu autem inter haec tantam multitudinem hominum interiectam non vides nec laetantium nec dolentium?* How elegant, balanced, smooth, and Ciceronian!

The abbey at Monte Cassino

View of Mount Vesuvius

"Then would you prefer," I asked him, "to debate rhetorically, rather than through dialectics?"

"As if uninterrupted speech were only appropriate for public speaking, and not also for philosophers!" he joked.

"That is the position held by Zeno the Stoic," I replied firmly. "He used to say that all meaningful speech was divided into two categories, as Aristotle had previously taught: *rhetoric* (which was like the palm of the hand), and *dialectic* (which was like the fist). He said this because rhetoricians use speech in a 'broad'[118] way, and logicians use it in a more 'compact'[119] manner. So I will follow your recommendation and speak, if I can, in a rhetorical manner; but it will be the rhetoric of the philosophers, and not forensic rhetoric.[120] Because forensic rhetoric is used in ways designed to sway public opinion, it sometimes needs to be a bit more coarse.

18. "Since Epicurus looks down on dialectic (which brings together in one place the science of examining things, evaluating their properties, and arguing in an ordered and rational way), he sabotages his own arguments, Torquatus. As I see it, he did not clarify in a systematic way the doctrines that he wanted to teach, as we are doing with the ideas we are discussing now. You[121] consider the Ultimate Good to be pleasure. What 'pleasure' is must be clearly defined, otherwise it is not possible to know what we are looking for. If Epicurus had defined his terms, he would not have gotten into so much trouble. He might have viewed pleasure in the same way as Aristippus (i.e., a condition in which the senses are aroused sweetly and delightfully, which is what

---

[118] *Latius*.

[119] *Compressius*.

[120] Forensic rhetoric (*rhetorice forensis*) was the kind of rhetoric used in jurisprudence and courts of law. The three kind of rhetoric are described by Aristotle in *On Rhetoric* (I.10 *et. seq.*)

[121] I.e., "You Epicureans."

sheep would call pleasure if they could speak). If he wished to use his own words, rather than using the words of

All the Danaans and Mycenaeans,
The manhood of Attica,[122]

and the rest of the Greeks invoked in this metrical line of verse,[123] he might have limited the term 'pleasure' to the condition of having no pain, and denounced Aristippus's conception of pleasure. If he endorsed both kinds of pleasure (as he certainly does), he should have combined both 'absence of pain' with 'pleasure' and made use of two Ultimate Goods.

19. "Many great philosophers have viewed the Ultimate Good as something unified. Aristotle connected the use of virtue with the prosperity of a full life; Callipho[124] linked pleasure with moral goodness; Diodorus[125] added freedom from pain to the same moral goodness. Epicurus might have done the same thing, if he had connected this opinion[126] (which is Hieronymus's) with the old viewpoint of Aristippus. These philosophers disagree among themselves; and for this reason, they each offer their own version of the Ultimate Good. Each of them speaks perfect Greek. Aristippus (who calls pleasure the Ultimate Good) does not consider 'lack of pain' as pleasure; and Hieronymus (who defines the Ultimate Good as 'lack of pain') does not use the word pleasure to

---

[122] The source of this quote is not known. "Danaan" is a Homeric term for "Argive" or Greek.

[123] The word used is *anapaestum* (anapest), a metrical foot used in classical poetry.

[124] Callipho (or Calliphon), a Greek philosopher (apparently of the Peripatetic school) who flourished in the second century B.C.

[125] Diodorus of Tyre (fl. c. 118 B.C.), a Greek philosopher who succeeded Critolaus as head of the Peripatetic school in Athens. Cicero mentions him in *De Oratore* (I.11) and *Tusc. Disp.* (V.30).

[126] I.e., that the Ultimate Good is something unified.

indicate this freedom from pain.[127] Indeed, Hieronymus does not even count pleasure among the things that are worth seeking.

VII. 20. "They are two different things, in case you were thinking it is just a matter of words. It is one thing to be without pain; it is something else to feel pleasure. From these two different things you try not only to design one label (for I could endure that more easily), but even to create one single entity from the two, which in no way can be done. Epicurus endorsed both types of pleasure, and ought to have incorporated both of them into his system. He in fact does this, but does not define the terms separately. When, at different places in his writings, he praises that 'pleasure' which we all call by the same name, he dared to say that he could not conceive of any Good that was disconnected from the kind of 'pleasure' proposed by Aristippus. This is what he says in his entire dissertation on the Ultimate Good. In another book containing his most important ideas in condensed form (where he is said to have composed the oracles of wisdom), he writes certain words that you know very well, Torquatus. Who in the Epicurean school has not memorized their master's *Kuriai Doxai* (i.e., the *Principal Doctrines*),[128] as these core ideas succinctly enunciate the rules for living a good life?

21. "Let me know, then, if I am interpreting the following passage correctly: 'If those things that promote wanton pleasures could free men from the fear of the gods, from fear of death, and from fear of pain, and could teach them to set limits for their

---

[127] Here and in other places, Cicero uses different terms to convey the idea of "absence of pain," e.g., *vacuitas doloris* (lack of pain), *non dolore* (not in pain), *indolentia* (freedom from pain). He worked consistently to expand the boundaries of the Latin language for philosophic discourse.

[128] The *Kuriai Doxai* (Κύριαι Δόξαι), the "Sovran Maxims" or "Principle Doctrines" was a condensation of forty of the master's most important doctrines. It is one of the few pieces of Epicurean literature that has survived and as such is of great value. It is transcribed in Diogenes Laertius X.138 *et. seq.*

desires, then we would have no cause to criticize them. For they would be furnished with pleasures everywhere they turned; and in no way would they ever experience suffering or distress, which are evils.'"[129]

At this point Triarius was unable to hold himself back. He demanded, "I have to ask you, Torquatus...does Epicurus really say this?" I had the impression that he knew this was true, but still wanted to hear Torquatus confirm it.

But Torquatus was not rattled, and replied clearly and confidently. "Those were his words," he said, "but you are not understanding what he meant by them."

"If he meant one thing," I replied, "and said something else, then I'll never know what he was trying to say. But he clearly says what he means. If he is saying that self-indulgent men should not be criticized as long as they are wise men, then he is speaking absurdly. This is like saying that those who kill their own relatives[130] should not be criticized as long as they are not greedy or have no fear of the gods, no fear of death, or no fear of pain. What purpose does it serve to give out some half-baked exemption for self-indulgent people? Why fantasize about other people who are living in excessive luxury, and who are not criticized by the 'wisest philosopher' for this lifestyle as long as they are avoiding other types of bad conduct?

22. "But wouldn't you, Epicurus, still find fault with these hedonists for the simple reason that they spend their lives chasing after all kinds of physical pleasures, when (according to you) the highest form of pleasure is to feel no pain? We will certainly find

---

[129] This quote is found in Diogenes Laertius X.142. *See also* X.35 *et seq.* of Diogenes Laertius (the "Letter to Herodotus") for a detailed description of Epicurean physics.

[130] The word used here is *parricida*, which can mean (1) someone who kills a relative or a leader; (2) a murderer in general; (3) a rebel; or (4) a traitor.

debauchers so profane that they would gulp down food from a *patella*,[131] and so unafraid of death that they are always parroting the following lines from the *Hymnis*:[132]

Six months of life are enough for me;
I promise the seventh to Orcus.

And from the medicine-chest they whip out this Epicurean remedy for pain: 'If it is serious, it is short; if it is light, it is long.' One thing I can't understand: if someone is a hedonist, how does he find limits to his desires?

VIII. 23. "How does it make sense to say, 'I have no cause to blame them if they set limits on their desires'? He could use the same logic to say that he doesn't have a problem with a morally corrupt man, as long as he is a decent person. This ascetic teacher[133] doesn't believe that extravagance *per se* should be condemned. By Hercules, Torquatus! If we are speaking frankly, I say that if pleasure is the Ultimate Good, then he is certainly correct. I definitely don't want to imagine—as you often do—sybarites who vomit at the dinner-table, who are physically carried away from banquets, and who plunge into the same behavior the next day while still disabled. I don't want to think about those who, as they say, have never seen either sunrise or sunset, or those who, having burned through their inheritances, are in dire financial straits. None of us thinks that these kinds of debauchers are leading a congenial life.

"Imagine opulent and highly refined men, with the best cooks, bakers, fish, birds, game meats, and every other exquisite thing;

---

[131] A *patella* was a plate on which were placed food offerings to Roman household gods. *See* Livy XXVI.36.6 and Ovid *Fast*. VI.310. To eat from one would thus be a disrespectful and profane act.

[132] The *Hymnis* was a play by Caecilius Statius.

[133] I.e., Epicurus.

imagine men avoiding indigestion, and for whom (as Lucilius[134] says) 'golden wine is poured from a full vessel, whose straining-bag catches anything offensive'; imagine men who arrange little performances and the things that follow (those things that, if we omit them, Epicurus claims not to know what 'Good' means); imagine handsome boys are present who attend to them; imagine fine garments, silver, Corinthian bronzes, and the dining room matching the sumptuousness of the scene: *I will never say that these hedonists are living happily or living well.*[135]

24. "All of this proves not that pleasure is not pleasure, but that pleasure is not the Ultimate Good. Laelius,[136] who as a young man studied under Diogenes the Stoic and then later under Panaetius, was not called 'the Wise' because he could not tell what foods were the most delicious (for it does not follow that when someone's intellect is powerful, his palate is therefore dumb), but because he did not think it was important.

O sorrel,[137] thrown away, how little are you known for what you are!
Laelius the Wise was in the habit of praising you,
Scolding our gourmands one after the other.

Wonderful, Laelius! How truly wise you are. Consider the truth of these lines:

---

[134] This is the satirist Caius Lucilius referred to in book one (III.7) above.

[135] This long sentence, rich in imagery and dripping with scorn, shows Cicero at his oratorical best. He paints an graphic picture of hedonism that—while not exactly a fair characterization of Epicurus's beliefs—is nevertheless quite effective in turning the reader against Epicurus.

[136] Caius Laelius Sapiens (c. 188 B.C.—?), Roman statesman and friend of Scipio the Younger (Aemilianus). He was a member of the so-called "Scipionic Circle," a group of artists and intellectuals.

[137] Sorrel (*lapathum*) is a perennial herb cultivated as a salad vegetable.

'O Publius Gallonius, O raging abyss, you are a miserable man,' he said.
'You have never eaten well in your life,
Though you spend everything on your prawns
And on gargantuan sturgeon.'

The person talking here places no value on pleasure. He does not think that someone who makes pleasure the focus of his life can ever dine well. He doesn't deny that Gallonius ate with gusto (for this would be false): he denied that he ate *well*. In this way he sharply and clearly separates the concepts of 'pleasure' and 'good.' We may conclude from this that everyone who dines well dines enjoyably, but those who dine enjoyably do not always dine well. Laelius always dined well.

25. "And what is 'well' supposed to mean? Lucilius would answer:

Cooked and flavored.

But if I then offer up the main course,

With good conversation.

And what is the end result?

If you ask, to dine with pleasure.

With a tranquil soul, he came to dinner to satisfy the normal desires of Nature. Therefore he is correct in denying that Gallonius had ever dined well and correct in calling him miserable, especially since all of his attentions were focused on consumption. No one denies that he dined with gusto. Why then not 'well'? Because 'well' means that he ate with propriety, with restraint, and with decency. Gallonius, however, ate corruptly, wickedly, and shamelessly: and for this reason he did not dine well. Laelius did not place the attractiveness of sorrel salad ahead of Gallonius's sturgeon: rather, he ignored gastronomical allure altogether. He would not have been able to do this if he thought pleasure was the Ultimate Good.

IX. 26. "Thus pleasure must be set aside, not only so that you follow the right path in life, but also so that you learn to speak in a civilized way. When all is said and done, can we consider something to be the Ultimate Good for our lives that we do not even consider the Ultimate Good for eating?[138] How does our philosopher respond to this? He says, 'There are three kinds of desires: natural and necessary, natural and not necessary, and neither natural nor necessary.'[139] As a matter of first impression, this division is awkward. There are only two categories of desires, but he makes three. This is not classifying something, but shattering it. Those who have acquired expertise in the subjects that Epicurus hated would put it this way: 'There are two types of desires, *natural* and *vain*.[140] And of the natural desires, there are two: necessary and not necessary.' This would have been a better arrangement. For it is a grave error of classification to treat a sub-category of something as a separate, co-equal category.[141]

27. "Yet we may reasonably grant him this point. He[142] looks down on the artistry involved in formal discussion. He writes fumblingly, but his style must be tolerated provided it expresses his ideas correctly. I can really only tolerate—indeed, I cannot very much respect—a philosopher sermonizing about 'putting limits' on our desires. Is it possible for desire to be demarcated? It must be seized and pulled up by the roots. What man who feels the pangs of desire can be considered 'rightfully desirous'? He

---

[138] I.e., how can pleasure be the Ultimate Good for life when it is not the Ultimate Good with regard to dining?

[139] See I.45.

[140] The word used is *inanis*, which can mean vain, foolish, or empty.

[141] *Vitiosum est enim in dividendo partem in genere numerare.*

[142] Epicurus.

will be stingy, but will have his boundaries; he will be an adulterer, but with some rules; he will be a libertine, but with an ordered program. What kind of philosophy fails to crush moral depravity unambiguously, and instead is content with 'regulating' our vices? Although I completely approve of the classification he proposes, I would like to see some refinement to it. Let him call the first category the 'requirements of nature.' Let the term 'desire' be used for something else—for that time when he discusses greed, intemperance, and the other major vices in order to indict them on capital charges.

28. "He was certainly in the habit of talking about this quite freely and often. Of course I don't blame him for it. It is expected for a philosopher of his standing to defend his ideas audaciously. Nevertheless, he often seems to embrace too enthusiastically the concept of 'pleasure' in the same sense as the popular meaning of the word, and this habit sometimes puts him in embarrassing situations. He vaguely implies that no act done for pleasure's sake might be so morally repugnant that it could not somehow be removed from the human conscience. Later, when the implications of his ideas make him uneasy (for the power of natural instinct is very great), he runs for cover by denying that anything can add to the pleasure of being free from pain.[143] But this condition of 'no pain' is not properly called pleasure.

'I don't split hairs about the terminology,' he says.

'Fine, but isn't it a completely different thing?'

'I can find many—no, even countless—more people who are neither as precise nor as annoying as all of you are, people whom I can easily persuade as I wish.'

---

[143] I.e., Epicurus takes refuge in the idea that "absence of pain" is the greatest pleasure.

'Then why should we hesitate to say that if absence of pain is the highest pleasure, then not feeling pleasure is the highest pain? Why isn't this true?

'Because the opposite of pain is not pleasure, but freedom from pain.'[144]

X. 29. "He is blind to the fact that a compelling argument against this sort of pleasure—the absence of which, he claims, makes him ignorant of the meaning of 'good'—now arises. He defines it as the things enjoyed by our taste and hearing, and even adds other pleasures to this list which one would have to ask forgiveness for mentioning. Yet he fails to see that this—which our harsh and austere philosopher recognizes as the only real 'good'—should not even be sought after. For according to Epicurus's own testimony, we should not feel any need for this kind of pleasure as long as we are free from pain! What a contradiction this is!

30. "If Epicurus had learned to define his terms, to make proper classifications, to appreciate the power of common speech, and to grasp the accepted uses of words, he would never have gotten himself ensnared in so many traps. And now you can see what he is doing. What no one ever previously called pleasure, he calls pleasure; where there are really two distinct things, he makes one. Sometimes he so denigrates the 'dynamic pleasure'[145] we discussed earlier (his term for the gratifying and delightful kind of pleasure) that you would think Manius Curius were speaking. At other times, he so praises it that he says he cannot imagine any other kind of 'good' existing. This kind of talk should be silenced not by another philosopher's arguments, but by a judge's

---

[144] This kind of hypothetical mini-dialogue (the preceding seven lines) is a rhetorical technique sometimes used by Cicero to illustrate a point or develop an argument.

[145] The *voluptas in motu* discussed in II.9 and II.16.

116

restraining order! Vice is found not only in speech, but also in behavior.[146] He does not condemn luxury, as long as it is free from uncontrolled desire and any fear of repercussions. With this point he seems to be trying to gain more followers: those who want to be hedonists first become philosophers.

31. "He traces the origin of the Ultimate Good, I believe, back to the advent of living organisms. As soon as an animal is born, it rejoices in pleasure and seeks it as a good; suffering is spurned as an evil. He claims these animals—since they have not yet been corrupted—are the ideal judges of what is good and evil. This is what you have proposed, and these are your words. Yet how many inadequate premises we have here! Through what type of pleasure (i.e., dynamic or static) will a crying child distinguish the Ultimate Good from the Ultimate Evil? After all, we learn to speak—if it pleases the gods—from Epicurus! If it is the static type, the organism's nature is obviously focused on self-preservation, as we both know. If it is the dynamic type (which is the position you are taking), then no pleasure will be so indecent as to be rejected. At the same time, an animal born in this way does not start from a point of the highest pleasure, which you have claimed to be the absence of pain.

32. "For this argument Epicurus could have consulted neither children nor animals (whom he thinks are an analogy to Nature as a whole); he could not say that Nature guides them to seek out the pleasure of having no pain. Neither can 'having no pain' arouse the soul's appetite. The state of 'having no pain' supplies no positive stimulus that arouses the senses; here was where Hieronymus also erred. *What moves the soul, rather, is that which stirs the positive sensation of pleasure.* Thus the argument

---

[146] *Non est enim vitium in oratione solum sed etiam in moribus.* Cicero is calling into question the character and morality of the Epicurean, not just his arguments.

Epicurus relies on to show that every creature in Nature seeks pleasure is that 'dynamic pleasure' entices animals and infants: they are not enticed by the 'static' variety of pleasure, which is really just the absence of pain. Who would agree with the statement, then, that Nature begins with one kind of pleasure, but places its Ultimate Good in another?

XI. 33. "On the other hand, I make no judgment with regard to the animals. Although they may not be depraved, they are still naturally capable of depravity.[147] Just as one stick is curved and bent by deliberate effort, and another one was formed that way naturally, the nature of animals is not corrupted by poor discipline: they are that way by their very nature. An infant's nature does not guide it towards seeking pleasure; its focus is to take care of itself, and is concerned with its own health and self-preservation. Every animal, as soon as it is born, holds itself and all its constituent parts dear. The two major divisions of this self-preservation instinct are mind and body; the constituent parts of each these two divisions come after this. Now certain special qualities are to be found in both mind and body. An animal gradually identifies these, and begins to distinguish them from each other, so that they *seek* the things granted by Nature and *reject* their opposites.

34. "Whether pleasure is included among these foremost natural desires is a critical question. But to think that there is nothing *except* pleasure—not our organs, our senses, our thought processes, our bodily integrity, nor our health—seems to me to be the height of ignorance. And from this source must flow every theory of Goods and Evils. Polemo[148] (and Aristotle before him)

---

[147] There is some word-play used in the original: *Quamvis enim depravatae non sint, pravae tamen esse possunt.*

[148] Polemo of Athens (?—270 B.C.), a Platonist philosopher and third head of the Academy in Athens after the death of Plato. One of his primary tenets was

identified the same foremost natural desires that I have just stated. Thus was born the doctrine of the Academics and Peripatetics that the Ultimate Good was to live according to Nature: that is, to enjoy what has been provided by Nature while making use of virtue. Callipho joined nothing to virtue except pleasure; Diodorus, freedom from pain...[149] For all of those philosophers I have named here, their End of Goods are logical conclusions. For Aristippus it is simply pleasure. For the Stoics it is to be in harmony with Nature; by this they mean virtue (i.e., to live in accord with moral goodness). They expand on this further by saying that this means to live in accord with what Nature provides, choosing the things that conform with Nature and rejecting the things that are their opposites.

35. "Thus there are three Ends that have no connection to moral goodness: one is that of Aristippus or Epicurus, another is that of Hieronymus, and the third is that of Carneades. There are three Ends in which moral goodness is combined with some other factor: those of Polemo, Callipho, and Diodorus. There is also one straightforward view of Ends (authored by Zeno) that is based completely on honor (i.e., moral goodness). The theories of Pyrrho, Aristo,[150] and Erillus[151] have long since been discredited. All of these philosophers just named (except Epicurus) were predictable in that their Ultimate Ends followed logically from their first premises. Thus for Aristippus the Ultimate End was pure pleasure; for Hieronymus it was absence of pain; and for Carneades it was to enjoy Nature's foundational principles.

---

that men should live in accordance with nature. *See* Diog. Laert. IV.10—21.
[149] There is lacunae in the text here, but it is not likely that much has been lost.
[150] Aristo of Chios (c. 320 B.C.—c. 250 B.C.) was a Stoic philosopher and contemporary of Zeno, although his views on Stoicism were in some ways different from Zeno's. *See* Diog. Laert. VII.2.
[151] Erillus (or Herillus) of Calchedon (fl. 3rd cent. B.C.), was a Stoic philosopher and follower of Zeno. *See* Diog. Laert. VII.3.

XII. "But when Epicurus, if he meant pleasure in the same sense as Aristippus, said pleasure was something of the first importance, he should have made pleasure the Ultimate Good just as Aristippus did. But if he meant pleasure in the same sense as Hieronymus, should he then have elevated that other kind of pleasure—the kind advocated by Aristippus—to be something of the first importance?

36. "When he says that the senses themselves should judge whether pleasure is a good and pain is an evil, he grants the senses more authority than our legal codes permit us in judging our own private litigation. We can judge nothing except that which is for us to judge. It really serves no purpose for judges to add the following qualification to their rulings: 'If this be something for the Court to decide.' For if it is not a matter for the court to rule on, then the decision itself is entirely void even if this clause is absent. What things do the senses judge?

Sweetness or bitterness, smoothness or roughness, proximity or distance, immobility or motion, squareness or circularity.

37. "This is why only Reason—summoned in the first place with knowledge of things both human and divine—will render a just decision and may truly be called wisdom. After this are added the Virtues, which Reason makes the mistresses of all things. Yet you wanted the Virtues to be the followers and lowly servants of the pleasures. With regard to all of these, Reason will deliver Her verdict first on Pleasure: *and She will say not only that Pleasure has no right to be uniquely crowned as the Ultimate Good which we seek, but also that it is unfit even for contact with Moral Goodness.* Her verdict will be the same with regard to the 'absence of pain.'[152]

----

[152] I.e., "freedom from pain" (*vacuitas doloris*) is equally unworthy: it has no right even to share the same company with moral goodness (*honestas*). The powerful passages that follow (i.e., II.37—47) are a beautiful exposition of

38. "Carneades's ideas will also be rejected. No theory of the Ultimate Good will be sanctioned that either: (1) includes 'pleasure' or 'absence of pain,' or (2) omits moral goodness. This leaves two remaining views for us to reflect on carefully. Either Her[153] final judgment is (1) that there is no Good except moral goodness and no Evil except moral corruption, and all other things are so inconsequential that they should be neither desired nor avoided, but only picked or rejected on a case-by-case basis; or (2) She will favor a theory She considers richly adorned with moral goodness, a theory buttressed by the foundational principles of Nature and by a human life more comprehensively perfected. Her final ruling on this issue will be clearer if She can discern whether the conflict between these theories is real, or simply a matter of semantics.

XIII. 39. "Following the example of Reason, I will proceed in a way that is consistent with Her authority. As much as possible I will focus our efforts. I will take it for granted that all these primitive theories having no connection to virtue must be entirely discarded from philosophy. The first of these theories is that of Aristippus and the Cyrenaics, who had no problem with placing the Ultimate Good in the kind of raw pleasure that arouses the senses with the maximum amount of physical delight, and who laughed at the concept of 'absence of pain.'

40. "These people did not understand that, just as a horse is born for running, an ox for plowing, and a dog for tracking, so too has man (as Aristotle tells us) been created for the twin purposes of thought and action. In this respect he is like a mortal god. In opposition to this, however, the Cyrenaics prefer to see this divine

---

Cicero's enduring belief in the superiority of reason and wisdom over the Epicurean concept of pleasure.

[153] Cicero is using "Her" and "She" to refer to Reason (*ratio*) personified, just as in the preceding section.

animal[154] as having been created to live like some lazy, stupid beast of burden, concerned only with the pleasures of grazing and reproducing. For me nothing could be more ludicrous.

41. "This is the essence of the case against Aristippus, the man who regarded pleasure (in the sense that we commonly use this word) as not only the Ultimate Good but also the *only good*. Your school[155] sees things differently. But Aristippus, as I have said, is degenerate. Neither man's corporal form nor his superior, innate reasoning abilities indicate that he was born for the sole purpose of entertaining himself with pleasure. Neither is it helpful to listen to Hieronymus, whose Ultimate Good is the same as that which you sometimes (or rather too often) say: the absence of pain. Even if pain is an evil, being free from this evil is not enough to provide us with a good life. Here the poet Ennius might say it better:

He who is completely without evil, has good without measure.[156]

Let us judge the good life not by the deflection of evil, but by the acquisition of good. Let us not sink into enfeebling inactivity, whether through physical joy (as Aristippus advises) or through freedom from pain (as Hieronymus counsels), but let us instead strive for positive accomplishment and productive thought.

42. "The same points can be made against the Ultimate Good of Carneades. He proposed it not in order to advocate it seriously, but instead as a weapon with which to attack the Stoics. However,

---

[154] I.e., man. Cicero's noble vision of man—that he was created for great purposes—is perhaps the most inspiring aspect of his philosophic outlook. Sallust had the same view; compare this sentence to the opening sentences of both the *Conspiracy of Catiline* and the *War of Jugurtha*.
[155] Meaning the Epicurean school.
[156] This quote is from Ennius's play *Hecuba*, itself modeled on a tragedy by Euripides of the same name.

it is of such a character that, if it were added to virtue, it would possess some authority. It would probably help in attaining a good life, which is the central topic of our discussion. Those who attach to virtue either pleasure (the one thing virtue cares about the least) or the absence of pain (which despite being free from evil, is not the Ultimate Good) are using an approach that is quite unjustified. I also do not understand why they make their arguments in such a stingy and restrictive way; it is as if they personally had to buy the things they want to attach to virtue. In the first place, they are adding the cheapest things possible to virtue. Instead of linking with moral goodness all the things first endorsed by Nature, they prefer to give out their additions[157] to virtue one at a time.

43. "These things were considered by Aristo and Pyrrho to be of no consequence. They said that there was no significant difference between the best health and the most serious illness, and for good reason disputes about them have not taken place for a long time now. They wanted virtue to be more important than anything else; they robbed it of its power to choose and gave it no place to begin and nothing to depend on. By doing this, they destroyed the very same virtue that they so ardently embraced. Erillus, by basing his entire system on knowledge, saw one distinct Good; but this was neither the Ultimate Good nor a Good that could function as a guide to life. Therefore his system has long since been discredited: no serious thinker has bothered to debate Erillus's ideas since the time of Chrysippus.

XIV. "So now only you are left.[158] A meaningful debate with the Academics is hardly useful. Having given up hope of acquiring definite knowledge of things, they are unwilling to

---

[157] By "additions to virtue" is meant "pleasure" and the "absence of pain" (see the previous two sentences).

[158] I.e., only the Epicurean school of thought remains (*Restatis igitur vos*).

confirm anything as fact, and prefer to be guided by whatever seems most likely to be true.[159]

44. "However, with Epicurus there is more difficulty because he is a compound of two different types of pleasure. There have been many defenders of his system besides himself and his supporters. It is not clear to me why, but the general public—the group that is least qualified to judge such things yet has the greatest power—apparently agrees with them. Unless we disprove the arguments of these people, all virtue, all dignity, and all true merit must be discarded. Once all other systems of thought have been set aside, the contest that remains is not between myself and Torquatus, but between virtue and pleasure.

"A man as sharp and diligent as Chrysippus took this contest quite seriously. He believed that the entire question of the Ultimate Good came down to a comparison between these two things. It is my view, however, that if I can show there is a Moral Goodness we should seek for its own sake and for its own value, then your entire system will be reduced to ruins. So I will define Moral Goodness as briefly as circumstances require. Unless my memory happens to let me down, Torquatus, I will then deal with each of the points you have raised.

45. "We understand Moral Goodness to have such a quality that, even though stripped of any practical utility, it can nevertheless be praised for its own sake, irrespective of material profit or benefit. Its essential quality can be understood not by the definition I am using (although this definition does help in revealing its nature), but by the judgment of our entire society and by the goals and deeds of its best members. Although they may see no immediate advantage in doing so, good people perform many actions because such deeds are proper, right, and morally good.

---

[159] Meaning that the Academics embrace probability rather than absolutes.

Views along the Amalfi Coast

"For although man differs from the unreasoning animals in many respects, the single most significant difference is that he possesses the faculty of Reason granted by Nature, together with a mind that is sharp, vigorous, and able to process many things rapidly. If I may state it this way: his reason is perceptive enough to detect causes and consequences, to make use of similar patterns and link disparate quantities, to connect future consequences with present events, and to comprehend the whole trajectory of his subsequent life.

"This same Reason causes man to seek out his fellow men, molding them together in groups by character, diction, and custom. Starting from the affection felt towards family and friends, Reason guides man along steadily from there to connect him first with his fellow-citizens, then with the society of all mankind. As Plato wrote in his letter to Archytas,[160] man should remember that he was not born for himself alone, but for his country and his people; and not much of a man is left over for himself after serving these purposes.[161]

46. "This same Nature has instilled in man a love for evaluating the truth. This is very clear when we are in repose and not oppressed by worldly cares; we wish to know the nature of those celestial objects that illuminate the night sky. Guided by these initial sentiments, we come to have a special regard for all truth: that is, all things honest, unaffected, and reliable. We likewise despise everything that is untrustworthy, false, or fraudulent, such as trickery, perjury, malice, and injustice. Reason carries within herself something inherently eminent and noble, so that She is better suited for leadership than for subservience; She regards all human

---

[160] A reference to the ninth letter (357d—358b) of the so-called "Platonic Letters," a series of epistles supposedly written by Plato. Their authenticity has been disputed. The ninth letter is addressed to Archytas of Tarentum.
[161] This beautiful section (II.45) is as eloquent an expression of Cicero's humanistic faith in reason as any that can be found in *De Finibus*.

vagaries not merely as bearable but also as trifling; and She carries with her something lofty and transcendent, fearing nothing, surrendering to no one, and never subjugated.

47. "After taking note of the three types of moral goodness, there follows a fourth one of equal allure that springs from the preceding three: this is the idea of *order and moderation*. We see this idea manifested in the beauty and excellence of physical forms; this idea is then applied to moral goodness of speech and action. It incorporates something from each of the three praiseworthy qualities that I mentioned earlier. It strongly disapproves of rashness; it has no desire to harm anyone through reckless words or actions; and it fears doing or saying anything that might be seen as insufficiently virile.

XV. 48. "You have here, Torquatus, a complete and comprehensive description of moral goodness in all its aspects. This description is formed from all four of the virtues that you have also discussed. Yet here your Epicurus claims to be entirely ignorant of the *specific quality* assigned to moral goodness by those who use moral goodness to evaluate the Ultimate Good. If everything relates back to moral goodness, and they say that there is no pleasure to be found in it, then he says they are speaking complete jibberish (these are the actual words he uses). He does not know or see what meaning could even be attached to the expression 'moral goodness.' As the term is commonly used, 'moral' means something that popular opinion regards very highly.[162] Epicurus says that although this public esteem may be more pleasant than some other pleasures, it is still desired for the sake of pleasure.

---

[162] Cicero is pointing out the subtle link between morality and honor. The word used for "moral" here is *honestum*, which has several shades of meaning. It signifies something morally honorable, as well as virtue, moral goodness, and moral rectitude.

49. "Do you see how significant his difference of opinion is? A major philosopher, influential not only in Greece and Italy but also in all barbarian lands, says he does not know what Moral Goodness is if it is not contained in pleasure—unless, perhaps, it is whatever the gossip of the common mob cheers on. I believe that what the general public celebrates is often indecent; and when it happens *not to be* indecent, it is only this way when whatever the crowd is praising is itself morally right and laudable. But it is not considered 'moral' because the crowd cheers it on, but because it has such a special quality that, even if men were unaware of it or never discussed it, it would still be praiseworthy due to its unique beauty and excellence. Boxed in by these logical conclusions that he cannot dodge, Epicurus says somewhere else in his books what you just said[163] a little while ago: *that it is not possible to live well unless one also lives in a way that is morally good.*

50. "What does the term 'morally' signify now? Does it have the same meaning as 'delightfully'? Does he mean that it is not possible to live morally unless life is lived in a moral way?[164] Or unless you judge everything by the opinion of the crowd? So is he saying that one cannot live agreeably without the consent of the mob? What could be more disgraceful than to make the wise man's life be dependent on the ignorant talk of fools? What was he thinking when he used the term 'moral' in this context? Clearly, he meant *nothing except that which can justly be praised for its own sake.* For if it is praised on account of pleasure, then of what value is this praise that can only be sought from a

---

[163] Referring to I.57.
[164] There is subtle word-play with the verb "to live" (*vivere*) in the original that requires some agility to convey in English: *Ergo ita: non posse honeste vivi nisi honeste vivatur?*

merchant's market?[165] Since he values moral goodness so highly that he claims one cannot live agreeably without it, Epicurus is not the man to conflate this moral goodness with what is popular and then say it is impossible to live well without the mob's approval. He does not understand anything morally good except that which is right in itself—that which is praiseworthy for itself, through its own intrinsic merit, its own character, and its own nature.

XVI. 51. "Therefore, Torquatus, when you say Epicurus sweepingly concludes that it is not possible to live well unless one lives honestly, justly, and wisely, I have the impression that you are boasting. There was a persuasive power in the phrases you used that came from the inherent dignity of the words; you climbed ever higher with your rhetoric, stopping occasionally to look down on us, as if you were trying to show us that Epicurus sometimes did praise moral goodness and justice. Perhaps it was right for you to use these words; if philosophers did not use them, we would have no need at all for philosophy. It was because of their irresistible love of these words—namely Wisdom, Courage, Justice, and Temperance, all of which are rarely mentioned by Epicurus—that men of the most exceptional character have applied themselves to the study of philosophy.

52. "Our sense of sight, Plato tells us, is our most acute sense—but it cannot discern wisdom. She would arouse our most ardent love if we could see her. Why do I say this? Is it because of her skill in being able to design pleasures in the most artful way? And why is justice praised? What is the source of that old adage, 'You can throw numbers at him in the dark'?[166] While this

---

[165] Meaning that to value morality simply as a gateway to pleasure is to commodify and cheapen it.

[166] A reference to the guessing game called *morra*, mentioned by Cicero in *De Officiis* III.19. See note 214 on p. 198 of my translation of *On Duties* (Charleston: Fortress of the Mind Publications, 2016). In *morra*, one had to

saying is particularly applicable to honesty, it may be given this wider relevance: *that with regard to every action we do, we should not be morally guided by the existence of an audience.*[167]

53. "The disincentives you talked about earlier are trifling and inadequate: namely, the wicked being tortured by a guilty conscience, the fear of punishment hovering over them, or at least the possibility of retribution oppressing their thoughts. We must not think of the evil man as having a fearful or fragile disposition who flagellates himself over his conduct and dreads the results of his actions. For him, everything is skillfully engineered for utility's sake. He is sharp, cunning, and highly experienced, deftly able to accomplish his purposes in the shadows, deceiving others without witnesses or accomplices.

54. "Do you think I'm talking about Lucius Tubulus? As praetor, he presided over murder cases. And he so openly accepted money in return for favorable verdicts that, during the following year, the tribune of the plebs Publius Scaevola brought the matter before the plebian assembly. Their intention was to investigate the issue. To implement this plebian resolution, the senate decreed

---

guess the number of fingers "flashed" out by the opponent. The meaning of the adage was that someone could be so honest that he would tell the number of fingers ("numbers") thrown out, even if it was dark and the other player could not see what was happening. *Morra* is described in detail in Polydore Vergil's 1499 treatise *De Inventoribus Rerum* (*On Discovery*). He writes (II.13.17) that "Guessing with the fingers is another game, played by calling out a number with both hands closed and then suddenly extending the fingers. When I hear the word, I put out three fingers, you the same number; I call four, you call six, and you win because your call guessed the number. And since the extended fingers appear so suddenly, the game is called flash by a figure of speech…This game is known in Italy where the people call it *mor*…A serious person does not flash." *See* Copenhaver, Brian, *Polydore Vergil: On Discovery*, Cambridge: Harvard University Press, 2002, p. 283.

[167] Meaning that our decision to act morally should not be based on whether someone is watching. Stated another way, one should act morally even if no one is observing.

that Cnaeus Caepius should conduct the inquiry; but Tubulus, lacking the courage to face the charges, immediately fled into exile. For there had been no doubt about the outcome.

XVII. "Thus we are not just describing a corrupt person, but a corrupt person who is also *devious*, just like Quintus Pompeius was when he abrogated the Numantine treaty.[168] We are also not describing someone who is fearful, but someone who first and foremost is untroubled by the pangs of conscience, someone for whom suppressing his inner voice is a routine matter. This man— whom we characterize as furtive and secretive—is so unlikely to betray himself that he will even pretend to be wounded by someone else's misdeed. Is this not the behavior pattern of a wily deceiver?

55. "I remember once being with Publius Sextilius Rufus when he brought up the following issue with his friends. He had been left as an heir to Quintus Fadius Gallus; Fadius's will instructed that he wished his heir to convey his entire estate to his daughter. Sextilius denied the existence of the testator's wish. He could do this without consequences, for who was there to stand in his way? None of us believed Sextilius. Since he had a vested interest in the matter, it was more likely that *he* was lying than was Fadius, who had written that he made the testamentary arrangements he was supposed to make.

"Sextilius also added that, having promised to comply with the Voconian law,[169] he dared not do anything to violate it unless

---

[168] Refers to an incident during the Numantine Wars (143 B.C.—133 B.C.) in Spain. Quintus Pompeius was consul in 141 B.C. and was sent to Spain to command Rome's efforts to subdue the Numantines. Pompeius was unsuccessful and signed an armistice with the enemy without senatorial authorization. He was relieved of command in 139 B.C. and recalled to Rome to answer for his misconduct.

[169] The *lex Voconia* was passed in Rome in 169 B.C. when Quintus Voconius

his friends thought he should act differently. I was only a young man at the time, but the others present were men of distinction; and none of these recommended that Fadia should be given more than she would be permitted under the Voconian law. Sextilius thus came into possession of a very large inheritance, not a single coin of which he would have touched if he had followed the counsel of those who place goodness and virtue ahead of all benefit and personal profit.

"Do you think after this that Sextilius's mind was disturbed, or that he was riddled with guilt? Not at all. In fact it was just the opposite: he was made rich by this inheritance, and he was quite pleased with the outcome. He figured he had acquired a large sum of money not only without violating the law, but also with its assistance. Indeed, as you Epicureans believe, a man should hunt for money even if danger is involved, since money is the enabler of a large number of wonderful pleasures.

56. "Therefore, just as those people who believe right and honorable things should be sought for their own sake must frequently risk danger to affirm honor and integrity, so you Epicureans—who measure everything by the standard of pleasure—must also risk danger to acquire significant pleasures. Suppose a major inheritance or a large sum of money is there for the taking. Since a great many pleasures can be acquired with money, your Epicurus (if he wants to acquire the Epicurean version of the Ultimate Good) will have to act in the same way that Scipio did when lured Hannibal back to Africa in order to attain enduring military glory.[170] What great dangers he risked to

---

Saxa was tribune of the plebs. This (apparently sumptuary) law limited the total value of property that could be bequeathed by inheritance to women. In practice, however, it was often evaded. *See* Aulus Gellius XVII.6.

[170] Referring to Scipio Africanus the Elder (236 B.C.—183 B.C.), who achieved enduring fame by defeating Hannibal in the Battle of Zama (202 B.C.) during the Second Punic War.

do this! His motivation in this supreme undertaking is to be found in *honor*, not in pleasure. When aroused by the opportunity for significant material gain, Epicurus's version of the 'wise man' will, for good reason, also fight ferociously if he has to.

57. "If he is able to keep his crime hidden, he will be happy; if caught, he will not trouble himself about any resulting penalty. He will have been taught not to worry about death, exile, and even pain itself. And with regard to pain: when proposing punishment for the evil man, you make pain out to be *intolerable*; but when you claim that the wise man will always have more of the Good, you choose to see the same pain as *tolerable*.

XVIII. "But imagine if the man who does evil is not only cunning, but also very powerful, as was Marcus Crassus,[171] who used to follow his own good character. Or consider our own Pompey,[172] who should have our gratitude for his consistently doing the right thing; he could have been as unjust as he wished without suffering any consequences. How many unjust deeds can be committed that no one would be able to reprimand!

58. "If your friend were dying and asked you to transfer his estate to his daughter, yet had neither written anything down (just like Fadius) nor mentioned it to anyone else, what would *you* do? Certainly you would carry out the transfer. Epicurus himself probably would have done this also. So did Sextus Peducaeus, son of Sextus, a learned man as well as the best and most just of men; he left behind him a son—our comrade—as a spitting image of his father's prudence and character. No one was aware that an eminent Roman knight named Caius Plotius of Nursia had made this very same inheritance request to Sextus.

---

[171] Marcus Licinius Crassus (c. 115 B.C.—53 B.C.), Roman politician and military leader of the late Roman republic.
[172] Cnaeus Pompeius Magnus (106 B.C.—48 B.C.), Roman general of the late republic who was defeated by Julius Caesar in the Civil War.

"Yet Sextus voluntarily chose to inform Plotius's astonished widow of her late husband's deathbed instructions, and then turned over the entire estate to her. I want to ask you this: since without doubt you would have done the same thing, don't you perceive from this the greater power of nature? You Epicureans say you measure everything according to your own pleasure and personal benefit, but in practice your actions make it clear that you are following not pleasure but duty. Is our natural capacity to do what is morally right stronger than the power of corrupted reason?

59. "Carneades said the following: if you know there is a poisonous snake hiding out of sight somewhere, and someone whose death would be a great benefit to you is unwittingly about to sit on it, then you are committing an evil act by deliberately failing to warn him not to sit there. Yet your act would still go unpunished. For who would be able to prove you had known? But we have lingered too long on these matters. It is clear that *unless good faith, equity, and justice originate from Nature herself, and if these concepts only have value for some temporary expediency, then it is not possible to find a good man at all.* This subject was fully discussed by Laelius in my treatise *De Re Publica*.[173]

XIX. 60. "Shift the same logic to the concepts of modesty and temperance. I am referring to the moderation of the desires and our submission to the power of Reason. Is a man upholding a true sense of honor if he surrenders to his baser passions without anyone noticing? Or can something be disgraceful *per se*, even if no dishonor follows in its wake? Which is the right answer? Do great men enter into battle and pour out their blood for their country only after performing detailed calculations about the

---

[173] Cicero's dialogue *De Re Publica* (*On the State*), which survives in incomplete form in six books. The character Laelius was one of the speakers of the dialogue.

pleasures that will follow, or are they roused by a passion and vigor of the spirit? If your ancestor Imperiosus[174] heard our conversation here, Torquatus (with me saying he had done nothing for his own sake but everything for the sake of the country, and you saying he had done everything for his own benefit), would he have heard *your* statements with more satisfaction, or *mine*? And suppose you wanted to justify your opinion, and spoke even more frankly by telling him that he had done everything for the sake of pleasure. How do you think your statement would have been received?

61. "So be it. If you want, let us say Torquatus acted as he did for his own utility (For a man of his greatness, I prefer to state it this way than to say he acted for his own 'pleasure'). What can we say about his colleague Publius Decius, the first in his family to be consul? When he consecrated[175] himself and charged into the middle of the Latin battle-line, riding his horse at full gallop, was he thinking about his own pleasure? If so, then where or when would he take it? He knew immediately he was about to die, and sought this death with more burning zeal than Epicurus believed we should have in seeking pleasure. Had Decius's act not been deservedly praised, it would not have been imitated by his son during his fourth consulship.[176] Neither would *his son in turn* have perished in battle while commanding troops as consul against

---

[174] Referring to the famous Titus Manlius Imperiosus Torquatus, who held three consulships and three dictatorships from 353 B.C. to 340 B.C. (mentioned above, I.23).

[175] Consecrate (*devovere*) in the sense of preparing himself for death. The reference is to Publius Decius Mus, who was consul in 340 B.C. According to Livy (VIII.9), he invited death in battle in accordance with the ritual of *devotio* (i.e., voluntary sacrifice of the leader in exchange for victory).

[176] This occurred at the Battle of Sentinum in 295 B.C., when the Romans fought a combined force of Gauls and Samnites. He had the same name as his father. *See* Livy X.28.

Pyrrhus, thereby becoming the third in his familial line to have fallen in battle for the sake of the nation.[177]

62. "Other examples are not necessary. The Greeks have a few: Leonidas, Epaminondas, maybe three or four in all. But if I were to collect a list of us Romans, I would show beyond doubt that 'pleasure' has been kept tightly restrained by virtue—and daylight would expire before the list was complete. Aulus Varius was known as a very stern judge. When witnesses had given testimony in his court, and then still others were called to the stand, he used to say to his fellow judge on the bench, 'Either the testimony we already have is sufficient, or I don't know what testimony might be sufficient.' So for me enough evidence to prove my point has already been given. What do you think? For you yourself—a most worthy inheritor of your ancestors' greatness—was it pleasure that compelled you, as a mere youth, to take the consulship from Publius Sulla?[178] You brought back that trophy for your father, that most courageous of men: and what a great consul he was, as well as a great citizen even after he left office! With his help I managed a crisis I knew was of vital importance, not just for myself, but for the entire state.[179]

63. "But how beautifully you phrased it when, on one side, you placed someone swimming in plentiful and superlative pleasures, feeling no pain either now or in the future; and then, on the opposing side, you placed someone whose entire body was

---

[177] This was the Battle of Asculum in 279 B.C. against Pyrrhus of Epirus. He also had the same name as his father and grandfather.

[178] In 66 B.C. Torquatus was defeated in the consular election by Publius Cornelius Sulla and Publius Autronius Paetus. Torquatus accused them of corruption and brought a successful indictment under the *Lex Acilia Calpurnia* (which banned candidates from holding office who had been convicted of corruption). They were removed from office and Torquatus himself made consul.

[179] A reference to the Catilinian conspiracy of 63 B.C., an event in which Cicero played a major role.

suffering from the most agonizing pain, with neither the present ability nor future hope of experiencing pleasure. You then asked who could be more miserable than the latter person, and who could be more fortunate than the former, finally arriving at the conclusion that the Greatest Evil is pain, and the Greatest Good is pleasure!

XX. "There was once a man named Lucius Thorius Balbus from Lanuvium,[180] whom you cannot remember. He lived his life according to the rule that no exotic pleasure existed in which he could overindulge. He had a surpassing lust for pleasures and a keen appreciation of their varieties and how to hoard them. He was so empty of religious feeling that he looked down on the many ritual offerings and temples located in his birthplace, and so unafraid of death that he was killed in battle while fighting for his country.

64. "He did not measure human desires by Epicurus's categorization schemes, but only according to his own gratification. Nevertheless he was prudent with his health. He exercised enough so that he would come hungry and thirsty to his meals; his foods were wholesome and quite simple in preparation, with wine sufficient for pleasure but short of causing harm. He made use of other pleasures too: pleasures that, if they were taken away, Epicurus says he would not know what Good is. Pain was entirely missing from his life. If he did encounter it, he would not have tolerated it easily, and would have chosen to see a doctor instead of a philosopher. He had an exceptional complexion, a robust body, and was extremely popular. To sum up, his life was crowded with all varieties of pleasure.

65. "You Epicureans believe his situation is a happy one; your logic compels this conclusion. But I place before him someone

---

[180] An ancient town about 32 km. southeast of Rome, known for its temple of Juno and other shrines. *See* Livy VIII.14.

whom I dare not identify. Virtue may speak on my behalf, and she would not hesitate to place Marcus Regulus ahead of this 'happy' man. On his own volition, and under no coercion except the guarantee he had given to an enemy, Regulus returned to Carthage after leaving his own country.[181] Yet despite being tortured with sleep deprivation and hunger, Virtue declares him to have been more fortunate than Thorius drinking himself to oblivion on a bed of roses.[182]

"Regulus had waged great wars, had twice served as consul, and had celebrated a triumph. And yet he considered these previous deeds neither as great nor as noble as what he did as a prisoner of the Carthaginians, an act that was inspired by honesty and unshakeable courage. To us—hearing of this incident long after the fact—this fate seems pitiable. But to the man who endured it at the time, it was agreeable. For often even the sad can become happy by displaying strength and firmness; they are not made happy by lightheartedness, nor by frivolity, laughing, or joking, which is the companion of shallowness.

---

[181] Marcus Atilius Regulus (consul in 267 B.C. and 256 B.C.) was captured during the First Punic War and released by the Carthaginians for the purpose of negotiating peace with the Roman senate. He promised the enemy he would return to Carthage at the conclusion of his mission. According to tradition, he asked the senate to refuse the Carthaginian peace terms, then returned to captivity in Carthage where he was tortured to death. This brave act made him a model of moral rectitude.

[182] The reference is apparently to Lucius Thorius Balbus, an obscure general who Cicero uses as a symbol of decadence. He was defeated and killed by the noted statesman Quintus Sertorius at Consabura in 79 B.C. *See* Plutarch, *Sertorius* XII. (Plutarch misspells his name as Thoranius, but this is likely a copyist error). The upper classes in Cicero's day would often decorate couches at dinner parties with rose petals for their fragrant and visual qualities. *See* Parsons, S.B., *The Rose: Its History, Poetry, Culture, And Cultivation*. New York: Wiley & Putnam, 1847, p. 17.

66. "Forcibly raped by the king's son, Lucretia took her own life after testifying to this fact before her fellow citizens.[183] The resulting sorrow of the Roman people—voiced by the leadership and initiative of Brutus—was the proximate cause of freedom for the state. In grateful memory of this courageous woman, both her husband and father were selected as consuls for the first year of the republic. Sixty years after our country had secured its liberty, Lucius Verginius, a poor man of plebian rank, slew his daughter with his own hand rather than deliver her into the lecherous embraces of the most powerful man in Rome, Appius Claudius.[184]

XXI. 67. "So you must either denounce these heroic deeds, or you must abandon your advocacy of pleasure. But what decent arguments can you make—what support can you bring to bear— when you can't summon any witnesses or advocates from the ranks of great men? We, for our side, can recall the great names from the chronicles of history, men who spent their entire lives in glorious undertakings and who never even cared if they heard the word 'pleasure.' In your arguments, history is entirely silent. In Epicurus's school I never once heard the names Lycurgus, Solon, Miltiades, Themistocles, or Epaminondas mentioned; and yet these names are heard in the discourses of every other philosopher.[185] Now that we have started to delve into this subject, how many more distinguished names will our good friend Atticus make available to us from his vast personal archives![186]

---

[183] See Livy I.57 et seq. and Boccaccio's On Famous Women, Ch. XLVIII. According to this famous story, Lucretia's rape and suicide set in motion a chain of events that led to the downfall of the Roman monarchy in 509 B.C. and the beginning of the republic.

[184] See Livy III.44 et seq. Lucius Verginius was a centurion, and this incident took place around 449 B.C.

[185] The individuals named are famous civil and military leaders from Greek history.

[186] Cicero's friend Titus Pomponius Atticus (110 B.C.—32 B.C.) collected historical information and published a book entitled Liber Annalis (Yearly

68. "Wouldn't it be better to talk about these heroic figures than to fill so many scrolls with talk about Themista?[187] This type of thing should be left to the Greeks. Although we learned philosophy and all the noble disciplines from them, there are still some things not allowed to us that may be permitted to them. The Stoics fight with the Peripatetics. Some say that there is nothing 'good' except moral rectitude; others place by far the greatest value on moral goodness, yet concede that good may still be found in bodily things and things external to the body. This is a respectable fight, and a splendid dispute![188] For the entire debate hinges on the actual worth of virtue. But when you are talking about these issues with your associates, you must listen to a great deal of talk about obscene pleasures—and Epicurus himself supposedly talked about them quite often.

69. "Believe me, Torquatus, if you take a close look at your inner thoughts and impulses, I think you simply can't defend these ideas. I say that you would be ashamed of the picture that Cleanthes used to paint so skillfully with his words. He would tell his listeners to draw a mental picture of Pleasure seated on a throne, outfitted with the most beautiful garments and royal accessories. Right next to Queen Pleasure would stand the Virtues as her fawning little servants; these Virtues should do nothing, and know they have no official function, except to cater to the whims of Pleasure. As necessary they would whisper into her ear (as well as this could be displayed by a painting), warning the queen to be

---

Accounts) in 47 B.C., a chronicle of great names and deeds in world history. See Cornelius Nepos's *De Viris Illustribus* XXV (*Atticus* 18).

[187] Themista of Lampsacus, a female student of Epicureanism and the wife of Leonteus. Diogenes Laertius (X.25) says that Epicurus "wrote letters" to Themista.

[188] There is a play on words with the use of the phrase "respectable fight" (*certamen honestum*). *Honestum* also conveys the meaning of moral goodness or rectitude, which is mentioned in the preceding sentence.

careful not to do anything by mistake that might disturb the feelings of the public, or to do anything that might cause pain. 'We Virtues were indeed created to serve you; we have no other function besides this.'

XXII. 70. "But Epicurs denies—and this is your key point—that anyone who does not live in a morally righteous way can live happily. As if I care what Epicurus admits or denies! What I ask is this: what is appropriate for a man to say who places the Highest Good in pleasure? What can you offer to explain why Thorius, or Postumius of Chios, or the leader of them all, Orata,[189] did not live wonderfully pleasant lives? As I said earlier, Epicurus maintains that the lives of pleasure-lovers should not be condemned unless they are obviously foolish: that is, unless they are tormented by desire or fear. *And since he promises a cure for both desire and fear, he is promising an endorsement of self-indulgent behavior.* Once desire and fear are taken out of the picture, Epicurus says he cannot find anything to condemn in the lives of debauchers.

71. "Therefore, by aligning yourselves with every kind of pleasure, you Epicureans are unable to safeguard or preserve virtue. For a man who refrains from evil deeds in order to avoid injury to himself should not be considered good and just. I believe you have heard this before:

No one is upright whose uprightness…[190]

Take care to remember that nothing is truer than this. A man whose actions are repressed by fear is not 'just': for as soon as he stops feeling fear, he will certainly stop being just. Furthermore,

---

[189] These were apparently famous sybarites. It is possible that the text is corrupt here, and that four names (not three) were originally intended.

[190] The author of this phrase (*Nemo pius est qui pietatem…*) is not known. The gist of the quote was likely that moral conduct should be based not on fear of punishment, but on sincere respect for virtue.

he will not feel any fear if he can hide his crimes, or if he can continue his bad acts with the help of vast material resources. And without doubt, he would prefer to be *thought of* as a good man instead of *being one*, rather than actually *being* a good man but not *thought of* as one. What is most certain is this: you Epicureans offer us a *simulation* of justice as a substitute for true and reliable justice. You teach us to think little of our own reliable consciences, and instead to be paying constant attention to the wrongheaded opinions of others.

72. "These same things can still be said about the other virtues. You base all their fundamental rationales on pleasure, which is equivalent to placing them on a foundation of water. Where does this lead us? With this logic, can we even say that that the legendary Torquatus was brave? Although I cannot 'corrupt' you (as you put it), I am fascinated—even awed, I can say—with your family and your name. By Hercules, how I can see before my eyes now that great and most beloved of men, my friend Aulus Torquatus. His exceptional devotion and loyalty to me during difficult times are things that both of you must be aware of.

"As for me—as someone who wants to be grateful and show gratitude—I would not have felt such gratitude had I not clearly seen that he was a friend who had *my* interests at heart, *not his own.* You might say his actions were for his own benefit, in the sense that it is in everyone's interest to act morally. But if you do say this, then I have won the argument: for we subscribe to this rule, and we maintain above all else, *that our profit from duty is the duty itself.*[191]

73. "Your Epicurus does not want to acknowledge this. He looks at everything with the idea that pleasure should be extracted from it, like some kind of reward. But I will go back to Torquatus

---

[191] *Offici fructus sit ipsum officium.* The same principle as "duty is its own reward."

again. If it were for the sake of 'pleasure' that he challenged that Gallic warrior to man-to-man combat near the Anio River—and as his reward for victory, stripped him of his torque and appropriated his surname for any other reason than that he sincerely believed such deeds were worthy of a true man—then I do not see Torquatus as courageous.[192] If our sense of decency, our discipline, our modesty, and our self-control itself were preserved only through fear of punishment or disgrace, and were not maintained for their own independent merit, then what kind of adultery, depravity, or sexual excess would not burst forth and rage out of control, since such things could now be done in secret, or with impunity, or with the tacit endorsement of others?[193]

74. "What do *you* think? What would someone conclude, Torquatus, if a man of your family name, character, and fame did not have the courage to explain to a group of people what you are doing, what you are thinking, what objectives you are working towards and how you intend to accomplish these plans, and finally what you judge to be life's ultimate good? What 'reward' are you looking for when you undertake the responsibility of a magistracy, or step in front of a public assembly? For you must state in advance what rules you intend to follow in office; and if appropriate, perhaps you will also say something about the customs of your ancestors and about yourself as well. What 'reward' are you expecting if you then say that everything you will do in office will be focused on pleasure, and that you have

---

[192] See I.23 above (and footnotes) for this incident.

[193] This is a sentence of great oratorical power, displaying Cicero's mastery of alliteration, balance, repetition, and emphasis in Latin. It would have been impressive to hear it spoken publicly: *Iam si pudor, si modestia, si pudicitia, si uno verbo temperantia poenae aut infamiae metu coercebuntur, non sanctitate sua se tuebuntur, quod adulterium, quod stuprum, quae libido non se proripiet ac proiciet aut occultatione proposita aut impunitate aut licentia?*

never done anything in life that was not for the sake of pleasure?

"Here you might say, 'Do you think I would be so insane as to speak that way in front of common people?' Well, then say the same words in front of a court tribunal; or if you are afraid of the audience there, speak before the senate. You will never do it! But why, if not because such talk is repulsive? And yet you think Triarius and myself are deserving enough for you to speak so disgracefully *before us*?

XXIII. 75. "Let us suppose you make a valid point. The word 'pleasure' itself does not have a very dignified ring to it, and perhaps we don't comprehend its true meaning. You are always saying again and again that we don't understand what you mean by 'pleasure.' As if the concept were a difficult or mysterious one to grasp! We understand *you* when you talk about indivisible atoms and the spaces between planetary worlds[194] (which do not exist and never can exist), and yet *we* cannot figure out the concept of pleasure, something that is familiar to every sparrow on earth? What if I make you concede that I not only *do know* what pleasure is (it is a delightful stirring of the senses), but I also know what *you want it to be*? In one situation, you want the word 'pleasure' to have the meaning I have just defined. You then tag it with the name 'dynamic pleasure' when it is or produces some changeable sensations. Then at other times you say it is a different feeling, some kind of 'ultimate pleasure' which is the highest pleasure that can exist. This state comes about when all pain is absent. You call this condition 'static pleasure.'

76. "This last feeling you refer to may indeed be pleasure. Tell any public assembly that you will only do what does not cause

---

[194] *Intermundia*, or the spaces between worlds. Cicero may have coined this word, as its only appearances in classical Latin literature (according to the Oxford Latin Dictionary) are here and in his *De Natura Deorum* (*On the Nature of the Gods*) I.18.

you pain. If you think saying this is not dignified enough, or not morally respectable enough, then tell your audience that while in office and for the rest of your life you will only act for your own benefit. You will do nothing except what is expedient, and nothing except what helps you personally. Imagine the outrage in the audience; think of what your chances would then be for success in a consular election (something that now appears quite certain for you in the future).

"Do you intend to use a school of thought for yourself and your friends that you dare not disclose in public? And yet the lofty words invoked by the Peripatetics and the Stoics are always flowing from your lips in the courtrooms and in the senate. Duty, justice, honor, fidelity, rectitude, moral worth, prestige of office, the stature of the Roman people, risking every danger for the republic, knowing how to die for one's country—when you talk about these things, we blockheads are awestruck. And of course you quietly laugh to yourself.

77. "For pleasure has no place among these glorious and lofty words. There is no place for what you call 'dynamic pleasure' (which is what every person, whether sophisticated or simple, calls pleasure, and every person who speaks Latin calls pleasure, I think). And neither is there any place for this 'static pleasure,' which no one considers 'pleasure' except you Epicureans.

XXIV. "Do you really think that you ought to use our words with your own special meanings? If you were to display some contrived facial expression or way of walking in order to make yourself seem more important, you would not be acting in a way that is true to your nature. So would you now create bogus words and say things you don't believe? Or will you have—just just like a changeable set of clothing—one opinion that is valid for the home, and another that is good for public consumption? Would you show one face openly, and keep your true beliefs hidden inside? I ask you to consider whether this is honorable. As I see it, true beliefs are those that are honest, creditable, and beneficent, beliefs that can be openly expressed in the senate, to the public,

145

and before any meeting and gathering, so that a man should not be ashamed to say openly what he is not ashamed to think privately.[195]

78. "What is the role of friendship here? Or rather, who can be a friend to anyone else if he does not love the other person for his own unique nature? What is the meaning of 'to love' (the verb from which the word 'friendship' is derived)[196] except to want the best things to happen to someone, even if such things give us no direct benefit? 'It is useful for me,' he says, 'to have this thought.'[197] On the contrary, it is useful *to appear* to think this way. You cannot appear to be such a sincere friend unless you really are one. Who can be a good friend without being motivated by genuine goodwill? True kindness does not usually come from a cold assessment of advantage to oneself: it germinates by itself, and blossoms through its own special vitality. Here you will say, 'But I follow the rule of expediency!' Then your friendship will endure just as long as the expediency endures; and if utility has created the friendship, then utility will ruin it.

79. "But what are you going to do when expediency ceases to be aligned with friendship, as often happens? Will you abandon the friendship? What kind of friendship is this? Will you preserve the relationship? How does this harmonize with your ideas? Remember when you laid down the rule that friendships should be pursued for the sake of expediency. 'If I abandon a friend, I might become an object of hatred.' First of all, why would such an action be worthy of hate unless it really was repellent?

---

[195] Here again is a sentence of great rhetorical beauty, constructed for oral delivery, which I cannot resist quoting: *Mihi quidem eae verae videntur opiniones quae honestae, quae laudabiles, quae gloriosae, quae in senatu, quae apud populum, quae in omni coetu concilioque profitendae sint, ne id non pudeat sentire quod pudeat dicere.*

[196] The verb "to love" is *amare*, and *amicitia* is friendship.

[197] I.e., the thought of wanting the best things to happen to someone, even if it provides no direct benefit to oneself.

"If you do not abandon a friend out of worry that severing the link would cause you problems, you will still hope that he dies, so that you are not chained to a profitless relationship. What if he not only brings you no advantage, but causes you to lose property, to take on unnecessary burdens, or to be at risk for your life? Indeed, will you even then not reflect on and think about the fact that each man is born to take care of himself and his own pleasures? Will you put up your own life as collateral to a tyrant for a friend, as a certain Pythagorean did to a Sicilian tyrant?[198] Or if you were Pylades, would you say you were Orestes in order to die on behalf of your friend?[199] Or if you were Orestes, would you contradict Pylades and disclose who you really were? And if you could not prove your real identity, would you protest if you were both ordered to be executed together?

XXV. 80. "Indeed, Torquatus, you would do all these things. I personally believe there is nothing truly praiseworthy that you would avoid out of fear of pain or death. However, the issue here is not what actions are in harmony with your personal nature, but rather what actions are consistent with your Epicurean beliefs. This school of thought that you defend, and these precepts you have studied diligently and endorse, completely subvert true friendship no matter how much Epicurus lauds friendship (as he does) to the skies. Here you may say, 'But Epicurus himself

---

[198] A reference to the story of Damon and Pylades (Pythias), also mentioned in *On Duties* III.45. Damon agreed to put his life up as surety for his friend Pythias, after the tyrant Dionysius of Syracuse accused Pythias of conspiring against him. Pythias honored his bond conditions and returned to face Dionysius's charges. The tyrant was so moved by this display of friendship that he pardoned them both.

[199] Reference to a scene from a lost play (*Orestes*) by Pacuvius. A king wished to execute Orestes, but did not know which of the two friends (Pylades and Orestes) was his intended target. This incident is also mentioned in V.22, below.

cultivated a good many friends.' Who, I ask, is denying that he was a good man, as well as a curteous and civilized one?

"In this debate we are talking about his intellect, not about his personal qualities. This perversity should be left to the shallowness of the Greeks, who denounce with bitter words those whose views of the world they find objectionable. Epicurus indeed may have been gracious in looking after his friends; nevertheless, if these points I'm making are true—for I don't claim to be infallible—then he was not very profound.

81. "You may say, 'But he was able to gain many adherents.' And maybe he deservedly had many followers. Yet the opinion of the crowd is not what is most important. In any art, area of study, or field of knowledge—and even when it comes to virtue itself— the best of each type is extremely uncommon. And in my view, the fact that he was a good man, that many Epicureans were (and are today) faithful to their friends, that they lived their lives with firm resolution and conscientiousness, and that they were guided in their decisions by a sense of duty instead of a desire for pleasure: all this actually *confirms* the greater worth of moral goodness and *discredits* the value of pleasure. Indeed, they live in such a way that their conduct refutes their professed philosophy. Most men are judged to have better words than deeds; but with the Epicureans, it seems to me that their actions are better than their words.

XXVI. 82. "But this is not directly related to our subject. Let us evaluate what you said earlier about friendship. From listening to your comments, I think I recognized one of Epicurus's principles: namely, that friendship cannot be separated from pleasure, and that it should be encouraged because without out it a man cannot live safely and free from fear (and therefore cannot live enjoyably). A sufficient response has already been given to this point. You quoted a different, somewhat more civilized saying from the modern Epicureans which—as far as I know— was never spoken by Epicurus himself. The adage is this: in the beginning we seek friends for reasons of expediency, but as familiarity habituates us to our friend, we begin to love him for his own sake—even if we have no expectation of personal pleasure. It is possible to find fault with this statement for several reasons. Nevertheless, I take what they say at face value: for me it is enough to make my case, and for the Epicureans it is certainly not enough. *For they are saying that sometimes moral goodness can exist without any expectation of, or demand for, pleasure.*

83. "You also suggested that other authorities say wise men make certain collective agreements with each other that they should have the same personal feelings towards their friends as they have regarding themselves. According to you, this is possible and has already been done; it is allegedly highly relevant in the acquisition of pleasures. If wise men have made such an agreement, let them also agree to this: *that they have a special regard for equity, modesty, and all the other virtues for their own sake, without any expectation of material benefit.*

But if we cultivate friends for reasons of profit, personal benefit, and utility—if there is no human sentiment that generates friendship for its own sake, through its own intrinsic power, and because it is inherently worth pursuing—is there any doubt that we will place real estate and apartment houses ahead of our friends?

84. "Here you may recall again those superlative words spoken by Epicurus in praise of friendship. I'm not asking for a verbatim quote of what he says, but rather what he can logically proffer that is consistent with his reasoning and thought processes. 'Friendship is sought for reasons of utility.' So do you think Triarius here is more useful to you than if you owned the granaries of Puteoli?[200] Collect all the Epicurean aphorisms you commonly

---

[200] Today known as Pozzuoli, a small city located about 8 km. west of Naples.

use. 'Friends are an armed garrison.' You can protect yourself. You can rely on the legal system. There is adequate protection in your regular friendships. You will not be able to be disrespected.[201] You will easily avoid hatred and jealousy: for lessons are given on these matters by Epicurus himself! And by spreading around your financial wealth so generously, you are protected and watched over splendidly by the goodwill of a great many people, without the need for any Pylades-type friendship![202]

85. "But with whom (as the saying goes) will you be able to share your serious or amusing thoughts, your intimate secrets, or your most personal reflections? You yourself are the best for this role; a non-threatening type of friend may also serve this purpose.[203] Let us agree that these benefits of friendship are not inconsequential. But what advantage do these benefits give us, when we compare them to huge sums of money? You can see, then, that if we measure friendship by the emotional bond it generates, there is nothing that surpasses it. But if you measure it purely in terms of financial reward, then you will conclude that the greatest human intimacies are eclipsed by the rent payment from a productive estate. *So if we are to be true friends, you should love me for myself, not for the things I own.*

XXVII. "But we are spending too much time on points that are self-evident. We have demonstrated conclusively that if everything is judged according to the 'pleasure' it brings, then

---

In Cicero's day it was a noted port city and trading hub; grain-ships from Egypt and other regions docked there.

[201] Meaning that a man of strong character cannot easily be denigrated by others.

[202] The last two sentences here are meant as contemptuous sarcasm. The reference to Pylades is from section 79, above.

[203] Cicero confided in Atticus in his personal letters, a non-competitive man with whom he could relax and let his guard down. He was the type of average, non-threatening confidant that Cicero is referring to here.

there is no place for the virtues or for friendships. Once this is understood, nothing else really needs to be said. Nevertheless, in order not to appear unresponsive to the points you've raised, I will say a few words in rebuttal to rest of your dissertation.

86. "While the entire of goal of philosophy is directed towards how to live a good life, and men seeking this one goal are united in devotion to this purpose, living happily has been interpreted in different ways by different philosophers. You place 'the good life' in pleasure; against this, you assign all wretchedness to pain. Let us first take a good look at what the nature of your 'good life' really is. I think you will concede that if happiness does in fact exist, it ought to be within the wise man's reach. For if a happy life can be lost, then a truly happy life is impossible. Who can have faith that something fragile and transitory will continue to endure with stability and permanence? The man who lacks confidence in the durability of his possessions must necessarily fear losing them and becoming miserable. No man who is in constant anxiety about life's most important things can be cheerful.

87. "No one, therefore, can be happy. A life is usually said to be 'happy' once its entire span has been surveyed, not just when looking at some particular segment of a life. Indeed a life is not properly called a life unless it is complete and consummated. A person also cannot be at one time happy, and at another time miserable; for he who thinks that he might be unhappy will not be content. For once the true Good Life has been attained, it is as permanent as wisdom itself (which is the creator of the Good Life). We need not wait until the end of our earthly lives, as Solon counseled Croesus to do, according to the historian Herodotus.[204]

---

[204] *See* Herodotus I.32. Solon's counsel to Croesus was that, because life was so uncertain and changeable, no man can be called happy until after he has died and his whole life has been evaluated. The same subject was specifically taken up by Montaigne in his *Essays* (I.19).

But here someone might point out—as you actually did—that Epicurus denies that longevity alone adds something meaningful to the Good Life. The pleasure experienced in a brief period of time, he says, may be just as much as the amount of pleasure felt in a period of infinite duration.

88. "These statements are entirely incompatible. While he places the Supreme Good in pleasure, he refuses to admit that the pleasure gained from an infinity of years would be greater than the pleasure felt in a finite period of time. If a man thinks the Highest Good is found in virtue, he can say that happiness is attained through the perfection of virtue; he does not believe that specific time periods can bring about the Highest Good. Then consider the man who thinks that happiness is attained through pleasure. How can he logically believe this if he doesn't think that the aggregate pleasure in our lives increases as time goes by?

"If aggregate pleasure does not grow with time, then neither does pain. And if the most terrible kind of pain is the pain that lasts the longest, should it not also be true that long duration optimizes pleasure? Why, then, is Epicurus always saying that God is 'happy' and 'eternal'? If Jupiter's immortality were taken away, he would be no happier than Epicurus: each of them is free to enjoy Epicurus's Highest Good, which is pleasure. Here you will say, 'But Epicurus might also experience pain!' Yet pain gives him no trouble. For he assures us that he would cheerfully say 'How delightful this is!' while being roasted alive.[205]

89. "So then in what way would God surpass Epicurus, if we were to take away God's immortality? And what good does immortality offer, except the highest and most long-lasting pleasure? What is the purpose of Epicurus's speaking so extravagantly, yet also so inconsistently? The ability to live a happy life is centered around bodily pleasure. If you want, I will

---

[205] See below, V.80 and V.85.

add 'mental pleasure' to this, as long as it too is acknowledged as being in the body (as you already have indicated). Who can assure the wise man that he will really receive this everlasting pleasure? For pleasures are created by variable causes that are not in the wise man's control. *Happiness is not to be found in wisdom itself; it is found by using the tools acquired by wisdom to produce pleasure.* However, all of this is external; and what is external is subject to chance. Thus Mistress Fortune is the final arbiter of the happy life: yet Epicurus claims that Fortune gives the wise man hardly any trouble at all.

XXVIII. 90. "Here you will say, 'Be reasonable! These criticisms are petty.' This same Nature enriches the life of the wise man, and Epicurus says Nature's treasures are easy to acquire. These words are true enough, and I do not oppose them; but Epicurus's positions are at odds with each other. He refuses to admit that the plainest sort of nourishment—that is, the lowliest kind of food and drink—might generate less pleasure than the most exquisite dishes at a banquet. As I see it, if he claimed that his happiness in life was not affected by the kind of food he ate, I would agree with him. I would also praise him for saying this, for he would be speaking the truth. On this point I will listen to Socrates—who reckoned pleasure to be unimportant—when he said that the seasoning for food should be hunger, and the flavoring for drink should be thirst.[206] But I will not listen to someone who makes everything in life about pleasure, someone who talks like Piso the Frugal[207] while living like Gallonius. I do not think he is saying what he truly believes.

---

[206] Meaning that neither food nor drink should be consumed to excess.
[207] Lucius Calpurnius Piso, tribune of the plebs in 149 B.C. and consul in 133 B.C., received the agnomen "Frugi" (frugal) for his parsimony with public funds. He also wrote an early annalistic history of Rome in seven books (now lost).

91. "He has said that nature's riches are easily procurable, because nature is content with little. No doubt this is true—if only you Epicureans didn't value pleasure so much! No less pleasure, he asserts, is gained from the cheapest things as from the most expensive. This displays not only a lack of judgment, but also very poor taste. Someone who looks down on pleasure may say that he doesn't value a sturgeon any more than an inexpensive fish.[208] But certainly for the man who places the Highest Good in pleasure, everything has to be judged according to sensation instead of reason; and the things that are most gratifying are inevitably called 'best.'

92. "Let us concede for argument's sake that what he says is true. If he can, he acquires the greatest pleasures not only for little expense, but (as I see it) for nothing. There is no less pleasure in the edible cress which (according to Xenophon[209]) the Persians regularly consumed as in the lavish Syracusan meals that were so harshly condemned by Plato. I concede that the acquisition of pleasure is as easy as you say it is. But what will we say about pain? If pain truly is the greatest evil, it can bring so many torments as to make a happy life simply impossible. The philosopher Metrodorus himself (who was practically another Epicurus) defined happiness with nearly these exact words: 'when the body has good health, and this condition is expected to persist.' But with regard to the state of one's body, can anyone have a guarantee of health? I don't say a year from now, but this very night! Therefore pain—the greatest evil—will always be feared even when it is not present, for its appearance is always possible. Who, then, can live in a state of happiness while in fear of the greatest evil?

---

[208] *Acipenser* is generally considered a sturgeon; *maena* is a small, cheap sea-fish, probably a sprat.

[209] *Cyropaedia* I.2. The cress named here is *nasturcium*, which according to the Oxford Latin Dictionary is likely *Lepidium sativum* or perhaps also watercress.

93. "Here someone will say, 'But a method of ignoring pain is taught by Epicurus!' Yet it is ludicrous to think that the greatest evil can simply be ignored. And what exactly is this method of his? He announces that 'the greatest pain lasts a short time.' First of all, what do you mean by 'a short time'? And what is 'the greatest pain' supposed to mean? Well, what? Can't the greatest pain last for several days? You might find out that it can last for months! Maybe you mean some random event that kills you as soon as it crosses your path. But who lives in fear of this sort of pain?

"I would prefer that you ease the pain suffered by that great and most humane man, my close friend Cnaeus Octavius (son of Marcus); and I want the pain lifted not just once or for a short time, but often, and for long durations. Immortal gods, what awful pain he went through! When every one of his limbs felt like it was on fire, he used to experience terrible suffering. Although he was going through a challenging ordeal, he was not 'miserable,' because pain was not considered the greatest evil. *But if he had inundated himself with pleasures in a life of dissipation and licentiousness, he certainly would have been miserable.*

XXIX. 94. "When you say, though, that intense pain is brief and mild pain long-lasting, I don't know what you mean by this. For I see pains that are intense and at the same time very lengthy. In order to tolerate them, it is better to do what you Epicureans—who do not love moral goodness for its own sake—are incapable of doing. There are certain precepts and rules of courage that forbid men to be effeminate in the face of pain. Thus it should be considered shameful not to be in pain—for this is sometimes necessary in life—but rather to 'defile the rock of Lemnos with the wailing of Philoctetes,'

Until he causes the silent rocks give off the sound of wailing,
Reverberating with his groaning, weeping, whimpering, and cries of sorrow.[210]

If he can, Epicurus can try to console a person who

Experiences horrific agonies in his blood-vessels and organs,
When injected with toxin from the viper's fang.

Here Epicurus would just say, 'Philoctetes, be calm! Remember that if the pain is extreme, it will be short!' But he has been in a cold tomb for ten years now. 'If the pain is prolonged, it will be light; it will come in intervals and diminish periodically.'

95. "Firstly, this does not often happen. And secondly, what good would this reprieve from pain be if the memory of the past pain is still recent, and if a man is still tormented by fear of imminent pain to come? Epicurus's response is, 'Let him die.' Maybe that is the best thing, but what happened to your motto 'Always more pleasure than pain'?[211] If this motto is true, don't you see that you are committing a foul act by telling him to die? Better would it be to say: *it is shameful and womanish for a man*

---

[210] This quote and the one that follows it are from the play *Philoctetes* by the early Latin dramatist Lucius Accius (also known as Lucius Attius) (170 B.C.—86 B.C.?). Substantial fragments of his works have survived. According to legend, Philoctetes was a warrior who, while on his way to Troy, was bitten by a snake. When the wound would not heal, he was abandoned on the island of Lemnos. His comrades eventually returned for him ten years later. The story is mentioned in Homer (*Iliad* II.720) and was the subject of Sophocles's play *Philoctetes*.

[211] *Plus semper voluptatis*, which could also be rendered "pleasure should always have the upper hand [i.e., over pain]."

to allow himself to be debilitated, shattered, and overwhelmed by pain. And with regard to your little epigram, 'Severe pain, short time; mild pain, long time,' it sounds like something dictated from a lesson-book. For pain is most effectively alleviated by the medicines of virtue, greatness of soul, endurance, and courage.

XXX. 96. "I don't want to wander too far away from our subject. But listen to what the dying Epicurus said, so that you can appreciate the gap between what he preached and what he actually practiced: *'Epicurus sends his greetings to Hermarchus.*[212] *I am writing this note on the last day—and also the happiest day—of my life. I am suffering from diseases of the bladder and colic*[213] *which could not possibly be more serious than they are now.'* Unfortunate man! If pain is the Greatest Evil, then nothing else can really be said. But let us hear what he actually did say: *'Even in the midst of all these physical hardships, I am still compensated by the spiritual happiness gained from reflecting on my doctrines and discoveries. In order to reflect honorably on me, and on the philosophy that you took up since your youth, look after Metrodorus's children.'*

97. "Not even the final scenes of the lives of Epaminondas and Leonidas would I value more highly than the picture presented by Epicurus's death. One of these men[214] defeated the Lacedaemonians at Mantinea and could see that he had been severely wounded; and the first thing he did after recovering his ability to speak was to ask whether his shield was intact. When his weeping men told him that it was, he asked whether the enemy had been defeated. When he heard the answer that he wanted to hear, he ordered the

---

[212] Hermarchus (c. 325 B.C.—c. 250 B.C.), an early disciple of Epicurus who succeeded him around 270 B.C. as head of the Epicurean school. Only a few fragments of his works are extant.

[213] *Torminum*, a griping pain in the bowels, or colic.

[214] Epaminondas defeated the Spartans at Mantinea in 362 B.C.

spear that had penetrated his body to be pulled out. And thus, with the emission of a great deal of blood, he expired in victory and happiness. Leonidas, the Lacedaemonian king who led his band of three hundred men from Sparta, confronted a foreign army at Thermopylae[215] and had to choose between an ignominious flight or a glorious death. A battlefield death for a military commander is heroic; philosophers, however, normally expire in their beds. Nevertheless it makes a difference *how* they die. Epicurus seemed to be happy as he passed away. I compliment him on this. He says, 'My terrible pain is cancelled out by the joy I feel.'

98. "Epicurus, I certainly listen to the words of a philosopher; but you have forgotten what should have been said at that moment.[216] Firstly, if the things that you claim to feel joy in recalling are true—that is, if your books and discoveries are true—then you cannot really be rejoicing. You have no physical sensation that relates to the body; but you have always insisted that the only way a man can feel either joy or pain is through the use of his body. Epicurus says, 'I rejoice in what happened in the past.' What past events are you talking about? If you are referring to things related to the body, then I would respond that *it is actually your philosophical ideas, not the memory of past pleasures your body experienced*, that are compensating you for your current physical sufferings. But if you are referring to the mind, then your belief that all mental pleasures ultimately relate back to the body is simply not correct. And finally, why are you concerned with providing for Metrodorus's children? What is there related to the body in this exceptional act (as I see it) of duty and faithfulness?[217]

XXXI. 99. "Torquatus, you Epicureans may skirt and dodge the point, but I say there is nothing stated in this well-known letter

---

[215] The famous Battle of Thermopylae against the Persians in 480 B.C.
[216] I.e., just before death.
[217] Meaning that Epicurus's telling someone to care for the children had nothing to do with bodily pleasure.

of Epicurus that is consistent and in accord with the teachings he advocated. Thus he refutes himself: his doctrines are defeated by his own honesty and good morals. The desire to provide for Metrodorus's children, the awareness and care he had for friendship, and the observance of these all-important duties in the final moments of his life, all show that there was an innate, unqualified decency in the man, an inherent goodness not motivated by physical pleasures or the inducements of material rewards. When we consider how great was his sense of obligation in his final moments of life, what more compelling evidence can we ask for to prove that moral goodness and virtue are desirable for their own sake?[218]

100. "While I believe that this letter—which I have precisely translated—is very much deserving of praise, and although it is in no way consistent with his philosophy, in a larger sense I think that his final testament is not only inappropriate for the dignity of a philosopher but also disconnected from his own statements. Indeed he expended a great many words to advance the following view (and so stated tersely and compactly in the book I named a short while ago): 'Death does not concern us. That which has been destroyed cannot feel anything; and that which has no sensation does not affect us at all.' He could have stated this idea in a more elegant and artful way. For when he said, 'that which has been destroyed cannot feel anything,' the phrase he uses does not make it clear just *what it is* that has been destroyed.

101. "Still, I understand what he is trying to say. But the question I have is this: if the physical body is destroyed—that is, when the senses are terminated by death and nothing remains that may have any effect on us—why is it that he makes such painstaking and detailed plans and mandates that '*my heirs Amynomachus and*

---

[218] Cicero adroitly manages to use Epicurus's good personal character as a weapon against Epicurean doctrines.

Timocrates shall, after discussion with Hermarchus, set aside suf-
ficient resources to celebrate my birthday every year in the month
of Gamelion,[219] *and will also make adequate provision for a*
group dinner for their fellow philosophy students on the twentieth
day of each month, in order to honor the memory of both myself
and Metrodorus?'

102. "I have to say that these are the words of a considerate and charitable man. But in no way should a wise man (especially a natural philosopher, which is how Epicurus presents himself) think that any day can serve as someone's birthday. How could this be? Could the same day arrive again and again? Certainly not. What about a similar day? This could not happen either, unless there was an intervening period of many thousands of years, when all the stars completed their revolutions and at the same time returned to their original positions.[220] Therefore, no person really has a birthday. Someone may say, 'But a day is customarily chosen.' Well, thank you for educating me about this! Even if this is so, should a birthday be celebrated after one's death? Speaking with the authority of an oracle, Epicurus taught that nothing can affect us after we die; yet he establishes a birthday memorial for himself in his will. An act like this is not exactly fitting for a man whose 'mind roamed thoroughly'[221] over innumerable worlds, infinite vistas of space, and regions without shores or boundaries. Did Democritus do something like this? (To avoid mentioning other Epicurean philosophers, I will only name the man whose doctrines Epicurus followed.)

---

[219] A month in the Attic calendar of ancient Greece. Gamelion (Γαμηλιών) was a winter month and roughly corresponds with our modern January and February.

[220] This point of Platonic astronomy (the "turning year" (*vere vertens annus*) or "great year") is discussed in Cicero's *Dream of Scipio* (book VI of his *De Re Publica*). *See* my *Stoic Paradoxes* (Charleston: Quintus Curtius, 2015), p. 98, note 73 for a detailed discussion of this topic. A "great year" (*magnus annus*) was traditionally believed to be between 12,000 and 15,000 years.

[221] A sly reference to the Lucretius's *De Rerum Natura* I.74.

103. "And if a day should have been chosen for his remembrance, was it better to pick the day on which he was born, rather than the day on which he became a wise man? Your response will be, 'He could not become wise unless he had first been born.' Following this logic, one could just as easily say 'unless his grandmother had been born.' Everything about wanting the memory of your name to be celebrated with a group dinner after your death is unworthy of educated men. How you Epicureans go about celebrating this day, and the degree of sophistication of the witty men you encounter there, I will not discuss.[222] There is no need to fight about this. I will only mention that it was more important for you to celebrate Epicurus's birthday than it was for him to make arrangements in his will that it be celebrated.

XXXII. 104. "But let us return to our original proposition— for we have been sidetracked by this testimonial letter. We may conclude the issue in this way. He who is gripped by the Greatest Evil is not happy at the time he is caught up in it; but the wise man, however, is always happy, even if he experiences pain now and then. Thus, pain is not the Greatest Evil. And what does it mean to say, 'the wise man should not forget the goods things that happened in the past, and should not remember the bad things'? Do we have the ability to control what we remember? Indeed, when Simonides or some other person proposed to teach Themistocles how to improve his memory, Themistocles bluntly responded, 'I prefer to learn how to forget. For I remember what I don't want to remember, and I can't forget what I want to forget.'

---

[222] This sentence and the two that follow are classic Ciceronian oratory: mockery mixed with a hint of scorn.

105. "Epicurus was a man of great natural disposition; but we cannot ignore the fact that it is too domineering for a philosopher to command us to forget something. If you insist on ordering me to do something I cannot do, keep in mind that adopting these imperious habits makes you as big a tyrant as your ancestor Manlius—perhaps even bigger.[223] And what happens if the memory of past evils is actually enjoyable? It goes to show that some proverbs are more true than the doctrines of the Epicurean school. It is commonly said that 'Completed labors are delightful.'[224] Euripides puts it quite well when he says (I will put it into Latin, if I can, but all of you know this verse in Greek):

> The remembrance of long-departed hardships brings satisfaction.[225]

But let us revisit the question of past Goods. If your school was referring to the kind of past Goods that Caius Marius[226] possessed after he had become a destitute exile wallowing in a swamp who alleviated his misery by musing over his old triumphs, then I might listen to you and agree enthusiastically. The happy life of the wise man could never be attained, or guided to its complete maturity, if all of his good deeds and wise designs were first purged entirely from his memory.

------

[223] Referring to Titus Manlius Imperiosus Torquatus, mentioned above in II.60.

[224] *Iucundi acti labores.*

[225] From Euripides's lost play *Andromeda*. Fragments of the play are preserved in several ancient writers. Details of the myth of Perseus and Andromeda are found in Ovid (*Metamorphoses* IV.604—803).

[226] Roman general and statesman (157 B.C.—86 B.C.), known for his unrelenting ambition and energy. He endured a period of exile before making a final (but short-lived) return to power. On his character, see my *Sallust: The Conspiracy of Catiline and The War of Jugurtha* (Charleston: Fortress of the Mind Publications, 2017), pp. 228—231.

106. "But for you Epicureans it is the remembrance of savored past pleasures that makes a happy life. And indeed you mean bodily pleasures: for if it were any other type of pleasure, then it is false that all pleasures of the mind are derived from their close connection with the body. If bodily pleasure is a source of delight even if it happened in the past, then I do not understand why Aristotle so ridiculed the epigram of Sardanapalus,[227] in which the Syrian king bragged that he had taken with him all the physical pleasures he enjoyed during life. How (Aristotle asked) could a pleasure sensation last after death that, even when he was alive, the king could not feel for a long time while he was enjoying it? Bodily pleasures, therefore, quickly fade away: each one vanishes in succession, leaving us more often with cause for regret than remembrance. For this reason Scipio Africanus should be considered happier when he told his country the following:

Be finished with your enemies, Rome.

He then finished with this wonderful sentiment:

My labors have produced your robust fortifications.[228]

Scipio derives satisfaction from his past hardships, but you are telling us to feel joy from our past pleasures. He evokes past experiences that had nothing to do with the body; but you insist on linking everything to the body.

---

[227] The text reads *Sardanapalli epigramma*. The word *epigramma* can mean inscription, short poem, or epigram. The reference is to a work of Aristotle that has not been preserved. Sardanapalus is the Hellenized name for a legendarily corrupt Assyrian king; the name is probably an amalgamation of two kings, Ashur-uballit II and Ashurbanipal. *See* Diodorus Siculus II.27.
[228] The source of this quote is unknown; it may be the poet Ennius.

XXXIII. 107. "Who can support this idea you Epicureans teach, that all pleasures and pains of the mind are derived from pleasures and pains of the body? Doesn't anything, Torquatus (I know with whom I am speaking), give you joy simply for its own sake? I will omit honor, moral goodness, and the splendor of the virtues (which were discussed earlier). I will propose these lighter topics: poetry and oratory (whether written or read); the study of past events and the world's various regions; statues, paintings, beautiful landscapes, sports, hunting; and Lucullus's country villa[229] If I talk about *your* villa, you will have a pretext to wriggle out of my point, by saying that you derive physical pleasure from your villa. Consider these pleasures I have just listed: do you really connect them to the body? Isn't there something that gives you joy by itself and on its own? If you insist on linking the pleasures I have just mentioned to the body, then you prove yourself to be totally unreasonable; and if you admit my point, then you repudiate Epicurus's entire notion of pleasure.

108. "You have advanced the idea that mental pleasures and pains are greater than those of the body, based on the fact that the intellect is active in three periods of time[230] while the body feels only things happening in the present. Yet who can agree with the idea that someone who celebrates on account of my own pleasure actually feels more joy than I do myself? [Pleasure of the mind comes about because of bodily pleasure, and mental pleasure is greater than bodily pleasure; therefore it follows that the person

---

[229] Lucius Licinius Lucullus (118 B.C.—c. 56 B.C.), general and politician of the late republic who distinguished himself during the Third Mithridatic War (73 B.C.—63 B.C.). According to Plutarch's *Life of Lucullus*, in later years he became notorious for his lavish banqueting and lifestyle. The adjective *Lucullian* has entered the English language as a synonym for luxurious gastronomy.

[230] The past, present, and future.

who congratulates is happier than the person being congratulated].[231] But if you try to demonstrate that the wise man feels the greatest mental pleasures, and that these are in every way superior to the pleasures of the body, you do not see the problem this creates for your argument. For you must also say, then, that the wise man feels mental pain greater in every respect than he feels bodily pain. Thus, he whom you want always to be happy must sometimes be stricken by suffering: *and you will never succeed in making him happy as long as you continue to evaluate everything in terms of pleasure and pain.*

109. "For this reason, Torquatus, something else must be found to serve as man's Supreme Good. We may allow physical pleasure as something for the beasts (whose testimony you Epicureans are in the habit of using when discussing the Supreme Good). But what if even animals, driven by their individual natures, do many activities that are mostly selfless and at their own expense (such as giving birth to offspring and rearing their young), so that one can easily see they are motivated by other impulses besides pleasure? Some animals find joy in running and ambling around; others love to assemble in communities and create social structures that simulate our idea of a 'state.'

110. "In certain types of birds we detect some indications of compassion towards their fellows and powers of recognition and memory; in many of them we even observe expressions of regret. So if the equivalents of the human virtues are unrelated to pleasure in the case of animals, will there be no virtue except for pleasure's sake in the case of human beings? And will we really say that man—who is so vastly superior to other living things—has been granted nothing unique from nature?

---

[231] This sentence appears in the Latin text but has been rejected by editors as a later interlineation by a scribe or copyist. It is apparently intended to reinforce the point made in the preceding sentence by showing the logical inconsistency of the Epicureans' ideas.

XXXIV. 111. "If indeed everything is about pleasure, we humans are greatly surpassed by the beasts. This earth generously grants them various and abundant pasturage with no exertions on their part, while for us the expenditure of great effort sometimes can—and sometimes cannot—accommodate our survival needs. Yet in no way can I consider the Supreme Good for a beast of burden and for a human being to be the same. What would be the purpose of the machinery we have created for the advancement of learning? Of what use would be the catalogue of honorable intellectual endeavors, or the noble fraternity of the virtues, if all of these things are sought for no other reason except pleasure?

112. "If Xerxes, when he crossed the Hellespont with such huge numbers of ships, cavalry, and foot soldiers, cut a passage through Mount Athos[232] and marched through seas and sailed over lands,[233] and if, when he arrived in Greece with this colossal force and someone asked him the purpose for all these forces bristling with weapons, he had answered that he only wanted to retrieve some honey from Mount Hymettus,[234] then of course his immense expedition would be seen as utterly pointless. Similarly, if we say that the wise man—trained and outfitted with all the most distinguished arts and virtues and not, like Xerxes, stumbling across the seas on foot and navigating mountains with ships, but instead mentally comprehending the heavens, land, and sea in all their aspects—has only pleasure as his goal, then we are saying that all the wise man's labor is expended for the sake of some honey.

113. "Believe me, Torquatus, we are born for greater and no-bler missions. This is clear not only from the mind's varied

---

[232] The Persian king Xerxes ordered a canal to be dug across the Athos isthmus during his invasion of Greece in 483 B.C. *See* Herodotus VII.24.

[233] The text actually reads *mari ambulavisset, terra navigavisset* ("marched through seas and sailed over land.")

[234] A mountain range near Athens. The honey near Hymettus was famous for its excellence. *See* Pliny, *Hist. Nat.* XI.13.

capabilities, which possess the ability to recall vast amounts of information. In your case, this power of memory is almost infinite. It is also shown by our ability to predict future events with a degree of accuracy not far removed from divination. It is found in our sense of shame that restrains our basic desires. It is displayed by our sense of justice that acts as a steadfast sentinel for human society; and it is revealed by our showing toughness and resolution when engaged in great labors and when wrestling with dangers, or by our showing contempt for pain and death. These are the capabilities of the mind. But you should also consider the body's limbs and organs of sense-perception: for these, like the other parts of the body, you will realize are not only the *associates* of the virtues, but also their *servants*.

114. "But if, with regard to the body, many qualities are given priority over pleasure (such as strength, health, swiftness, and beauty), what will you then think about the intellect? The most learned men of ancient times taught that that the intellect contained an element of the divine and the celestial. If the Supreme Good were found in pleasure (as you Epicureans say), the most desirable thing of all would be to spend one's days and nights—with no interruption—surrounded by the most intense pleasure, with every bodily sense so stimulated as if to be practically drenched in bliss. But who is worthy of being called a man, who would want to spend one single day experiencing this kind of 'pleasure'? Indeed the Cyrenaics[235] do not object to this form of indulgence. You Epicureans are more modest in these matters; but the Cyrenaics, perhaps, are more consistent.

115. "But let us not be distracted by a discussion of these very important arts. We note that our ancestors would have considered a man who lacked such arts to be useless. Instead I ask if you

---

[235] The adherents of the hedonistic school founded by Aristippus of Cyrene.

167

believe Phidias, Polyclitus, and Zeuxis—as well as Homer, Archilochus, or Pindar—practiced their arts for the sake of pleasure.[236] Would an artisan, therefore, have a better awareness of the beauty of forms, than a distinguished citizen would have of the beauty of good deeds? What cause could there be for a mistake so chronic and so pervasive? It is the fact that he who thinks pleasure to be the Supreme Good does not use the part of his mind controlled by reason and rational deliberation, but rather the part ruled by desire—the most capricious part of the mind. I would also like to know this: if the gods really do exist (as you Epicureans believe), how can they be happy if they are unable to feel bodily pleasure? Or if they are happy without this kind of pleasure, why do you refuse to believe that a wise man could experience something similar, namely, a pleasure of the mind?

XXXV. 116. "Torquatus, read the written tributes not of the men eulogized in the pages of Homer—not of Cyrus, Agesilaus, Aristides, Themistocles, and not Philip or Alexander. Read instead the panegyrics composed about our own men; read the encomiums written to honor your own family. You will see no one praised for being an adept master in the art of acquiring pleasures. Neither do inscriptions on grave markers show this. Consider the one beside the city gate:

HERE LIES ONE WHOM MANY DIVERSE NATIONS ACKNOWLEDGE
WAS A MAN OF THE FIRST RANK.

---

[236] Phidias (c. 480 B.C.—430 B.C.) was a famed Greek sculptor and painter; Polyclitus of Argos was a Greek sculptor of the fifth century; and Zeuxis of Heraclea was a fifth century Greek painter. Homer should require no explanation; Archilochus of Paros was a seventh century Greek lyric poet; Pindar of Thebes (c. 522 B.C.—c. 443 B.C.) was a famed early lyric poet.

117. "Did many diverse nations acknowledge that Calatinus[237] was a 'man of the first rank' because he had been superb in amassing pleasures? Will we say, then, that strong character and true potential are found in those young people whom we judge to be ruled by their own self-interests and whatever actions are expedient for them? Do we not see what turmoil, what demoralizing social upheaval, such an ethic would create in the natural order of things? Kindness is removed; gratitude is removed; and these are the very bonds of social comity.[238] It should not be considered benevolence when you lend money to another person for your own benefit, but usury;[239] no gratitude is owed to him who, for his own profit, makes money available to another. When pleasure holds the dominant position, all the virtues will eventually be reduced to ruins. *Unless moral goodness is made dominant as a natural principle, it is difficult to refute the proposition that there are many morally depraved actions consistent with the behavior of a wise man.*

118. "Rather than present additional examples—there are indeed many—it is sufficient to say that truly authentic virtue must not allow pleasure to gain a foothold in its domain. Do not expect me to lay everything out for you; examine your own conscience. After careful and extensive reflection, ask yourself this: would you prefer to bask in the enjoyment of perpetual pleasures and—as you so often talked about—live all your years in tranquility without any pain or even the fear of pain (a condition you Epicureans add but which can never occur), or would you rather serve the needs of all mankind, bringing prosperity and hope to the downtrodden, even if this may seem at times to be like the brutal toils of Hercules?[240] It was this truly somber word—

---

[237] Aulus Atilius Calatinus (?—c. 216 B.C.), Roman general of the First Punic War and politician who was consul in 258 B.C. and 254 B.C.

[238] *Tollitur beneficium, tollitur gratia, quae sunt vincla concordiae.*

[239] *Faeneratio.*

[240] Referring to the famous "twelve labors" of Hercules from Greek

toils[241]—that our ancestors rightly used to describe labors that could not be avoided, even by someone who was a god.

119. "I could bait you and force you to respond, were I not so worried that you might say the labors of Hercules—shouldered for mankind's salvation—were performed for the sake of pleasure."

I was now finished. Torquatus then spoke. "I have specialists to whom I can refer your arguments," he said. "Although I could present a rebuttal myself, I prefer to find learned experts to handle this."

"I think you are referring to our good friends Siro and Philodemus," I replied.[242] "They are both good men, and very well-read in these matters."

"I definitely agree," he said.

"So be it," I answered. "But it would be more objective to let Triarius issue a final ruling on our debate."

Smiling, Torquatus said, "I would object to that! He is hardly impartial on this subject. Your views are moderate, but Triarius would really bludgeon us with a Stoic cane!"

To this Triarius responded, "Certainly after this discussion I will be even more bold, for the arguments I have heard will be right at my fingertips. But I won't become truly aggressive until I can confirm you've been prepared by these experts you talk about."

And with that, our walk and our dialogue came to an end.

———————————

mythology.

[241] *Aerumnas*, as distinguished from *labores*.

[242] Philodemus of Gadara (c. 110 B.C.—35? B.C.), an Epicurean philosopher who studied under Zeno before moving to Rome. Substantial portions of his works—long buried by the Vesuvius eruption—have miraculously been unearthed at Herculaneum in the so-called "Villa of the Papyri." These works are now being gradually published. Siro "The Epicurean" (fl. 50 B.C.) resided in Naples and is credited with having been one of the poet Virgil's teachers.

COMMENTARY ON BOOK II

In Book II, Cicero makes a dedicated effort to refute Epicurus's ethical system. He begins with the Epicurean conception of pleasure, which he argues is ill-defined and confused (II.4). It is futile to search for the End of Goods, he says, when we do not even have a clear definition of what pleasure is (II.5). Pleasure is not just pain avoidance; there is a difference between sensory pleasure and the avoidance of pain. The arguments found in II.6 through II.15 elaborate on this point. What Epicurus never grasped is that "lack of pain" is not really pleasure, but a sort of middle-ground between true pleasure and true pain (II.16).

This failure to pay attention to definitions and fine-line distinctions, Cicero says, is one of the main reasons why Epicurus arrived at flawed conclusions. Instead, he mistakenly conflated "pleasure" and the "absence of pain." Epicurus also attempted to classify desires into three categories (II.26): natural and necessary, natural and not necessary, and neither natural nor necessary. But this scheme is confusing and unnecessary. There are, in fact, only two kinds of desires (II.26). The problem is that Epicurus could never really make up his mind whether he thought absence of pain was the End of Goods, or whether he thought pleasure was.

Worse yet, Epicurus's fixation on pleasure opened himself up to allegations of endorsing moral corruption. We must look at the primary impulses of human nature (II.34). Any consideration of the End of Goods must give the central position to human reason, not to our senses. When all is said and done, Cicero reminds us, virtue is the all-important source for the Highest Good; the virtues are based on reason and are our best guide (II.45—47). Epicurus did not speak enough of the virtues; he glosses over the importance of justice, courage, temperance, and courage. Various examples from history (Epaminondas and Leonidas) tell us what is truly important in human affairs (II.62). The impression Cicero gives of Epicureanism is that it remains a cowardly, negative, inward-looking philosophy, a thought system unworthy of a great man (II.67). No man of affairs could embrace it and hope to be successful (II.74). Epicureanism sees the virtues as little more than appendages to be used to acquire pleasure, instead of the character-building fortresses of strength that they really are (II.69). Epicurus paid lip-service to the idea of virtue, but in fact he had little faith in its redemptive power.

Cicero believes that Epicurus's ideas corrupted the idea of friendship (II.78), but his reasons for saying this are not convincing. He believes that Epicurus's ideas encouraged a mercenary conception of friendship, a conception grounded in temporary expediency. This is too harsh an indictment; in fact, friendship was one of the most positive aspects of Epicureanism.

No wise man can make pleasure his focus; pain will always be present, and he must learn to deal with it (II.90). It is no use looking for ways to escape something that will always be a fact of life. Cicero at least has good words to say about Epicurus's personal conduct. Although the philosopher may have been wrong in his ideas, he at least lived an exemplary life. In fact, the example of his life proves that courage and virtue are more important than pleasure (II.96). Brilliantly focusing on Epicurus's will and testament, Cicero nevertheless finds a way to turn the philosopher's own words against him (II.99—102). Pleasure may have its modest place, but when all was said and done, an End of Goods must be found that is based on something more solid and enduring than pleasure.

Cicero's attack on Epicureanism may not be entirely fair, but it certainly resonates. He harps again and again on: (1) Epicurus's flawed definition of pleasure; (2) the critical error of basing a theory of the End of Goods on pleasure; (3) Epicurus's timid downplaying of the importance of the masculine virtues; (4) the unsuitability of Epicureanism for a man of affairs; and (5) Epicurus's allegedly flawed theory of friendship. Except for the last one, these criticisms are reasonable. It is difficult for the reader not to conclude that Epicureanism is not quite up to the task of providing us with a worthy conception of the Supreme Good.

BOOK III

BOOK III

I. 1. If Pleasure had to argue on her own, Brutus, and did not
have such obstinate advocates arguing *for* her, I am convinced that
at this point—having been routed by the soundness of the
arguments in the preceding book—she would admit defeat. She
would indeed be impudent if she continued to fight against virtue
by placing physical pleasures ahead of moral goodness, or by
insisting that bodily delights and the sense of satisfaction they
produce are more important than seriousness of mind and
steadfastness of character. Let us, therefore, dismiss Pleasure
from our presence, and direct her to stay within her proper
boundaries, lest the importance of this discussion be undermined
by her charms and enticements.

2. This is what must be asked: where can we discover that
Supreme Good we are searching for? Pleasure has been removed
from our analysis; and the same criticism can be leveled against
those who try to equate the End of Goods with "the absence of

pain."[243] Ultimately, any conception of the Supreme Good that excludes virtue cannot be recommended, for there is nothing more transcendent than virtue. Although we were not ineffective in our debate with Torquatus, an even more imposing challenge now lies before us with the Stoics. Pleasure, when it is made a subject for discussion, does not exactly produce the most sophisticated or profound kind of dialogue: those who advocate for pleasure tend to be unable to handle logical debate, and those who argue against it are not confronting a very formidable enemy.

3. Actually Epicurus advises against having protracted debates about pleasure; he believes it is more appropriately judged by our bodily senses. It is enough for us, he says, to be reminded of pleasure: beyond this nothing more need be proven. This was why our discussion focused on presenting the basic arguments of both sides. There was nothing obscure or excessively complex in Torquatus's presentation; and my statements were, I believe, quite transparent. But as you well know, the Stoics have a tortuous and finely-tuned dialectical style. The Greeks certainly consider them difficult, and we Romans must find them even more so, since new Latin terms must be coined and a new philosophical parlance established for unfamiliar concepts. This will come as no surprise to someone of even average learning. Such a person will remember that in every field of knowledge beyond the layman's ken and purview, there will always be a good deal of lexical innovation when new words are created for its specialized phraseology.

4. Therefore, natural philosophy and the study of logic both use words that are unknown even to the Greeks. Geometry, music, and grammar also employ their own specialized jargons. Even the

---

[243] I.e., the same objections that were made against "pleasure" being the End of Goods can be made against "absence of pain" being the End of Goods.

art of rhetoric—which is entirely public and universal[244]—still uses its own idiosyncratic and distinctive vocabulary when training students.

II. And even if I omit these elegant and distinguished arts, it is clear that not even common artisans would be able to sustain their profession unless they used a specific nomenclature that is foreign to us, but quite familiar to them. Even agriculture, which is averse to bookish notions of sophistication, has constituted new terms to handle the specifics of its activities. The philosopher must do the same thing, and has even more justification for doing so: for philosophy is the art of life, and it cannot conduct its inquiries with words from the market-place.[245]

5. Of all the philosophical schools, the Stoics have been the most willing to break with tradition; yet Zeno, their founder, was not so much an inventor of new doctrines as he was a creator of new terms. If the Greeks have allowed their learned men— speaking a tongue generally considered more abundant in vocabulary than Latin—to discourse on arcane subjects using abstruse terminology, should it not be even more justified for us Romans (who are daring to grapple with these subjects for the first time) to take such creative liberties with our own language? We have often said—and we have directed this complaint not only against the Greeks themselves but also against those who would

---

[244] Classical rhetoric was divided into three broad categories: *forensic* (or judicial), *epideictic*, and *deliberative*. *Forensic* rhetoric was for the courtroom and focused on the justice or merits of a case; *epideictic* rhetoric was the speech that focused on praise or condemnation, such as invectives, encomia, and panegyrics; and *deliberative* rhetoric was speech designed to persuade an audience.

[245] This section (4) and the previous one highlight Cicero's awareness of the need for creating new words in Latin to deal with subtle philosophical concepts. This creativity remains one of his great legacies.

like to be considered Greek—that we Latin speakers are not only *not bested* by the Greeks when it comes to richness of vocabulary, but are in fact *their superiors*.[246] We must strive relentlessly to demonstrate our true worth, not only in our own arts, but also in those fields considered the exclusive domain of the Greeks. Those words that have been incorporated into the Latin lexicon through recognized custom (such as "philosophy" itself, as well as "rhetoric," "dialectic," "grammar," "geometry," and "music"), we may consider as belonging to us. Although these concepts could be expressed with new Latin words, the foregoing Greek terms have already been assimilated into our vocabulary by established tradition. These, then, are my views with regard to philosophical terminology.

6. As for these subjects, Brutus, I often fear I will be scolded for writing about them to you, a man who has advanced so far not just in the general study of philosophy, but specifically in the best category of philosophy.[247] If I were pretending to give you lessons, I would be justly reproached. But this is absolutely not my intention. I am sending you these books not to teach you

---

[246] This sentence and the one that follows it are significant. As stated in the Introduction, Cicero is throwing down the gauntlet to those upper-class Romans who slavishly imitated Greek culture and undervalued their own. In Cicero's day, Greek was considered the premier language of education and scholarship. For a learned Roman like Cicero (himself educated in Greek and speaking it fluently) to insist that Latin was not just *equal* to Greek, but actually *superior* to it, was something boldly iconoclastic. Some may disagree with his statements, but it cannot be denied that he set out single-handedly to refashion the Latin language. In his hands Latin would come to rival—and then surpass—Greek as the language of education in Western Europe until modern times. His linguistic nationalism shows him at his scrappy, competitive best, and proves that he could be a visionary thinker in his own right.

[247] Meaning ethics, which Cicero considered the most important branch of philosophy.

subjects you are already thoroughly familiar with, but because I take great solace in inscribing your name here, and because I consider you a fair-minded judge and arbiter of those ethical studies with which you and I share a common bond. You will therefore listen closely, as you always do, in order to mediate this debate I had with your uncle, a man of unrivalled brilliance and inspired vision.

7. I happened recently to be in Tusculum,[248] and wanted to make use of some books in young Lucullus's library. I paid a visit to his villa, as I often did, to find the materials I was looking for. When I entered the residence, I found Marcus Cato—whom I had no idea would be there—sitting in the library, encircled by a large number of volumes on Stoic philosophy. As you know well, he had a craving for books that was almost never satisfied; indeed, never afraid of the disapproval of the crowd (yet not neglecting his duties to the state), it was his habit to read in the Curia itself while waiting for the senate to convene its session. Thus it was fitting to find him buried amid such copious rolls of books, ensconced in "lettered gluttony," if this phrase is indeed appropriate.

8. When we both happened to see each other, he stood up immediately. Then came the standard questions we usually asked each other when meeting.

"So why are you here?" he said. "I'm guessing you came from your villa. If I'd known you were there, I would have paid you a visit!"

"The games started yesterday, so I left the city and arrived here in the evening. I came here to pick up some books. Without doubt, Cato, our friend Lucullus really should get to know this wonderful library; and I hope he gets more satisfaction from these books than from any other furnishing in his house. Although of

---

[248] Tusculum was a town in Italy's Latium (modern Lazio) region, located in the Alban Hills near Rome, about 6 km. south of the modern town of Frascati.

course it is your own responsibility, I'm very much concerned that he becomes as learned as his father and our friend Caepio—and as well as you yourself, who are so closely related to him. I have good reason for taking an interest in this. I have a very high regard for his grandfather's memory. And you certainly know how much I thought of Caepio, who would in my view be one of the greatest men of our day if he were still alive. Lucius Lucullus is someone I can never forget; he was a giant among his peers, and he was linked to me in friendship, purpose, and shared ways of thinking."

9. "It is a beautiful thing," Cato said, "for you to honor the memory of men who entrusted their children to you as their legacy. Just as admirable is your special regard for young Lucullus. I don't recuse myself from what you call my own responsibility, but I'd like to have you as a partner in this duty. I can also say that the boy already gives many indications of humility and solid character—but you can see how young he still is."

"I can indeed see this," I replied. "But he ought to be imbued with those humanistic arts which he will readily absorb while still of tender years; such a program will fortify him for greater challenges as he grows older."

"Exactly," he rejoined. "We will certainly talk about this in greater detail several more times, and implement a joint plan of action. But let's sit down, if you'd like."

We both then took a seat.

III. 10. Cato then asked, "What books would you need here, since you already have access to so many?"

"I came here to borrow some Aristotelean note-books[249] that I knew were here, hoping I might read them in my free time. I do not often get such time for myself."

---

[249] This term is explained more fully in V.12, below. The word used is *commentarius*, which can mean note-book, journal, treatise, or textbook. In context here it describes a type of literary work.

"How I wish you would lean towards the Stoics!" he chuckled. "If any man could appreciate it, you certainly would know that the only real good is virtue."

"But it is rather *you*," I said, "who should not have bandied about a lot of new words, when in fact you see things the same way I do. Our reasoning is in harmony, but our words conflict.[250]

"Our reasoning is not in harmony at all," he retorted. "If you say that there is something besides moral goodness that should be sought after, and treat anything except moral goodness as a true good, then you wipe out the idea moral goodness itself—which is the very light of virtue. You are effectively demolishing the idea of virtue."

11. "Those are lofty-sounding words, Cato," I replied. "But don't you know that the grandeur of your words was echoed by Pyrrho and Aristo,[251] who gave an equal value to all things? I want to know what you think of their ideas."

"Do you really want to know what I think?" he shot back. "I think men who were strong, good, just, and self-controlled (whom we either learned about from history or witnessed ourselves during public service), men who accomplished great deeds by following Nature's law without any formal philosophical training—*I believe these men were better molded by Nature than they ever could have been shaped by philosophy had they adopted any doctrine other than the one telling us that there is nothing truly good except moral goodness, and that moral corruption is the only evil.* All other schools of philosophy (some more than others, but still all of them) say that something having no virtue can be either a good or an evil.

---

[250] A memorable aphorism: *Ratio enim nostra consentit, pugnat oratio.*
[251] See II.35, above.

Scenes along the road from Frascati to Tusculum

"I think these schools not only do nothing to help us or strengthen us in our quest for self-improvement, but they actually degrade our characters. Unless we unequivocally uphold the idea that moral goodness is the only true good, it is impossible to prove that the good life is achieved through virtue. And if we can't even establish *this*,[252] then I have no idea why we should spend our time studying philosophy. For if any wise man can be miserable, I don't see why I should place such a high value on your glorious and exalted virtue."

IV. 12. "The statements you've made so far," I countered, "could easily have been spoken by an adherent of Pyrrho or Aristo. As you know, this moral goodness you refer to is for them not only the *highest* good but also the *only* good, just as you yourself say; and if this is true, it follows that all wise men are happy—a conclusion I believe you endorse. So do you agree with the view of these philosophers, and believe we should adopt it?

"No, I don't think you should accept their view," he told me. "The most critical aspect of virtue is that one has a degree of choice among the things that are in accordance with nature. Those who make everything equal—so that all things revert to a bland uniformity and nothing stands out as worthy of selection— succeed only in destroying virtue itself."

13. "You certainly make the point convincingly," I nodded. "But I wonder whether you're doing the same thing they are if you insist that only what is morally right and honest is good, and remove all differences between everything else.

"This would indeed be true," he asserted, "if I were removing all differences between everything else. But I am not doing this."

---

[252] The text literally here reads *quod si ita sit*, or "if this is so," referring to the point made in the previous sentence. A more relaxed style in English sometimes better matches the tone of the text.

14. "But how are you *not* doing it?" I pressed him. "If virtue is the *one thing*, that *sole thing* which you say is morally good, right, praiseworthy, and respectable (for its meaning is better elucidated by using a number of descriptive words)—if, I say, this virtue is the *only* good, then what else will you have to seek besides this? Or if there is nothing bad except what is indecent, shameful, ugly, depraved, scandalous, or hideous (here also we make our point by using an assortment of terms), what else besides this do you think should be avoided?

"You can guess what I am going to say," he rejoined. "But since I suspect you would love to take advantage of my words if I give a brief response,[253] I will not answer you point by point. And because we have the leisure time, I will instead set forth the complete philosophical system of Zeno and the Stoics—unless you have an objection to my doing so."

"Of course not!" I exclaimed. "Your explanation would be of tremendous value in helping us resolve the questions we have been asking."

15. "Well, then let us put it to the test!" he cried. "But remember that there is more difficulty and obscurity in the Stoic system than might be expected. Even in Greek, the words for its new concepts were not at first generally acceptable; regular use of its terminology, however, has worn away this initial resistance. So what do you think will happen in Latin?"

"I think it will be a simple matter," I told him. "If Zeno was allowed to impose some bizarre new word when he invented an unfamiliar concept, why shouldn't Cato be given the same privilege! Nevertheless it is unnecessary to reproduce every word with a precise equivalent (as uncouth translators often do) when there is already a more recognizable word that denotes the same thing.

------

[253] Meaning "you would exploit the brevity of my response by latching on to what I did not say, or how I expressed myself."

Indeed my own method—if no other way is possible—is to propose several words in Latin when encountering one Greek term. However, I still believe we ought to have the right to import a Greek word when no equivalent can be found in Latin. Why should it be more acceptable to see the words *ephippia* and *acratophora*, than the words *proëgmena* and *apoproëgmena*?[254] These last two words, however, may be correctly translated as 'approved' and 'rejected.'

16. "What you're doing is much appreciated," Cato told me. "I will use the Latin terms you have just stated, and you'll help me in other situations when you see me having problems."

"I'll pay close attention," I nodded. "But fortune favors the brave,[255] so I'd ask you to make an effort. What could we be doing that is more divinely inspired?

V. "According to the philosophy of those whose school[256] I endorse," Cato began, "every animal at the time it is born (for this is where the analysis must begin) seeks to preserve, protect, and maintain itself in its current condition, and tries to acquire those things that may help maintain it in security. Conversely, however, it is also repelled by destruction and by those things that may cause extinction. To prove this point, they say that babies seek out what is healthy for them and reject the opposite of this before they are even know what pleasure and pain are. This would not happen unless they had a special regard for their own condition and at the same time feared destruction. They would not be able to feel desire for something unless they had a sense of self-awareness and a sense of self-love. One should conclude that the operative principle here is self-love.

---

[254] *Ephippia* means "saddles" and *acratophora* are vessels for unmixed wine. They are originally Greek words that have been incorporated into Latin. Cicero's point is that we should not be squeamish about adopting Greek philosophical terms since we have already done so in other fields of endeavor.
[255] *Fortuna fortes.*
[256] I.e., the Stoics.

17. "Most Stoics, however, do not believe pleasure should be counted as one of the fundamental principles of nature. In this I very much agree with them; for if pleasure were considered one of the chief goals to be sought, a great deal of moral debasement would be the predictable consequence. This point seems sufficiently proved just by noting that we instinctively favor those things first adopted by nature; and there is no man who, if he were presented with either option, would not prefer to have a body whole and functional in all its parts, rather than an impaired or deformed body, even if he could make use of it.

"As for the operations of human thought (we may call them comprehensions or perceptions or, if these words are irksome or hazy, use the Greek term *katalepseis*[257]), we think these should be adopted for their own sake, since they have something innate that contains and encircles the truth. This can be observed in the case of infants, who we see are delighted with themselves when they discover something new through their own powers of reasoning, even if it brings them no tangible benefit.

18. "We also believe the arts and sciences should be sought for their own sake, since there is an aspect of intrinsic merit in their pursuit. They also are based on active cogitation,[258] and contain facts proven by reasoning and inference. The Stoics believe that acquiescing in something false is more objectionable than other things that are contrary to nature.

["As[259] for our limbs, some parts of the body seem to have

---

[257] The Greek word κατάληψις, which means "grasping."
[258] The phrase used is *tum quod constent ex cogitationibus*, giving the meaning that the sciences are based on or correspond to active thoughts.
[259] Editors of the Latin text have claimed that this bracketed paragraph may be an interpolation by a later copyist. This judgment is based on its supposed lack of logical connection to the context. But Cicero sometimes does jump abruptly from one topic to another, so we cannot be certain.

been given us by nature for their own inherent utility, such as our hands, legs, feet, and internal organs; the extent of their usefulness is disputed even by physicians. Other bodily parts seem to have ornament as their sole purpose, such as the peacock's tail, the variegated plumage of the dove, and the male human's whiskers and nipples.[260]]

19. "Perhaps it has been unproductive to dwell on these points. In essence these are the fundamental elements of nature, for which refinement of speech can hardly be employed. And for my part I hardly wish to exert the effort to do so. But when you are discussing loftier themes, the words used tend to harmonize with the gravity of the topic; and as the subject becomes more serious, so does the style of speech become more lustrous."

"What you say is true," I replied. "But nevertheless, when speaking about an all-important subject, I think anything said clearly has been said eloquently. It is puerile to wish this kind of topic discussed in a fancy way: a man of learning and intelligence is capable of explaining himself plainly and lucidly."

VI. 20. "Let us move on then," he nodded. "We have digressed from the subject of nature's principles; what follows from these first principles ought to be consistent with them. What comes next is this first classification. The Stoics call 'valuable' (I think this is the term we may use) something that is either itself in accordance with nature, or creates something that is. For this reason something worthy of selection is something important enough to possess value (value the Stoics call *axia*). And what is contrary to this they call 'valueless.'

---

[260] The word used is *mamma*, which means breast. "Nipple" is a better translation, since the male breast obviously has muscular utility, while the male nipple serves no function.

"Thus, having laid down the principles that those things in accordance with nature should be sought for their own sake, and those things not in accordance with nature should be avoided, the first 'proper action' (for this is what I call the Greek term *kathekon*[261]) is to preserve oneself in one's natural condition. The next responsibility after this is to retain those things that are in accordance with nature, and to reject the opposites. Once this principle of choice and rejection has been discovered, there then follows choice based on 'proper action.' After this, such selection becomes a matter of routine usage; ultimately it becomes unchanging and fully in harmony with nature. It is at this point that what can truly be called 'good' first makes itself known, and is understood for what it is.

21. "Man's first inclination is towards those things that are in accordance with nature. But as soon as he has understanding (or rather 'awareness,' something the Stoics call *ennoia*), and grasps the underlying order and harmony (if I may use this word) that regulate human actions, he values this natural harmony much more than all those things that first attracted him. And so he concludes, by using cognition and reason, that here one can find man's Ultimate Good, the thing that is meritorious and desirable for its own sake. This is found in what the Stoics call *homologia* (which we may call 'concord,'[262] if you like); and in this resides that Good which is the moral end that everything else aims for.[263] Right conduct and moral goodness itself—which (although it

---

[261] καθῆκον. Cicero uses the word *officium* for this Stoic term. English terms that have been used include "appropriate behavior" and "proper function." The thrust of the term is acting in accordance with nature.

[262] The term used is *convenientia*, meaning harmony, concord, consistency, or agreement. *See also* Seneca's *Epistulae* 74.30.

[263] I.e., in this resides that Good which is the ultimate end to which all else is a means (*id bonum quo omnia referenda sunt*, literally "that Good to which all else relates back to").

arose later) is alone considered a good—is still the only thing desirable because of its own special power and excellence. None of the primary objects of nature, on the other hand, is desirable for its own sake.

22. "Since the things I have called 'proper actions' originate from nature's initial principles, it follows that 'proper actions' should aim towards these principles. It may rightly be said that all 'proper actions' are ways for us to acquire the necessities described by nature's primary laws. But this acquisition is not the End of Goods, because moral action[264] is not one of the primary desires of nature. It is a *consequence* of these things and, as I have already explained, is something that arises later. Nevertheless, moral action is in accordance with nature and triggers our yearning far more than all the other things that previously came to our attention.

"We should identify a potential pitfall here at this beginning stage: this is the mistaken view that there are *two* Ultimate Goods. If we imagine a man decides to take aim with a spear or arrow at some target, we may refer to this purpose as the 'Ultimate Good.' In this example, the man would do everything possible to ensure proper aim. It is this exertion of maximum effort towards his purpose that would be his 'ultimate end' (so to speak)—and it is basically the same as what we call the Supreme Good in life. The actual hitting of the target is, we could say, something 'to be selected' but not something 'to be desired.'[265]

VII. 23. "But since all proper actions originate from nature's principles, it follows that wisdom itself proceeds from these same principles. And just as it often happens that, when a man is introduced to someone else, he gravitates to this new person more

---

[264] The phrase used is *honesta actio*.

[265] This last sentence and the three that precede it are one long (and likely corrupt) sentence in the original. I have adopted the suggestions of earlier editors of the Latin text to make it comprehensible.

Scenes in the Alban Hills on the road from Frascati to Tusculum

than the friend who made the introduction, so it comes as no surprise that even though we are first introduced to wisdom by nature's initial principles, this same wisdom thereafter becomes more precious to us than those initial principles which first introduced us to wisdom. Just as our internal and external organs were given to us with the intent that they be put to use for a certain way of living, so also our 'soul's desire' (called in Greek *horme*[266]) was not given to us for just any sort of life, but rather was bestowed on us for a specific mode of living. The very same thing can be said for reason and for perfected reason.[267]

24. "Just as the movement of an actor or dancer must be done in a specific way and not in any random fashion the performer desires, so also must one's life be lived a certain way, and not just however one pleases. This way we call 'appropriate' and 'agreeable.'[268] We do not think that wisdom is similar to nautical skill or the art of medicine, but rather more like the arts of dancing and acting I have just mentioned. Its goal—the practice of the art—lies within the art itself, and is not sought outside this activity. There is also another difference between these arts and wisdom. With acting and dancing, movements that are performed correctly do not contain all the constituent parts that form the underlying art itself. But with wisdom, however, the things we may call (if you agree) 'right conduct' or 'rightly done actions' (the Greek term is *katorthomata*) contain all the elements of virtue. Only wisdom is completely self-supporting; the same cannot be said for the other arts.[269]

---

[266] Ὁρμή. Cicero translates this as *appetitio animi*, which in English can mean "intellect's desire," "soul's desire," or "spirit's desire." The essence of the word is the idea of an inner, dynamic impulse to carry out a goal.

[267] *Perfecta ratio* (perfected reason, or reason that has been completed or developed to its full extent).

[268] The words used are *conveniens* and *consentaneus*, respectively.

[269] *Sola enim sapientia in se tota conversa est, quod idem in ceteris artibus non fit.*

25. "Yet we should not try to compare the Ends of medicine or seamanship with the End of Wisdom. For wisdom embraces greatness of soul, justice, and an attitude that any misfortune befalling a man cannot adversely affect him; this is not found with the other arts. Indeed, no one will be able to attain any of the virtues I have just mentioned *unless he has grasped that the only things separating or distinguishing one thing from another are moral goodness and moral corruption.*

26. "We may now see clearly how the premises I have demonstrated will lead to certain logical conclusions. Since the final goal—you know, I think, that all this time I have rendered the Greek term *telos* as 'final' or 'ultimate' or 'highest'; one may also use 'end' instead of 'final' or 'ultimate.' Since this final goal is to live in harmony and congruence with nature, it necessarily follows that every wise man always lives happily, unreservedly, and accompanied by good fortune. He is hindered by nothing, impeded by nothing, and is in need of nothing. The rule that embraces not only the philosophical system I am describing now, but also our very lives and fortunes, is this: *that we should judge moral goodness to be the sole good.* Indeed this rule could be decorated and expanded with the various artifices of rhetoric, while reciting all the choicest and most serious words abundantly and with fluidity. But the syllogisms[270] of the Stoics please me far more with their brevity and acuteness.

VIII. 27. "Their arguments are contained in these propositions: everything good is praiseworthy; whatever is praiseworthy is morally right; therefore, whatever is good is morally right. Does this conclusion appear to be satisfactory? It is: you can clearly see what has been concluded as a logical result of the first two propositions. The customary rebuttal to the conclusion drawn from the

---

[270] *Consectaria*. "Conclusions" or "consequences" also convey the same meaning.

first two premises above is to point out that not everything good is praiseworthy. For it is normally conceded that what is praiseworthy is morally righteous. But it would be completely ridiculous to say that something good is not also desirable, or that something desirable is not also pleasing, or if pleasing, not also favored. It is therefore commended; thus it is also praiseworthy. However, the praiseworthy is morally right.[271] Thus it must follow that what is good is also morally right.

28. "Finally, I ask who can be content with a life that is unhappy or miserable? Therefore contentment exists only with a happy life. From this it follows that the happy life is something worthy of pride (if I may phrase it this way); and this condition exists only when one is leading a life of moral rectitude. Therefore, the morally good life is the happy life. And because the man who is deservedly praised possesses special badges of distinction and renown, so that on account of these honors he can rightly be called happy, the life of such a man can similarly be said—with absolute correctness—to be happy also. Thus, if the happy life is determined by moral rectitude, then moral rectitude must be the only good.

29. "What do you think? Can it be denied in any way that no man who is steadfast, resolute, and possesses greatness of soul—someone whom we would call a strong man—could exist unless it were proven that pain is not an evil? For just as he who considers death an evil constantly lives in fear of it, *so can no man in any situation ignore or despise that which he believes to be an evil.* Having established this with the weight of general agreement, the following rule is next adopted: *he who possesses a great and lofty soul has contempt for, and thinks absolutely nothing of, all the possible misfortunes that can happen to a man.* This leads us to the conclusion that nothing is evil that is not morally corrupt.

---

[271] Referring back to the second proposition in the syllogism in the first sentence of the paragraph.

"This noble and outstanding man, who possesses a great spirit, who is truly courageous, who believes all petty human affairs are beneath him—this man, I say, whom we wish to create and who represents the ideal we seek, must believe absolutely in himself, his life, his actions and their consequences, and must hold himself in high esteem, fortified by the knowledge that nothing evil can happen to the wise man. From this we arrive at the same conclusion as before: that the only good is moral rectitude, and that to live happily is to live morally—that is, to live with virtue.

IX. 30. "I know very well that there has been a variance of opinion among the philosophers; more specifically, among those who place the Supreme Good (which I call the ultimate goal) in the intellect. The efforts of some of these thinkers were deeply flawed. Nevertheless I place a higher value on all those philosophers—no matter who they are—who believe the Supreme Good is found in the intellect and in virtue. Not only do I consider them superior to the three philosophers who, when they equate 'pleasure' or 'the absence of pain' or the 'basic principles of nature' with the Supreme Good, completely cut out virtue from consideration as the Supreme Good; but I also consider them better than the other three philosophers, who believed virtue would be crippled without some assistance, and therefore attached to it one or another of the three things I just mentioned above.[272]

31. "But those philosophers who say that the End of Goods is found in the pursuit of 'knowledge,' and those who believe that all things are indistinguishable, are also completely wrong. Equally mistaken are those thinkers who claim that the wise man will gain happiness by not favoring one thing over another in the slightest way, as well as those who teach (as some of the Academics are said to have believed) that the wise man's ultimate

---

[272] The six views of the Supreme Good mentioned here are discussed in V.12—22.

and supreme good is to resist deceptive appearances and refuse to endorse them in any way.

"The usual practice is to respond at length to each of these positions I have just mentioned. Yet things that are obvious do not need to be tiresomely discussed. If there is no choice between those things that are *contrary* to nature and those things that are *in accordance* with nature, could it be any more obvious that Prudence (that much-praised and sought-after virtue) would then be rendered meaningless? Therefore, if we disregard those doctrines I have just specified and any others that are similar, we must conclude that the Supreme Good *is to live by applying our knowledge of nature's causative forces, selecting the things that are in accordance with nature and rejecting the things that are not*. In other words, the Supreme Good is to live in conformity and alignment with nature.

32. "But[273] when we talk about something done 'artistically' in a creative field of endeavor, this attribute must be viewed as subsequent to, and as a consequence of, the endeavor. The Stoics call this quality *epigennematikon*.[274] When we say an act has been done 'wisely,' this descriptive label is most correctly affixed at the time the act is done. Whatever action the wise man does ought to be immediately perfected[275] in all its parts, since what we identify as 'desirable' is found in his action. Just as it is a sin to betray one's country, to commit violence against one's parents, or to rob a temple (where the sin in these examples lies in the result of an act), so also is it a sin to be swayed by fear, grief, and lust,

---

[273] Some editors believe this section to have been inserted here incorrectly, as having little connection to the context.

[274] This Greek term has been equated with the word "supervenient" (i.e., a condition existing when a system's higher-level attributes are determined by its lower-level characteristics. *See* Dillon, J. *Alcinous: The Handbook of Platonism*, New York: Oxford Univ. Press, 2002, p. 198.

[275] I.e., completed or fulfilled.

even when these emotions produce no external effect. These passions just mentioned do not become sins at the time we observe their consequences; they become sins the moment we first feel them. *In the same way, actions that have their origin in virtue must be judged as morally correct from the time of their commencement, and not at the time of their final completion.*[276]

X. 33. "The term 'Good'—which has figured so prominently in this dialogue—is also illustrated by definition. Their[277] definitions do not differ from one another very much, and they all gaze at the same objective. For my part I concur with Diogenes, who defined the Good as that which is by nature fully perfected. Following this idea, he said that what was 'useful'[278] (let us use this term to describe the Greek term *ophelema*) was a motion or a condition resulting from something fully perfected by nature. Notions in our mind are created when something has become known by either experience, a convergence of ideas, analogy, or logical reasoning. The fourth (i.e., the last) technique listed here is the one that provides us with an image of the Good. *When the mind, using logical reasoning, ascends from those things that are in accordance with nature, it will then arrive at a conception of the true Good.*

34. "However, this same Good can in no way be compared to anything else. It gets its special quality not by the addition or aggregation of other things, but by virtue of its own uniqueness: this is why we feel it is 'good' and call it so. Just as honey, although it may be extremely sweet, is judged to be sweet because of its own unique flavor profile and not by comparison with other things, so this Good which we are talking about must indeed be

---

[276] *Sic ea quae proficiscuntur a virtute, susceptione prima, non perfectione, recta sunt iudicanda.*

[277] I.e., the definitions of the Stoics.

[278] The term used is *quod prodesset*, literally meaning "what is useful" or "beneficial."

prized above all else. But its value is based on its *special identity*, not on some physical characteristic like size. 'Value' (in Greek *axia*[279]) should not be considered as either a good or an evil; no matter how much you add to it, it will always remain the same type of thing. Thus virtue's value is of a very special type: it is grounded in identity, not quantity.

35. "Disturbances[280] of the mind confer a miserable and bitter life on the foolish. The Greeks call these *pathe*, a word I might have translated literally as 'diseases;' although the word does not really harmonize with every context. Who is in the habit of calling pity or rage a 'disease'? Yet the Greeks do use the word *pathos* to describe them. Thus let us use the term 'emotion,' which by its very name seems to suggest a vice. These emotions are not generated by some natural force. All emotions are separated into these four categories (with many subcategories): grief, fear, desire, and that emotion that the Stoics apply equally to the body and the mind, *hedone* (pleasure). I prefer to use the term 'joy'[281] for this emotion; it is something like a pleasurable ecstasy of the mind when in a state of jubilation. However, emotions are not inflamed by any force of nature: they are—all of them—personal beliefs and superficial judgments. Thus the wise man will always be untroubled by them.

XI. 36. "The idea that everything morally good is desirable for its own sake is a principle we share with many other philosophical schools. With the exception of three schools that exclude virtue from the Supreme Good, this idea is endorsed by all other philosophers; this is especially true of the Stoics, who stress that only moral goodness should be considered a good at all. Defending this position is, indeed, quite easy and uncomplicated.

---

[279] ἀξία.

[280] *Perturbationes* can mean disturbance, commotion, or emotion, as here.

[281] The word used is *laetitia*, indicating joy, delight, or happiness.

A column fragment outside the ruins of Tusculum

Excavations in progress at Tusculum

For is there anyone—or has there ever been anyone—possessed of such burning greed, or of such uncontrolled desires that, although willing to commit any crime to achieve some purpose (and even knowing he would not be caught), he would still not prefer to use a non-criminal method of arriving at the same objective?

37. "Indeed, what utility or profit are we looking for when we explore the hidden mysteries of nature, or probe the mechanisms and causes of the movement of the celestial bodies? Who lives with such a primitive mentality, or whose mind is so obdurately set against the study of nature, that he recoils from learning about worthy subjects and clings to the vulgar belief that only what brings him 'pleasure' or 'profit' is useful? Whose spirit remains unmoved by a sense of awe when learning about the surpassing deeds, words, and ideas of our ancestors, or the Africani,[282] or that man—my great-grandfather—whose name you constantly mention, and the other exceptional men of courage and virtue?

38. "What man raised in a morally sound household, and having a decent background and education, is not offended by moral corruption, even if it may not be affecting him personally? Who can look on a man who wants to live a life of depravity and dissolution without feeling an extremely negative emotional reaction? Who does not despise the filthy, the vain, the trifling, or the worthless? If we conclude that moral corruption is not something that should be shunned for its own sake, how would we be able to dissuade people from using covert means and secretiveness to avoid shame resulting from their behavior, unless they were deterred by the inherent vileness of this moral corruption? Countless arguments could be advanced to support this view, but it is unnecessary to do so. *Nothing could be less subject to doubt than the idea that moral goodness should be sought for its own sake, and conversely that what is morally wrong should be shunned for its own sake.*

---

[282] Meaning both Scipio Africanus the Elder and the Younger.

39. "To this general rule we discussed earlier—that moral goodness is the only true Good—we must add the following logical consequence: that what is morally good must be reckoned as having more worth than the average things that are accumulated by it.[283] However, when we say that stupidity, cowardice, injustice, and intemperance must be avoided because of the predictable consequences that result from them, we do intend for this assertion to conflict with this principle that has already been established: that the only evil is what is morally corrupt. This is so because these things[284] are not related to bodily harm, but are connected to the morally corrupt actions that spring from human vices. The Greeks call this *kakia*;[285] I prefer to translate this word as 'vice' instead of 'wickedness.'[286]

XII. 40. "Cato," I said, "you make your points with clear words, and what you want to convey certainly shines through! In fact it seems to me you are teaching philosophy to speak Latin, and are practically giving her Roman citizenship. Until now philosophy has felt like an outsider in Rome, unwilling to use our vocabulary; and this is especially true of the Stoic creed, due to the refinement and subtlety of its ideas and terms.

"I know there are some thinkers who can philosophize in any language. But they use no classifications or divisions; and they themselves say that they only endorse those ideas that have the tacit approval of nature. Thus, because there is very little obscurity in their ideas, they do not need to exert much effort in explaining

---

[283] *Quam illa media quae ex eo comparentur*, meaning that moral goodness has more value than the ordinary things that it allows one to get.

[284] I.e, the consequences that result from stupidity, cowardice, injustice, and intemperance.

[285] Κακια (in Latin, Cacia) was also the name of a personified spirit (or goddess) of vice. *See* Xenophon's *Memorabilia* II.1.21.

[286] *Malitia*, meaning ill-will, badness, or wickedness.

them. So I am listening to you very carefully, and am memorizing whatever terms you use to identify the ideas of this dialogue; perhaps I myself will need these same words that you have been using. I believe you are most correct in naming vice as the opposite of the virtues; this also aligns with the general practice of how we speak. That which by its own nature 'deserves vituperation'[287] is properly called a 'vice,' I think. Or the word *vituperabilis* comes from the word for 'vice' (*vitium*). But if you had translated *kakia* as 'wickedness,' customary Latin usage would lead us to different specific vice. At present, vice is designated as the opposite term for virtue in its broadest sense.

41. "Now that we have laid down these principles," Cato said, "we reach a very significant point of contention. It was not handled very rigorously by the Peripatetics. Actually their style of speaking was not precise enough for the task, due to their ignorance of dialectic. But your Carneades, with his outstanding ability in dialectical logic and his great eloquence, brought the issue to a crisis point. With regard to the entire so-called 'question of good and evil,' he always maintained that the dispute between the Stoics and Peripatetics was not a conflict of ideas, but rather a conflict of terminology. As I see things, however, it is quite clear that the positions of these philosophers differ from each other in more than just words. I say that, between the Stoics and the Peripatetics, there is a much greater discrepancy of doctrines than of words. The Peripatetics say that everything related to what they call 'goods' assists us in living a happy life; but we Stoics do not believe that the happy life contains everything that has some value attached to it.

XIII. 42. "In fact, can there be anything more certain than that, under the reasoning of those who consider pain an evil, it is

---

[287] *Vituperabilis* means "able to be blamed or censured."

impossible for the wise man to be happy when his body is being twisted on the rack?[288] However, the reasoning of those who do not consider pain an evil certainly requires the conclusion *that the wise man maintains a happy life even amid the harshest torments.* Indeed the same sufferings are more tolerable when they are endured for patriotic reasons than when they are endured for some trifling cause. The magnitude of the pain is greater or lesser not because of the pain's inherent nature: it depends on the mental state of the one who is suffering.

43. "According to the position of the Peripatetics, there are three kinds of goods; and the more bodily goods or external goods a man has, the happier he is. We[289] cannot endorse this same position, and will not subscribe to the idea that the more of those highly-valued things a man has, the happier he is. For the Peripatetics believe that the happy life contains bodily benefits; we reject this view entirely. Our position is that the abundance of those things that we correctly identify as goods does not make life more happy, desirable, or valuable. A multitude of bodily benefits[290] certainly has very little connection with a happy life.

44. "Indeed, if it is desirable to have wisdom and health, a combination of both these qualities should be more desirable than wisdom alone. Nevertheless if each of these is worthy of value, their combined value is not greater than the value of wisdom separately by itself. We judge health to be worth some value, but we do not place it in the category of 'goods'; at the same time, we do not think anything is of such a high value that it may be placed ahead of virtue. The Peripatetics do not hold the same view. *They insist on saying that a morally good action that is physically*

---

[288] Meaning tortured on the rack.

[289] We Stoics.

[290] The phrase used is *multitudo corporis commodorum*, where the word *commodum* can mean profit, benefit, convenience, or advantage.

Ruins of a structure at Tusculum

Latin inscription located near the structure
in the preceding photograph

painless is more desirable than the same morally good action that involves physical pain. We do not see things this way. Whether we are correct is a question we will take up a bit later. But could the divergence between our views[291] be any greater?

XIV. 45. "Just as the light emanating from an oil lamp is obscured and overwhelmed by the light of the sun, and just as a drop of honey is subsumed in the expanses of the Aegean Sea's waters, and just as a single bronze coin[292] means nothing in comparison to Croesus's[293] riches, and just as a single step along the road from here to India is insignificant, so also, if we agree with the Stoic concept of the End of Goods, will all the value placed on these bodily benefits be necessarily obscured, overwhelmed, and crushed by the splendor and greatness of virtue. And just as 'opportunity'[294] (for so we will translate the Greek term *eukairia*) does not become greater with the extension of time, since those things we call 'opportune' have reached their natural ripeness, so 'right achievement'—I will use this term to translate *katorthosis*, since the term *katorthoma* represents a single right deed—right achievement, indeed, as well as decorum, and finally Good itself (which is defined as 'being in conformity with nature'), cannot be made greater or augmented.

46. "Just like opportunity, these things I have just mentioned do not become greater with the extension of time. For this reason it makes sense to the Stoics that a happy life is not better or more

---

[291] The views of the Stoics and Peripatetics.

[292] *Teruncius*, a bronze coin valued at three *unciae* or 1/4th of an *as*.

[293] Ancient king of Lydia from 560 B.C. to 546 B.C. who was legendary for his vast wealth.

[294] *Opportunitas* is the word used. It is a bit elusive in English. According to the Oxford Latin Dictionary, it can mean "the quality of favoring one's needs or purposes, advantage, suitability, etc." or "the quality of appearing or happening at the right moment, opportuneness (of an event, etc.), reasonableness (of an action).

desirable if it is longer than if it happens to be shorter. They make use of the following metaphor. If a boot's worth is that it fits the foot well, many boots would not be better than few boots, nor would larger ones be better than those that are smaller. Similarly, with regard to things whose goodness is determined by decorum and advantageousness, a large quantity of them is not considered better than a few; nor will things of longer temporal duration be valued more highly than those lasting for a shorter period of time.[295]

47. "Neither is this statement very convincing: if good health must be worth more when it lasts a long time than when it is brief, then the longest practice of wisdom must bring the greatest value. Those who say this do not understand that the value of health is judged by its duration, but the value of virtue is measured by its reasonableness in context.[296] Those who take this flawed position would be just as likely to say that a good death or a good child-birth are better when they last long than when they are brief. They cannot grasp that some things are more valued by their brevity, and other things by their longevity.

48. "Thus it is consistent with the line of reasoning already established that, if we accept the logic of those who think that the End of Goods (which we call the Supreme or Ultimate Good) can 'increase,'[297] one man can therefore be wiser than another, and also that one man can sin more or do more good than another. But those of us who *do not* believe that the End of Goods can 'increase' will refuse to make these statements. For just as a man submerged in water can no more easily breathe when he is a short

---

[295] An elegant and wonderful sentence in the original: *Sic quorum omne bonum convenientia atque opportunitate finitur, nec plura paucioribus nec longinquiora brevioribus anteponentur.*

[296] "Reasonableness in context" is the phrase used to translate *opportunitas*. It is a better choice than advantageousness, suitability, or opportuneness.

[297] I.e., that the End of Goods is variable, and can increase or "become larger" (*crescere*).

distance from the surface (so that he could at any time rise out of it) than when he is engulfed in a watery abyss, and just as a puppy preparing to open its eyes is not more discerning than a pup just born, *so the man who has made some progress on virtue's path is no less distressed than he who has made no progress on the path at all.*

XV. "I recognize that this conclusion seems astonishing. But since our earlier deductions are unquestionably well-reasoned and valid, and as these final judgments are consistent and rational progressions from those deductions, the veracity of these ultimate judgments cannot be doubted. But although the Stoics believe that neither virtues nor vices can be 'increased in grade,'[298] they nevertheless assert that both of them can be, in a way, enlarged or broadened.[299]

49. "Diogenes[300] thinks that wealth not only provides the means for gaining pleasure and good health, but that it also sustains[301] them; but he thinks it does not perform this function with regard to virtue and the other arts. Money may serve as a guide to these things, but it cannot sustain them. Therefore if pleasure or good health are considered goods, wealth must also be considered a good. But if wisdom is counted as a good, it does not

---

[298] Traditional Stoic theory held (rather severely) that something was either a virtue or a vice, and that there were no degrees or gradations of goodness or badness. As stated in the previous paragraph, a man is either virtuous, or he is not; something is either good, or it is not; and it made no difference if a man was a partially virtuous. A man on the path of virtue was still "miserable." Until he arrived at his final destination, he would remain as miserable as a novice.

[299] Meaning that the practice of virtues or vices can have an effect on more or less people.

[300] Diogenes of Babylon (c. 230 B.C.—145? B.C.), a Stoic philosopher who led a school in Athens.

[301] "Sustain" (*continere*) should be taken to mean "to be a vital component of."

follow that we must also consider wealth to be a good. Neither can anything that is *not* a good sustain something that *is* a good. Thus, because acts of thinking and comprehension (from which the arts are produced) arouse desire, since wealth is not a good, no art can be sustained by wealth.[302]

50. "If we permit wealth to be a vital component of the arts, the same rationale could not be used with regard to virtue, because virtue demands a great deal of mental preparation and practice. The same level of exertion is not required with the arts. Virtue requires steadiness, strength, and perseverance for the full duration of a man's life; we do not see the same level of emphasis placed on these traits in the artistic disciplines.

"At this point we undertake to explain the differences between things. For if we say that there are no differences between various things, then all of life would become a confounding blur—which is just where Aristo's arguments lead us. No function or role would be found for wisdom, since there would be no differences among the things that relate to the conduct of life, and thus no need for an ability to select the right thing. It has been sufficiently proven that moral goodness is the only good and moral corruption the only evil. But with regard to those things that are completely unrelated to happiness or sorrow, the Stoics wanted there to be some difference between them, so that some things would have a positive value, others an opposite value, and still others a neutral value.

51. "With regard to things that have value (such as health, fully functioning senses, freedom from pain, fame, riches, and similar things), some of them have sufficient justification for being placed ahead of other things, while others are not of this type. In the same way, some things that have no measurable worth

---

[302] When Cato says "no art can be sustained by wealth" (*nulla ars divitiis contineri potest*), he means that wealth is not an essential component of the artistic process.

may justifiably be rejected, such as pain, sickness, the loss of the senses, poverty, disgrace, and similar things; but this may not be true for other things with no measurable worth. Here is the original source for what Zeno called *proegmena*, together with the opposite *apoproegmena*. He was making use of his abundant language to create new words as he needed them, something that is not allowed to us with Latin's meager lexicon—although you are in the habit of saying that our own language is richer than Greek! To understand the full significance of this word, it will be helpful to explain the reasoning Zeno used in creating it.

XVI. 52. "Zeno said that in a palace no one refers to the king has having been 'promoted'[303] (this is what the word *proegmena* means) to his regal station. The word 'promoted' is properly applied to those who occupy a position that is next in rank just below the monarch. Similarly, when we speak of human life in general, the word 'promoted' is not used in connection with things in the highest position, but rather with things that occupy the second-highest place. We may call such things 'promoted' (this would be a literal translation of the word), or we may call them 'preferred'[304] or 'debased'[305]; or we may fall back on words previously used, the terms 'favored'[306] or 'exceptional.'[307] For the opposite we may use 'rejected.' We should avoid nit-picking in our choice of words when the meaning is clearly understood.

53. "However, because we say that everything good holds the highest position, we must conclude that what we call 'foremost' or 'exceptional' is neither good nor evil. Thus we define it as

---

[303] *Producere*, meaning "promoted" or "brought out."
[304] *Promota*, a "preferred thing."
[305] *Remota*, something removed, withdrawn, debased.
[306] *Praeposita*, something placed in command, preferred, or in the lead.
[307] *Praecipua*, particular or special.

'indifferent,'[308] but with an average value. It has occurred to me that I can use 'indifferent' as the correct term for their word *adiaphoron*.[309] So it must be true that the class of 'medium' things should contain some things that are in accordance with nature, and some things that are not. Furthermore, it is inevitable that this class should have some things of average value, and that some things in this class should be 'preferred.'

54. "Thus this distinction has been correctly made. In order for this to be more clearly understood, the Stoics present the following analogy. Suppose, they say, that our end and final objective is to throw a knuckle-bone so that it stands upright.[310] A bone thrown in such a way that it *stands* upright will be in some way 'preferred' with respect to its final objective; but a bone that falls in some other way will be the opposite of this. Yet this 'preferred status' of the knuckle-bone will not represent the end I have described. Thus those things that are 'preferred' are certainly *relevant* to the intended end, but are *not vital constituents* of the end's essential nature.

55. "We now come to the following division of goods. Some goods are 'constituents of the Ultimate End'[311] (this is my translation of their Greek term *telika*). Here we may decide—on a case-by-case basis—to use several words to convey the proper meaning in situations where one word is insufficient. Other goods,

---

[308] *Indifferens*, neither good nor bad; indifferent, neutral.

[309] ἀδιάφορα, meaning "indifferent" in the sense of an action that is neither morally required nor prohibited.

[310] The four-sided sheep's knuckle-bone (*talus*) was used in games of chance (see Ovid's *Tristia* II.473; Quintilian VI.1.47). The game played with such bones—similar to modern dice or jacks—was called *tali*. There were several varieties of the game, all of which involved throwing or catching the bones. The analogy here makes the point that "preferred" things are relevant to attaining the good life, but are not critical components of it.

[311] *Pertinentia*.

however, are 'productive'[312] of the Ultimate End (my rendering of the Greek term *poietika*). Still other goods are both of these things. There are no goods from the 'constituent' class except morally good actions; and the only good from the 'productive' class is a friend. Yet the Stoics teach that wisdom is both constituent and productive. Now because wisdom is a harmonious action, it falls into the 'constituent' category that I have just described. However, because wisdom both causes and produces morally good actions, it can be said to be productive.

XVII. 56. "These things we call 'favored' are so called sometimes for their own sake, sometimes because they produce something, and sometimes for both of these reasons. When called 'favored' for their own sake, it may be due to a certain expression of the mouth and face, or because of a posture or movement—things that may be in themselves favored or rejected. Other things are called 'favored' because they produce a certain outcome, such as money. Still other things are called 'favored' for both of these reasons, like well-functioning senses or good health.

57. "As for 'honorable fame'[313] (what the Stoics call *eudoxia* is better rendered here with the phrase 'honorable fame' than with the word 'glory'), Chrysippus and Diogenes denied that it had any meaningful utility, and taught that a man should not even stretch out a finger in pursuit of it. I fully concur with them. However, the philosophers who came after them (since they were incapable of responding to Carneades's ideas) announced that honorable fame should be favored and sought for its own sake. They said a free-born man of liberal education[314] would want the acceptance of his parents, family relations, and other good men in society, and that he would want these things for their own sake, not for any material benefit. They insist that, just as we try to provide for

---

[312] *Efficientia.*

[313] *Bona fama*, meaning a man's good name or reputation.

[314] *Liberaliter educati*, a liberal education in the classical sense, which is different from its modern meaning.

the well-being of our children for their own sake, even if they happen to be born after we die, so should a man be mindful of his posthumous reputation for its own sake, even if it does not bring him any material reward.

58. "But even though we say that moral goodness is the only thing worthy of being called good, it is still proper to perform an appropriate act,[315] even if we consider such an act to be neither a good nor an evil. There is something justifiable[316] in these things, in that the influence of reason can be detected; reason can therefore be found in a justifiably performed action. An appropriate act is an act carried out with a justifiable basis for its commission. It follows from this that an appropriate act is something 'in the middle,'[317] in the sense that it can be considered neither a good nor the opposite of this. And because those things that are neither virtues nor vices nevertheless have some quality that can be useful, this quality should not be discarded. A certain kind of action is also included in this class;[318] it is of such a kind that reason requires us to do or to make something in this 'medium' class. Something that has been done reasonably we call an appropriate act; therefore, an appropriate action belongs to the class of things that are neither good nor the opposite.

XVIII. 59. "It is also evident that, in the category of these intermediate things, the wise man carries out some actions. Therefore, he determines whether it is an appropriate act at the time he does it. Because he is never incorrect in his judgment, appropriate action will be found in this category of medium things. This conclusion is proved by the following reasoning. We see something that we call a 'rightly performed action,' but this is

---

[315] "Appropriate act" is the better translation of *officium* in this context, as it is more neutral than "obligation" or "duty."

[316] *Probabilis*, meaning justifiable, commendable, reasonable.

[317] Meaning "neutral."

[318] I.e., in the class of neutral intermediates, things "in the middle" that are neither virtues nor vices.

Memento mori: a skull being excavated at Tusculum

an appropriate action that has been completed.[319] There must also be such a thing as an appropriate act that is 'inchoate.'[320] So if lawfully returning a deposit of money is a right action, then returning a deposit of money must be considered an appropriate act. The use of the added term 'lawfully' makes the action a 'right' action; but the simple act of returning the monetary deposit is considered an appropriate act.

"There is no doubt that, in this class we call 'medium,' there are some things that are desirable and some things that are undesirable. Thus anything we describe in this way is included in that category we call appropriate action. From this it can be understood that, since all men have a natural fondness for themselves, both the wise man and the fool will seek out what is in accordance with nature and will reject that which is contrary to it. Thus there exists a certain type of appropriate action that is common to both the wise man and the fool. We can see from this how appropriate action is related to that category of things we have called 'medium.'

60. "But since all appropriate acts proceed from these 'medium' things, it is validly said that all of our thinking is connected to these things, among them the desire to live and the desire to die. When there is in one's life an abundance of things in accordance with nature, it is an appropriate act to continue to live; but when there is (or imminently will be) an abundance of things in life that are contrary to nature, then it is an appropriate act to exit such a life. From this it is clear that, under certain circumstances, it is an appropriate act for the wise man to end his life voluntarily even if he is happy, and for the fool to continue living even if he is miserable.

---

[319] *Perfectum*, meaning completed or fully performed.
[320] *Inchoatum*, meaning inchoate or incomplete.

61. "As has already been stated, the concept of good and evil should be considered a later development. But the primary things of nature—whether they are favorable or the opposite of this— fall under the judgment and preference of the wise man, and constitute the subjects and 'raw materials' of wisdom. Therefore, the reasons for remaining alive and for ending one's life must always be evaluated according to the primary things of nature that I have discussed previously. The man of virtue need not always continue in his life, and those who lack virtue do not always need to encounter death. Often it is an appropriate act for a wise man to abandon his life when he is at a point of great happiness, if a favorable opportunity for this presents itself. For the Stoics believe that living happily—meaning to live in conformity with nature—is a matter of having the right timing.[321]

"Thus the wise man may be instructed by Wisdom herself to take his leave from her, as the circumstances may require. Although vices are not powerful enough to provide a sufficient justification for suicide, clearly it is an appropriate act even for fools (who are also unhappy) to remain alive, as long as they have a preponderance of those things that we say are in conformity with nature. Since the fool is equally miserable whether he stays alive or chooses to quit this life, and since the lengthening of his life does not make it any more unsatisfactory, it is said for good reason that those who can enjoy a plurality of nature's gifts should stay in this life.

XIX. 62. "The Stoics believe it is important to appreciate that nature sees to it that children are loved by their parents. From this beginning we may perceive the evolution of human social systems. This ought to be immediately clear from inspection of the human physical form and the body's organs. These themselves

---

[321] *Sic enim censent [Stoici], opportunitatis esse beate vivere quod est convenienter naturae vivere.*

announce that the human method of procreation had its origin in nature. It would not be congruent with these observations that nature would want procreation yet not provide for offspring to be loved. Even among the animals, the power of nature in this regard can be perceived; when we note the labor involved in the birthing and raising of their young, we seem to hear the voice of nature herself. Just as it is obvious that nature predisposes us to be averse to pain, so it is clear that we are by nature impelled to love those to whom we have given birth.

63. "From this also is born the collective and natural esteem that man shares with his fellows; this common bond inclines every man to see his counterpart not as a stranger, but as a peer. For just as some organs (such as the eyes and ears) are created for their own sake, while other bodily parts (such as the legs and hands) assist the functioning of different limbs and organs, so are some huge animals born for themselves alone. But then consider the marine animal called the *pina*,[322] in its spacious shell, and the organism that people call the *pinoteres*[323] because it protects the *pina*. The *pinoteres* ventures out of the *pina*'s shell, and then encloses itself inside the shell after returning to it, so that it appears to 'warn' the *pina* of any surrounding dangers. In the same way, ants, bees, and storks do certain things for the sake of other animals. Human beings are even more communally bonded. We are therefore by nature suited to form associations, cooperative unions, and states.

64. "However, the Stoics believe that the world is ruled by the will of the gods. It is a kind of communal city or state inhabited by men and gods, and each one of us is a part of this shared world. The natural consequence of this arrangement is that we place the common good ahead of our own personal advantage. Just as the written laws place the security of all before the security of the individual, so does a good, wise, and law-abiding man, aware of

---

[322] A bivalve mollusk.
[323] A pea crab.

his social obligation to the state, contemplate the public good more than that of any one person, or himself. The man who is a traitor to his country should not be condemned any more harshly than the man who willfully turns his back on the common good or security for the sake of his own personal good and security. This is why we must praise one who meets with death for the sake of one's country: because it is right for us to value our country more than ourselves. Just as we consider a man malicious and criminal who announces that he could care less if, after his death, the entire world is consumed by fire (this thought is usually stated by using a certain Greek verse), so it is true that we must be unselfishly cognizant of the interests of those who will live after us.

XX. 65. "From this inner emotional impulse are born the covenants and commitments of those who are facing the prospect of death.[324] Since no one wants to spend his life in extreme solitude, even if he could enjoy an infinite abundance of pleasures, it is not difficult to understand that we have been created for fellowship and association, and for the natural community of mankind. We are, in addition, compelled by nature to want to help our fellows, especially by teaching them what we know and passing on the principles of wisdom.

66. "Thus it is not easy to find someone unwilling to teach another person what he himself knows. We are eager not only to learn things, but also to teach them. And just as bulls have been given the greatest powers and vigor by Nature to protect their calves from lions, so are men of singular ability and achievement (as we hear in the old stories about Hercules and Liber[325]) inspired by Nature to serve the human race. When we grant Jove the names Supreme, Great, Savior, Provider of Hospitality, or Upholder, what we mean to say is that the well-being of mankind is under

---

[324] Meaning the drafting of wills and trusts.

[325] Liber (or Liber Pater) was a traditional patron deity of the Roman plebian, and one of the three gods of the "Aventine Triad," along with Ceres and Libera.

Another view of the excavated skull

An excavated building at Tusculum. Note the remains
of the wall painting at center left.

his guardianship. But it would be most inconsistent for us to expect the immortal gods to care for us and grant us special affections, when we ourselves are cruel and uncaring with each other. Therefore, just as we make use of our limbs before having a real understanding of their functional purpose, so have we been connected and closely bonded by Nature in a civil community. If this were not so, there would be no place for justice or mutual kindness.

67. "In the same way that the Stoics believe men are linked together by the unifying power of law, so do they deny that any such connection exists between men and beasts. For Chrysippus clearly said that physical things were created for the sake of men and gods. However, these things are intended for their community and society, so that a man may use animals for his own advantage without committing any wrongdoing. Human nature operates in such a way that a kind of civil law intercedes between the individual and the human race. He who preserves this compact will be considered just, and he who abandons it will be viewed as unjust. Although we consider a public theater to be owned by the community, we can correctly say that the individual seat a man occupies belongs to him. Similarly, in a civil polity or the world at large—things we look upon as community property—it is not offensive to the law if someone should own something for himself.

68. "Since it is clear that man is created for protecting and assisting others, it is consistent with his nature that the wise man should want to play a role in the management and direction of public affairs. And in order to live in accordance with nature, he will desire to find a wife and have children with her. Indeed, as long as passions are sacred, they are not considered to be averse to the wise man.[326] Some Stoics say that the ideas and lifestyle of

---

[326] *Ne amores quidem sanctos a sapiente alienos esse arbitrantur.* The meaning is that love is acceptable for a wise man as long as it is pure and inviolable.

the Cynics are suitable for a wise man, if by chance the situation arises where a man must adopt that life. Other Stoics, however, disagree with this.

XXI. 69. "In order that all social concord, fellowship, and affection is preserved between one man and another, the Stoics wanted benefits and detriments (which they identified with the Greek terms *ophelemata* and *blammata*) to be held in common. Benefits are advantageous, and detriments cause harm. The Stoics said they were not only 'common,' but also 'equal.' They wanted disadvantages and advantages (called in Greek *euchrestemata* and *duschrestemata*) to be held in common, but they did not want them to be equal. Things that produce benefits and things that produce harm are either goods or evils, as the case may be; and these must be equal. But advantages and disadvantages belong to the class we call 'preferred' or 'rejected.' And these cannot be equal. Benefits[327] are said to be held in common; rightly-done actions and moral offenses, however, are not thought to be held in common.

70. "However, they believe that friendship should be something diligently pursued, since they consider it from the class of 'benefits.' In the matter of friendship, some Stoics say that the wise man will regard a friend's interests as equal in value to his own interests. Others, though, say that a man should treat his own interests as more important; but even the Stoics in this latter category concede that to take another's property for the purpose of self-enrichment is an act foreign to that sense of justice imbued in us from birth. The philosophical school I am speaking of here does not endorse the view that friendship and justice should be adopted or maintained for some situational advantage they might bring. For indeed, these same utilitarian reasons could undermine or

---

[327] Some texts insert the words "and detriments" (*et detrimenta*) after the word "benefits."

overthrow them. In fact neither justice nor friendship can exist at all unless they are sought for their own sake.

71. "However, what can be called or designated 'law' exists according to nature. To harm someone else, or even to commit a wrong against him, is for the wise man something completely foreign. Neither is it right to conspire in misconduct with one's friends or supporters; and it is strongly and truly argued that justice can never be separated from utility.[328] Whatever is equitable and just is also morally good; likewise, whatever is morally good will also be equitable and just.

72. "The Stoics also add logic and the natural sciences to these virtues we have been describing. They place both of these disciplines in the category of 'virtue.' Logic is classified in this way because it provides a means to avoid the inadvertent endorsement of untruths, and it prevents us from being misled by fallacious probability. It allows us to hold and safeguard what we have learned about good and evil: for the Stoics believe that without this critical art a man may be enticed from the truth into a wilderness of falsehoods. If indeed impetuosity and ignorance are vices in every situation, then the art which removes them is rightly called a virtue.

XXII. 73. "Not without good reason, the same honor is also conferred on the natural sciences, since he who would live in conformity with nature must go about this task with due consideration of the operative principles of the entire world. Nor can anyone form sound judgments on good and evil except through an understanding of nature's laws and of the life of the gods, and unless one knows whether man's nature is in alignment with these natural laws. Without an understanding of the physical sciences, no one can appreciate the power (and they truly do have

---

[328] Meaning that fairness or equity should always be mindful of practical, real-world utility, which is sound advice for any courtroom judge.

great power) of those ancient sayings of the wise men, where they counsel us to 'adapt to your circumstances,' 'follow God,' 'know thyself,' and 'have nothing in excess.' An understanding of the natural sciences can provide an appreciation of nature's power in cultivating justice, preserving friendship, and perpetuating the rest of our affections; neither can one truly comprehend the sentiment of piety towards the gods, nor the debt of gratitude that we owe them, without an awareness of nature's design.[329]

74. "But I sense that I have been carried far beyond the reasoning needed for our purposes here. In fact the wonderful architecture of the Stoic school of thought, and the extraordinary arrangement of its axioms, have led me happily along. By the immortal gods, are you not enthralled by the Stoic system? Nothing is more inherently proper, or more organized, than nature: but can anything be found in nature, or is there any product of human artifice, that is as well-arranged or as finely constructed? What deduction does not follow logically from the premise that came before it? What conclusions do not proceed from earlier observations? What other structure has its components so tightly bound together that, if you disturb one letter, the entire structure comes crashing down? Yet of course there is nothing in it that could conceivably be revised.

75. "How austere, how magnificent, and how steadfast is the ideal wise man so designed! Since reason has demonstrated that moral rectitude is the only good, the wise man must therefore always be happy, and that he truly is the possessor of all those noble titles which ignorant people love to mock. He will more rightfully be called 'king' than Tarquin,[330] who was able to rule

---

[329] This brilliant and inspiring passage is perhaps Cicero's most evocative statement of the power of the natural sciences as an aid to ethical philosophy. Not until Francis Bacon would such sentiments find comparable eloquence.
[330] Tarquinius Superbus, the notoriously inept last king of Rome who ruled

Excavating a paved road at Tusculum

from 535 B.C. to 509 B.C., and who was ousted by a popular revolt that established the Roman republic.

neither his subjects nor himself. He will more rightfully deserve the appellation 'master of the people' (which is what a dictator is) than Sulla,[331] who was the master of three pernicious vices— extravagance, greed, and cruelty. More rightly would he be considered rich than Crassus,[332] who, had he truly been in need of nothing, would never have wanted to cross the River Euphrates to start a war for no reason. He will rightly be seen as the master of all things, since he alone will know how to use all things; rightly also will he be called beautiful, since the features of the soul are more beautiful than those of the body. He will rightly be called the only free man, as he yields to the authority of no other mortal, and is not subservient to his desires; and rightly will he be called unconquerable, as his soul will never be enchained even if his body is subject to physical restraint.

76. "Nor would he have to wait until some specific point of his life, so that a final judgment on whether he is 'happy' could be rendered only when he crowned his last day of life with death. In was in these terms that one of the Seven Wise Men so unwisely warned King Croesus.[333] For if Croesus had ever been happy, he

---

[331] Lucius Cornelius Sulla (138 B.C.—78 B.C.), general and dictator famous for his ruthlessness.

[332] Marcus Licinius Crassus (c.115 B.C.—53 B.C.), general and politician. As governor of Syria, he was guilty of excessive hubris and tried to conquer Parthia to the east. Crossing the Euphrates, he and his army were crushed by the Parthians at Carrhae in 53 B.C. The historian Dio Cassius (XL.27) says that the Parthians, in mockery of his greed, poured molten gold into his mouth after he had been slain.

[333] A reference to a story in Herodotus (I.32). *See also* Ovid, *Metamorph.* III.135 and Montaigne's *Essays* I.19. Solon, one of the so-called Seven Wise Men, warned the fabulously rich Croesus that no man could be considered "happy" until after he died, since Fortune could at any time change his circumstances. Until he actually died, Solon said, a man could only be considered lucky.

would have maintained his happy life right up to the moment when he mounted the funeral pyre erected for him by Cyrus.[334] If it is true that no one but the good man is happy, and that all good men are happy, then what should be more encouraged than the study of philosophy, and what could be more divine than virtue?"

_____

[334] The funeral pyre story is related in Herodotus (I.86).

COMMENTARY ON BOOK III

Book III is devoted to explaining the ethics of Stoicism. Cicero was not, strictly speaking, a Stoic philosopher; but he did have strong sympathies for its moral code. It is thus remarkable that he is able to argue so persuasively both for it (in Book III) and against it (in Book IV). He respectfully takes note of the Stoic love for terminology (some might say hair-splitting) in III.4; and he uses their predilection for new words as justification to create his own new words in Latin. In III.7 he places the location of the dialogue in the charming town of Tusculum, nestled in the Alban Hills outside Rome. The photographs included within the text give the reader an idea just how suitable this locale is for philosophical disquisition.

Cato wastes little time in getting to the heart of the matter: moral goodness, he announces, is the only thing that is desirable; if it were otherwise, then virtue would be rendered useless (III.10—11). Cato then sets out to describe the fundamentals of Stoic doctrine. He candidly acknowledges the difficulty and abstruseness of Stoic terminology (III.15). Cicero reminds us that it may on occasion be necessary to import Greek words directly into Latin (III.15); like all good translators and linguistic innovators, he refuses to be bound by rigid rules. Sometimes he coins neologisms in Latin, and other times he simply Latinizes Greek words. We can never forget his decisive influence on the course of the Latin language.

Organisms, Cato says, do not hunger for pleasure, but for self-preservation. Later in life, organisms conform their behavior to the requirements of nature (III.20—21). Our "appropriate acts" are derived from nature's fundamental impulses. Our lives are not performances to be lived out any way we please. Just as an actor or dancer has a special role to perform on stage, so must our lives be conducted in a certain way (III.24). Seen in this light, it is clear that moral rectitude is the only true good (III.25). The Ultimate Good of the Stoics is precisely described in III.31: "Therefore…we must conclude that the Supreme Good *is to live by applying our knowledge of nature's causative forces, selecting the things that are in accordance with nature and rejecting the things that are not*. In other words, the Supreme Good is to live in conformity and alignment with nature." The Peripatetics saw things differently; for them, the wise man might not always be happy, and there could be "degrees" of virtue (III.42—43). The Stoics took the hard line: there were no degrees of wisdom (III.48). A man was either wise or he was not. A drowning man is still unable to breathe no matter how close to the surface of the water he finds himself (III.48).

The Stoics are indifferent to those things that are neither virtue nor vice. Cato seeks to lay out various Stoic classifications and categories (III.58—60). His presentation becomes more interesting with a discussion of family and society (III.62—66). These noble passages are the high point of Book III; they show a finely-tuned awareness of the common social good. Friendship is part of this social equation, and should be seen as something desirable for its own sake (III.70). Cato concludes his discourse with praise for the greatness of the wise man (III.75); he will always be happy, because he is possessed of moral goodness. He will need nothing else.

Compared with Torquatus's explanation of Epicureanism, Cato's presentation strikes the reader as more tightly composed and logical. Although Cicero will attack Stoicism in Book IV, we are left with the impression that Stoic thought is more "socially responsible" than the monastic, corruptible ethic of the

Epicureans. While some of the Stoic classifications appear artificial, the social ethics described in III.62—67 inspire more confidence than the individualist, somewhat depressing Epicurean view of man's place in society and the world.

BOOK IV

BOOK IV

HOMINES IUNGIT CONCORDIA BLANDA

I. 1. These words concluded Cato's discourse. At this point I spoke up. "You have expounded on many little-understood things from memory, Cato, and in a very clear way. Obviously I should either set aside what I want to say in response, or take some time to think these matters through. It is not easy to grasp fully a system so complicated—yet still one so firmly grounded and elaborately constructed—even if the system happens to be flawed. For on this point I do not yet wish to speak."

"Do you think so?" Cato answered. "Do you really think you should be given additional time to reply in my case here, when under this new law I know you can respond to the prosecutor on the same day with a speech taking no more than three hours?[335] You will see that the material you have to work with here is no better for you than what you might find in those cases you sometimes win. So approach this debate of ours with the same spirit, especially since the issues have already been debated by others and also by you. It is highly unlikely that you have nothing significant to say in response."

2. "By Hercules!" I said. "I'm not in the habit of going against the Stoics. Not because I agree with everything they say, but because I'm held back by a sense of propriety. They say much that is incomprehensible to me."

"I admit there are parts of the system that are obscure," he replied. "But they don't deliberately make obscure statements: the obscurity lies in the ideas themselves."

"Why is it then," I ventured, "that when the Peripatetics talk about the same ideas, not a single word is incomprehensible?"

"The same ideas?" he responded sharply. "Haven't I explained enough to show that the Stoics and Peripatetics differ not only in their words, but in their entire systems and in everything they teach?"

"Cato, if you can demonstrate that to my satisfaction," I smiled, "then you will convert me to your entire system."

"I thought that I had already said enough," Cato rejoined. "If it's agreeable to you, we will consider this topic first. If you'd rather start with some other issue, we can postpone it until later."

"On the contrary," I said. "I'll use my own judgment and consider each subject in its appropriate place, unless what I'm proposing is unfair to you."

---

[335] Cicero was known to represent the defense in public prosecutions. A law passed in 52 B.C. set time limits for speeches by the prosecutor and the defense; the prosecutor would have two hours, and the defense three, and both speeches had to be delivered on the same day.

"As you wish," he answered. "I thought my offer made more sense, but it is better to allow each man to decide for himself."

II. 3. "Well then, Cato," I said, "I submit to you that those old followers of Plato—Speusippus,[336] Aristotle, and Xenocrates,[337] and eventually their own students Polemo[338] and Theophrastus—constructed an impressively rich and elegant system of thought. When Zeno became the pupil of Polemo, there was no reason for him to dissent from Polemo's teachings or from the ideas of the philosophers that came before Polemo. We will now describe their doctrines. As we do this, I would like you to object if you think some point needs modification; do not wait until I have responded in full to every issue you have raised. For I think their entire belief system will necessarily be in conflict with the entirety of your own.

4. "Those thinkers believed that we have been created with an inborn proficiency for these distinguished and highly prized virtues. I am talking about justice, temperance, and others in the same category; all of them are similar to the rest of the arts, yet are different in that they surpass the arts in their material and their treatment of it. They also saw that we seek these virtues with more passionate nobility than we do the arts; that we have an innate or naturally constituted lust for knowledge; that we have been designed by nature for human congregation and social organization

---

[336] Speusippus (c. 408 B.C.—339 B.C.) was Plato's nephew and inherited the Athenian Academy after his uncle's death. He departed from some of the Master's teachings, especially the "theory of forms." After eight years as head (scholarch) of the Academy, he passed on its leadership to Xenocrates.
[337] Xenocrates (c. 396 B.C.—314 B.C.) was the successor of Speusippus as head of the Academy. His views aligned with those of Plato.
[338] Polemo (or Polemon) (?—270 B.C.) was a pupil of Xenocrates and succeeded him as the third head (scholarch) of the Academy. His views apparently aligned with those of his teacher Xenocrates. For the lives and views of all three of these successors to Plato, *see* Diog. Laert. IV 1—20.

with our fellow man; and that these impulses are most clearly manifested in those persons having the greatest traits of character. They divided all of philosophy into three parts, a classification system that we know was preserved by Zeno.[339]

5. "Of these three parts, one is said to be devoted to the study of moral actions. For the moment I will forego speaking about this category, which is the basis of our current debate. We will soon enough deal with the question of what is the End of Goods. For now, I need only mention that this subject—which I believe was rightly called 'politics' (in Greek *politikon*)—was discussed in detail and at great length by the old Peripatetic and Academic philosophers. And despite differing in the vocabulary they used, they were in general agreement with regard to the subject matter.

III. "How much they wrote about politics, and how many books they penned about the law! How much they left behind for posterity, not only in the principles of the rhetorical arts, but also in actual examples of oratorical practice! Firstly, they wrote with refinement and precision on those subjects that needed to be discussed with great subtlety. They laid out definitions and marked out topical boundaries, just as you Stoics do; but your manner is cruder,[340] while their style tends to be a bit more polished.

6. "How masterful, how truly awe-inspiring, was their language when dealing with topics that required convoluted and

---

[339] These three parts are logic, physics, and ethics. This tripartite classification was a cornerstone of Stoicism. As for how these three branches related to each other, David Sedley explains, "There was less agreement about how the three parts related to each other. One favored model compared philosophy to an orchard in which logic was the protective outer wall, physics the soil and trees, and ethics the fruit. Posidonius favoured the analogy to a living animal, in which logic was the bones and sinews, physics the flesh and ethics the soul." *See* "Stoicism" in *The Routledge Encyclopedia of Philosophy*.
[340] *Squalidius*, implying more coarse or more rough.

serious treatment! With regard to justice, temperance, fortitude, friendship, the management of one's life, the study of wisdom, and service in public office, there is no pedantic plucking at hairs, nor any scraping everything down to the bone,[341] as we encounter in the Stoic system. Instead they prefer their grand themes to be discussed in ornate fashion, and their minor subjects to be treated plainly. In this way did they write their consolations, their exhortations, and even their guidance and admonitions, for the most distinguished men of their era! Their oratorical exercises were twofold, just like the nature of the subjects they handled. Every question put forward for debate can be treated in two ways: (1) in a general sense, without regard to people or specific circumstances; or (2) after looking at the specifics of the case, by treating some discrete issue of fact, law, or terminology. Thus they were well-studied in both of these approaches. And this training was what produced their striking adroitness in both of these rhetorical styles.

7. "Zeno and the Stoic thinkers who came after him either could not, or would not, give their attention to these subjects. What is undeniable is that they left them unstudied. Although Cleanthes and Chrysippus wrote something on the art of rhetoric, their works are of such quality that anyone who fervently desires to lose his speech should read nothing else but these books. You can draw your own conclusion by the way they write: they pointlessly invent new words while abandoning ones that are commonly accepted. Yet some people say, 'But they are dealing with so many topics! This entire world is our town.' You can imagine how much work a Stoic thinker must do to persuade a man from Circeii[342] that the entire world is his neighborhood. You might say, 'He passionately inspires those who hear him.' What?

---

[341] *Ossa nudantium*, literally "stripping down to the bone" or belaboring a point over and over again for no reason, much like "beating a dead horse."
[342] The modern town of Monte Circeo, about 100 km. southeast of Rome. Perhaps its people had a reputation for parochial skepticism in Cicero's day.

He ignites the passions of listeners? He would be more likely to extinguish the passion that someone already possessed.

"You certainly deliver your little sayings—that the wise man alone is king, dictator, and truly wealthy—in a crisp and smooth way. Of course you do: for you got them from the rhetoricians. But how lame are the sayings of the Stoics themselves when speaking about virtue's power! They cling to the idea that virtue has such power that it can, by itself, provide a happy life. They jab at you with arguments that feel like little thorns. Even those who agree with them are not really convinced in their souls; and they depart no better off than when they first started studying. Their doctrines perhaps are true, and certainly of great importance; but they are not handled as they should be, and are somewhat tinged with narrow-mindedness.

IV. 8. "Logical reasoning and the natural sciences come after this. (As I have said, in due course we will take up the question of the Ultimate Good, and will analyze this topic in detail). In these two disciplines there is nothing that Zeno would have wanted to change; indeed, everything was already laid out very clearly in both subjects. What was still worth discussing in logic that the ancients had overlooked? They defined a large corpus of terms and left us studies of the art of definition. On the art of dividing something into its constituent parts (which is the art of definition's companion science), they provided specific examples and showed how it ought to be done. The same is true for the rules of contradictories, from which they crafted genera and the patterns of the various genera.[343] As for deductive reasoning, they begin by laying out what they consider to be obvious premises. Logical inferences follow from these; and the conclusion at the end is what is true in each individual case.

---

[343] Meaning the different species within the various genera (*Item de contrariis, a quibus ad genera formasque generum venerunt*).

9. "How many varieties of logical argument they offer, and how different these are from the quibbling ratiocinations used by the Stoics! How often they warn us not to place our trust in sense-perception without the guidance of reason, or in reason without the help of sense-perception, and that we must not separate one from the other! Don't you agree? Weren't they the ones who established the rules that logicians now teach and bequeath to their students? Chrysippus devoted a great deal of effort to formulating the rules of logic, but Zeno himself accomplished much less in this area than the ancient thinkers. In fact, some parts of Zeno's work barely progressed beyond the point reached by his antecedents. Some aspects of logic he failed to address at all.

10. "Now there are two subjects that entirely make up the disciplines of reasoning and oratory. One of these is discovery,[344] and the other is argumentation. The Stoics and Peripatetics both spent time on argumentation; yet although the Peripatetics capably handled discovery, the Stoics entirely neglected it. You Stoics were unaware that arguments could be picked out, so to speak, from a well-ordered mental repository as needed; but your predecessors taught a systematic approach and method for doing this. The art of discovery frees the speaker from constantly having to mouth the same generic arguments on the same subjects as if he were scanning a lesson-book and slavishly adhering to one's notes.

"He who knows where an argument is located (and how to work his way towards it) will always be able to pluck it out no matter how hidden it may be. And he will always be effective in debate. There do exist speakers of great natural ability who

---

[344] By "discovery" Cicero is referring to *inventio* (the "discovery of arguments") which is one of the five canons of classical rhetoric (the others being *dispositio, elocutia, memoria,* and *pronuntiatio*). It is basically the process by which a speaker organizes and constructs an argument.

achieve proficiency without formal study; nevertheless, training is a surer guide than nature.[345] It is one thing to spew out a torrent of words like the poets do. But to formulate what you wish to say using reasoning and applied craftsmanship is something entirely different.

V. 11. "Similar things can be said about the study of the natural world. It occupies the attention of both your school and the Peripatetics, and not just for the twin purposes (identified by Epicurus) of freeing men from the fear of death and religious doctrine. An appreciation of the universe's workings promotes a humility in those who can perceive the guidance and organizing principles of the gods; and an understanding of divine actions and works cultivates greatness of soul. A man's sense of justice is kindled when he grasps some awareness of the will, guidance, and purpose of the Supreme Guide and Ruler, to whose nature both true reason and the supreme law—so we are assured by the philosophers—are admirably adapted.

12. "There is, in this same study of nature, a limitless pleasure in the act of learning; in this activity alone we can honestly and congenially devote our attentions once the necessary responsibilities of life have been fulfilled. In this entire field of learning the Stoics followed the lead of the Peripatetics on nearly all the leading topics: they believed that the gods existed and that all matter could be reduced to four elements. Yet they sought an answer to the difficult question of whether a 'fifth element' existed from which arose reason and intellect. From which of these elements came the human soul was a question that readily followed.

"Zeno believed that this element was fire. On some issues (but only a few) his opinions were different from those taken by the Peripatetics; but on the most important question, he agreed with them that the entire universe and the plurality of its components

---

[345] A memorable saying: *ars tamen est dux certior quam natura. Ars* here indicates trained craftsmanship, not "art" in its regular sense.

Views of the countryside from Tusculum

are administered by a divine mind and nature. On these matters, however, we find the Stoics to be thin in material and depth of analysis. Their Peripatetic counterparts, in contrast, are quite fecund.

13. "How much they discovered and collected about all types of organisms, and how much on their growth, anatomy, and life cycles! How much on the variety of plant life! How plentiful and multifarious were their explanations of why things happen in nature, and their demonstrations of how these natural processes occur! From this vast corpus of knowledge are obtained copious and trustworthy arguments to explain the nature of each individual thing they wish. Thus, as far as I can see, there seems to have been no reason for the change of name.[346] Just because Zeno did not agree with the Peripatetics on every point does not alter the reality that he originally came from their ranks. For that matter, I actually consider Epicurus the offspring of Democritus, at least when it comes to physics. He modifies a few things, or perhaps more than a few; but on most issues—and certainly on the most crucial ones—he simply repeats the views of Democritus. The leading Stoic thinkers do the same thing, but do not pay adequate homage to the originators of the ideas they advocate.

VI. 14. "But enough of this. I suggest that we take up the matter of the Ultimate Good, which is philosophy's foundational question. What innovation did Zeno make that would account for his break with his predecessors, who had invented the doctrine of the Ultimate Good? On this point, Cato, you provided a concise explanation of the 'end of goods' doctrine and in what sense the Stoics used the phrase. Nevertheless, I will render my own summary, so that we may discern, if we can, what new element Zeno added to the philosophical picture.

_____

[346] I.e., no reason for Zeno to call his school "Stoic" instead of using the existing term "Peripatetic."

"Our predecessors (of whom Polemo was the most straight-forward) taught that the Supreme Good was to live in accordance with nature. The Stoics say that this credo can be understood in three ways. The *first* of these is: to live by applying a knowledge of the natural world's happenings.[347] They say that this version of the Supreme Good was the very same one taught by Zeno, and it elucidates the formula you used earlier, 'to live in conformity with nature.'

15. "The *second* explanation of this Supreme Good credo is that it means one should live with an awareness of all (or most) of one's 'medium duties.'[348] So described, this definition is different from the first interpretation. The first definition is talking about 'right action' (what you call *katorthoma*), and only the wise man can accomplish it. But the second explanation applies only to duties that are incomplete, that is, those not fully perfected, and it can be achieved even by the simple-minded. The *third* explanation of the Supreme Good definition is 'to live by enjoying all (or most) of those things that are in accordance with nature.' This ideal is not dependent on our conduct alone. It is dependent on: (1) having the type of life that enjoys virtue, and (2) having those things that are in accordance with nature but which we do not control.

"However, this 'third version' of the Supreme Good, and the life on which it is based, is only attainable by the wise man, since it is linked to virtue. This is the doctrine of the End of Goods which we find described in the Stoic books themselves, as it was established by Xenocrates and Aristotle. They describe the fundamental structure of nature (the point from which you also began) with words similar to these that follow.

---

[347] I.e., a knowledge of the causes and effects that happen in nature.
[348] Discussed in III.59 (*officia media*).

VII. 16. "Every living thing in nature desires to be its own protector, in order that it may be safe and preserved within its own species. For this purpose, they say that certain arts are needed to help nature. The first among these is the art of living, which is needed both to protect what has been gifted by nature, and to acquire what may be missing. They also divided man's nature into soul and the physical body; and they stated that each of these divisions was desirable for its own sake. The virtues of each of these parts, they taught, were also desirable for their own sake. Since they believed that the soul infinitely exceeded the physical body in inherent value, they readily placed the virtues of the soul ahead of the goods of the body.

17. "Since they intended wisdom to act as the custodian and sentinel for the complete man (meaning that wisdom should operate as nature's partner and helper), they stressed that the purpose of wisdom for an organism composed of both mind and body was to assist and preserve both parts of his being. After setting down their system's basic principles, they proceeded to describe the rest in greater detail. They believed that the goods of the body were governed by rather simple rules; but they analyzed the goods of the soul more meticulously. For in these goods they discovered the seeds of justice. They were the first philosophers to teach that it is a basic attribute of nature for offspring to be loved by their parents. They said that the joining of men and women in marriage arose from nature, and that it predated the love of parents for their offspring; from this root, they said, arose the bonds of family.

"From these initial propositions they proceeded to investigate the origin and progression of all the virtues. The concept of 'greatness of soul'[349] also arose from this exploratory process: for this quality had the ability to deflect or resist the cruelties of

---

[349] *Magnitudo animi*, a consistent motif in Cicero's writings, as we noted in *On Duties*.

fortune. This is so because the most important things in life are within the wise man's power; and a life guided by the rules of the old philosophers can easily overcome the randomness and injuries of fortune.

18. "Once these basic impulses were bestowed on us by nature, a certain bounty of goods was generated; this was partly a result of the contemplation of nature's designs, since a love of learning is embedded within the human mind. From this arises the love of reasoned discussion and debate. Man is the only animal born with a sense of shame and modesty, and he instinctively wishes to associate with, and form communities with, his fellow man; and he is careful in all he says or does, so that nothing morally repugnant or dishonorable may occur. From these foundational principles—or, as I called them earlier, these 'seeds'—that were given to us by nature, temperance, modesty, justice and moral goodness grew to complete development.

VIII. 19. "Cato," I said, "You've laid out the basic beliefs of the philosophers I've been talking about. Now that all this has been explained, I want to know why Zeno turned his back on this old system. Which of the old doctrines did he dissent from? That every living thing seeks to act as its own protector? Did he disagree with the idea that every animal practices self-love to the extent that it desires preservation and security among its own kind? Did he dislike the conclusion that, since the end[350] of every art is something nature very much demands, the same rule should be applied to the art of life in general? Was it that, since we are composed of soul and a physical body, these two things and their associated virtues should be accepted for their own sake? Did it displease him that such superiority should be granted to the virtues of the soul? Or could he simply not stomach what they said about prudence, the acquisition of knowledge, the fellowship of humanity,

---

[350] "End" here meaning ultimate purpose or final objective.

Near the Croce di Tuscolo can be found this carved-out rock cavity

or about self-discipline, greatness of soul, and moral goodness in general? The Stoics will readily admit the brilliance of all these things that have been said, and that *they were not* the reason for Zeno's defection.

20. "I believe there are other things they will say are major errors committed by the old sages, errors which that devotee[351] of investigating the truth could not in any way tolerate. What could be more warped, intolerable, or idiotic than to categorize good health, absence of all pain, and the proper functioning of the eyesight and other senses, as 'goods'? It would almost make more sense to say that there is no difference between these things and their opposites. All those things that the old philosophers called 'good' were not 'good,' but 'preferred.'

"Likewise it was ridiculous for the old thinkers to have said that superior bodily functions should be sought for their own sakes. They were things that should be 'accepted,' not things that should be 'sought out.' To summarize: a life that abounds in all the *other things* that are in accordance with nature (in addition to virtue) is not more worth *seeking*, but more worth *accepting*, than a life containing only virtue. Although virtue may make life as happy as it can possibly be, some things may still be missing from the wise man's life even when he is most happy. For this reason they take action to defeat pain, disease, and the infirmity of age.

IX. 21. "O, what incredible force of personality! What just cause Zeno had for founding a new discipline! Continue on a bit more. What is coming is the subject that you so expertly explained. By this I mean the doctrine that (1) all human folly, injustice, and vices are the same, and all sins are equal; and (2) that those who, through nature and instruction, are progressing on the road towards virtue are still entirely miserable unless they

---

[351] Zeno.

have actually *achieved* virtue, and that there is no difference at all between their lives and the lives of the most evil men.[352] Thus the renowned thinker Plato—if he never achieved the state of virtue—lived a life that was no better and no happier than the most despicable crook.

"This, then, is your correction and improvement of the old philosophy: a new rendition that could never be put to use in real society, in the courts of justice, or in the senate. Who would be willing to hear talk like this from a person who announced himself an expert on wise and right actions? Who would let him change the names of things while holding the same views as everyone else? Who would condone the foisting of different terms on concepts he assigns the same meanings that everyone else does, maybe tweaking the words a bit, but in no way altering their sense?

22. "Would an attorney arguing a case try to deny, in his closing argument, that exile and confiscation of property are evils? That these things 'should be rejected' instead of 'should be avoided'? Would he suggest that a judge should *not* know how to show clemency? Imagine an attorney were speaking in front of an audience, and Hannibal were camped outside the city gates and flung a javelin over the walls. Would he then deny that being subjected to capture, slavery, death, and foreign conquest are evils? Or could the senate, when ordering a triumph for Africanus,[353] use the phrases 'because of his virtue' or 'because of his good fortune' if no one except the wise man can be said to have virtue or good fortune? What kind of philosophy is this that in the market-place uses the vernacular of the common man, yet in its books employs a vocabulary entirely its own? Especially

---

[352] In other words, there are no degrees of virtue. One is either virtuous, or one is not.

[353] Referring to Scipio Africanus, who defeated Hannibal at Zama in 202 B.C.

since they produce no new ideas with their words; the doctrines are the same as before, just presented in different form.

23. "What difference does it make whether you classify wealth, power, and health as 'goods' or as 'preferred' things, when the person calling them 'goods' values them no more than you, who calls these same things 'preferred'? Panaetius, a man of the highest caliber and importance, was worthy of the close friendship of Scipio and Laelius. When he wrote to Quintus Tubero on the topic of enduring pain, he never offered his best argument—assuming it could have been proven—that pain is not an evil. What he actually did was define pain and its characteristics, discuss how foreign it is to our natural bodily condition,[354] and finally offer a method for coping with it. It seems to me that the emptiness of your words has already been affirmed by Panaetius's own verdict, since he himself was a Stoic.

X. 24. "But Cato, in order for me to approach more closely the things you've said, let's take it one step further, and compare the ideas you've stated with the ideas I believe are more convincing. We will, therefore, concede the ideas you hold in common with the old philosophers. But we can debate—if it is acceptable to you—those other ideas which are contested."

"I would be willing," he responded, "to scrutinize the issues even more rigorously—to take things one step further, as you have said. Until now, what you have offered are standard, mainstream opinions; but I really need something more polished from you."

"You want this from me?" I cried. "No matter, I will move forward. And if not enough points come to mind, I won't hesitate to use the material you consider to be mainstream.

---

[354] The text seems somewhat vague here: *quantumque in eo esset alieni*, where the demonstrative pronoun *eo* could refer to nature or the human body. I have chosen to interpret it as a reference to our natural bodily state.

25. "It must be established at the outset that we are committed to our own survival, and that the first imperative nature gives us is to uphold this fundamental desire to preserve our own lives. This is not disputed. It follows from this that we must learn who we are, so that we can base our conduct on the type of person we ought to be. We are human organisms. We are composed of body and soul, and these have a particular quality. As our first natural instinct requires, we ought to cherish these two halves, and from them establish this End, this Ultimate and Supreme Good. And if our initial propositions are true, *this End of Goods should be found in gaining as many as possible of the most crucial things that are in conformity with nature.*

26. "So this was what they considered to be the Supreme Good. What I have explained using many words, they explained concisely with these few: *to live in accordance with nature.* This was their view of the End of Goods.

XI. "Now ask the Stoic philosophers (or preferably you, for who is better suited for the job!) to tell us how, if we begin from these same first principles, one concludes that the Supreme Good is found in living honestly? For indeed this corresponds with 'living in conformity with virtue' or 'to live by following nature.' How or at what point did you abruptly remove 'body' from your analysis, as well as all those things that are in conformity with nature but beyond our control, and eventually even duty itself? What I would like to know, then, is this: how did it happen that so many things approved by nature were unexpectedly discarded by wisdom?

27. "Even if we were not searching for man's Supreme Good, but for the Good of some hypothetical organism that consisted of nothing but intellect (we may create such an animal here to advance our goal of discovering the truth more easily), this End of yours would still not be suitable for such an intellectual being. For the organism would also want good health and freedom from pain; it would seek to preserve itself and safeguard its own vital

interests; and it would make living in accordance with nature its ultimate End. And as I have previously stated, this means having all—or almost all—of the most important things that are in accordance with nature.

28. "Although we can imagine such a hypothetical animal as having no body, nevertheless, no matter how you envision such an animal, its mind would have qualities similar to those possessed by a body. Thus, there would be no way to establish an End of Goods for such an organism except by using the guidelines I have already described. However, Chrysippus—in his treatise on the various species of animals—says that some kinds of organisms excel in bodily power, others excel in strength of mind, and a few have both attributes in equal measure. Finally he discusses what ought to be the Supreme Good for each classification of animal. He placed mankind among the type of species that excels in strength of mind. Yet he described man's Supreme Good in such a way that he makes it look like man is *nothing but* intellect, rather than as if the intellect has the upper hand over his bodily attributes.

XII. "The only situation where it would be proper to place the Supreme Good in virtue alone would be if we were dealing with an organism that was totally composed of mind. It would also have to be true that this intellectual being had nothing in itself that was in accordance with nature (such as good health).

29. "It is impossible to form a picture of an organism like this that is not self-contradictory. But if they say that some things are overshadowed, and not worthy of consideration due to their relative prominence, we too concede this fact. Epicurus takes the same position with regard to pleasures; when pleasures are comparatively small, they are often outshined and forgotten. But the advantages of the body are of such magnitude, longevity, and quantity that they do not belong in this category. Thus in cases where the smallness of a pleasure causes it to be overshadowed, we are often forced to admit that their presence or absence is

irrelevant to us. It is just like you said earlier: neither lighting an oil-lamp in broad daylight, nor adding a single copper coin to the vast wealth of Croesus, make any meaningful difference at all.

30. "While such 'overshadowing' does not happen to some things, it may still be true that they do not make a big difference in the larger picture. If a man who has been living happily for ten years were granted another month of equally pleasurable life, it would be a good thing, since the durational increase in his enjoyment might have some significance. But if this extra month of happiness were not accepted, the man's happy life would not suddenly be cancelled out. Goods of the body are more like this latter kind of thing. They have some value that makes their attainment a labor that is worthy of our exertion. To me the Stoics sometimes appear to be joking when they say that, if asked to choose between a plain life of virtue and a life of virtue with an *ampulla* or strigil[355] added to it, the wise man would select the option with these added accessories. *Yet he would not be any happier for having them.*

31. "Is this comparison appropriate? Shouldn't it be refuted with laughter, rather than with reasoned argument? Who doesn't rightly deserve to be ridiculed who fusses over whether he has an *ampulla*? But he who restores someone's limbs to health and takes away another's agonies of pain, is deserving of immense gratitude. If this 'wise man' you talk about was forced by a tyrant to visit the torturer's rack, he would not carry the same expression as if he had lost an *ampulla*. He would have the countenance of a man who knew a great and difficult struggle was coming, and he would realize that he must now fight against a mortal adversary called pain.

---

[355] An *ampulla* was two-handed bulbous flask, often used for holding bath oils. A strigil was a curved scraper used to remove sweat, dirt, or skin oil during bathing.

"He would activate all the reserves of strength and endurance needed for protection in the great contest that lay before him. Finally, we do not worry whether something is so small that it may be 'overshadowed' or blotted out completely, *but whether that thing helps to complete the whole picture*. One pleasure may be overshadowed by many others in this life of pleasures; but this one pleasure, although it may be small, is still a part of this life which is grounded in pleasure. A single coin is eclipsed by the vast wealth of Croesus, yet it remains a part of his holdings. In the same way, *things we designate as being 'in accordance with nature' might be overshadowed by other things in a happy life, but they are still a part of that happy life.*

XIII. 32. "And if—as you and I both ought to recognize— there is a natural human inclination to want things that are in conformity with nature, then all of these must be collected to form some kind of comprehensive total. Once this fact is grasped, we may at our leisure probe into the relative value of each thing, the importance each one has in promoting a happy life, and the nature of this 'overshadowing' effect we spoke of earlier (which may or may not be noticeable due to the relative smallness of the pleasure).

"What about a point that is undisputed? No one will disagree with the statement that the ultimate target, the final objective to be pursued, is similar for all living organisms. Every organism is by nature diligent in taking care of its own interest. What animal ever lived that disregarded itself or any part of itself, or any essential action or capability thereof, or any of the other things (whether techniques or conditions) that are in accordance with nature? What organism has ever forgotten the original, formative principles of its creation? Certainly there is not a single one that does not maintain this kind of capability from its inception to its death.

33. "How does it happen, then, that it is only man who forgets his nature, forgets his body, and places the Supreme Good not in

the *whole* man but only in a *part* of him? How can we preserve the belief, which is admitted and upheld by all, that this End we are investigating is similar for all natures? We would consider it 'similar' if, when considering all the rest of the natures,[356] the Supreme Good for each nature is that aspect in which each nature excelled. This is how the Stoics view the Supreme Good.

34. "Why, then, are you so unwilling to change the principles of nature? You say that every animal, from the time it is born, is dedicated to its own interests and occupied with preserving itself. Wouldn't it be better for you to say that every animal is dedicated to that which is best in itself, and is focused on the preservation of that quality alone, and that other natures[357] do nothing but preserve that element which is best in each? But in what way is it the 'best' if there is no good besides it?

"However, if other things are also worth striving for, why shouldn't the foremost desire be the acquisition of all of them, or of the largest number and most important of them? A Phidias[358] can produce a statue from its inception and finish it completely, or he can receive and finish someone else's incomplete work. Wisdom is similar to this; she herself did not create man, but received him in rudimentary form from nature. She should, therefore, pay close attention to nature, and carry out her design as if she were completing the final work on a statue.

35. "What sort of man, then, has nature outlined in primitive form? And what is the role and objective of wisdom? What should be performed and accomplished by it? If there is nothing to be completed except a certain operation of the intellect (that is,

---

[356] The word *natura* is used here, but the meaning in this sentence and in the previous one implies a living organism.

[357] Meaning animal or organism.

[358] A renowned Greek sculptor, architect, and painter (c. 480 B.C.—430 B.C.).

reason), then its Ultimate Good must be to act in conformity with virtue. For virtue is reason's completed form.[359] If there is nothing but a body, then good health, the absence of pain, beauty, and all the rest will be the Ultimate Goods.

XIV. 36. "The question at present is this: what is the Ultimate Good for man? Do we doubt that the right way to answer this is to ask what has been accomplished in man's entire nature? It is generally accepted that the purpose and function of wisdom is to be occupied with man's refinement. Others (lest you think I am only speaking against the Stoics) propose theories that place the Supreme Good in that category of things that are beyond our power, as if they were talking about some inanimate being. Still others, however, only pay attention to the mind, as if man had no body at all. Yet the mind is not some vacant, unknown entity: this is a view that makes no sense to me. It is actually a certain type of body. It is not content with having virtue alone, but also seeks freedom from pain. So each philosophical school, so to speak, abandons the left side of its body in order to protect its right side; or they follow Erillus's lead when talking about the mind, in that they embrace abstract cognition but neglect the importance of action. They will pick out one thing while passing over a great many others, and this produces conclusions that are decidedly skewed. *Without doubt, the most comprehensive and accurate system is to be found in those thinkers who, when investigating man's Supreme Good, took care to provide for every aspect of man's body and mind.*

---

[359] *Rationis enim perfectio est virtus. Perfectio* here means completion or final form.

The amphitheater at Tusculum

A view of the area surrounding Tusculum

37. "Since virtue, as we all agree, carries the highest prestige and is of supreme significance, and because we believe that those who are wise have achieved perfection and complete development, you, Cato, want to overwhelm our powers of judgment with the splendor of virtue. In every living thing, such as horses or dogs, there is something great and noble; but they still require freedom from pain and bodily health. The same, therefore, is true for man: this 'completed form' referred to earlier[360] finds its greatest glory in what is man's best quality (i.e., virtue). I suspect that you do not pay enough attention to nature's scheme and her method of progress. When nature produces crops, she guides the process from seedling to the final ear of grain; she then discards all but the grain as being of no value. The same thing, however, does not happen in the case of man once nature has guided him to the destination of rational thought. Indeed she always adds something, so that she does not abandon what she first granted.[361]

38. "In this way nature added reason to the bodily senses and, once reason was created, did not abandon sensation. Consider the cultivation of grapevines, whose purpose is to put the grapevine with all its constituent parts in the best possible condition. Let us imagine this to be true—we are allowed to do this, just as you are in the habit of proposing a hypothetical for teaching purposes.

"If this art of grapevine cultivation was a quality belonging to the grapevine itself, then it would want, as before, those things that are related to grapevine cultivation. However, it would favor itself over all other parts of the vine, and would conclude that no other quality of the vine was superior to itself. In the same way, when an organism has acquired the faculty of sensation, it indeed

---

[360] In IV.35, above. "Completed form" is *perfectio*. It could also be translated as consummation or perfection.
[361] A beautiful sentence: *Semper enim ita assumit aliquid ut ea, quae prima dederit, non deserat.*

protects the organism; but sensation also protects itself. But when reason is then added, it occupies such a commanding position that all those fundamental principles of nature are placed under its tutelage.

39. "Therefore reason never withdraws its support of previously-established principles: it should govern the whole of life. I could not be more amazed at the inconsistency of the Stoics on this point. They want natural appetite (which they call *horme*), duty, and even virtue to be counted among the things that are in accordance with nature. But when they want to reach the Ultimate Good, they sidestep all of these and leave us with two tasks instead of one. They want us to 'accept' some things, and 'desire' other things, rather than just combining both of these under one 'End.'

XV. 40. "Yet you say that virtue cannot be established if things other than virtue are held to be essential ingredients of the good life. But the truth is the exact opposite: *virtue can by no means be introduced unless everything that she keeps and rejects relates back to one Supreme Good.* For if we neglect ourselves altogether, we would be guilty of Aristo's faults and mistakes, and would lose sight of what we said were the basic principles of virtue herself. If we do not neglect these things, and also do not relate them to the purpose of the Supreme Good, then we will not be deviating much from the shallow ideas of Erillus. We would have to accept two different rules of life simultaneously. For Erillus creates two separate Supreme Goods, which he should have joined together if they were both valid. They are so divided as to be completely segregated; and nothing could be more abnormal than this.

41. "So the reality is opposite of what you are saying. Virtue can in no way be established *unless it interprets the fundamental principles of nature in a way that they remain pertinent to the Ultimate Good.* We are searching for a virtue that does not renounce nature, but rather embraces it; the virtue you find appealing is one that embraces part of nature, and throws away

the rest. If it could speak, man's deepest instinct would say that its first objectives were focused on preserving itself with the constitution that it possessed from birth.

"But what nature herself wanted had not yet been announced at that time. So let it be announced. What happens then? What else can be understood from this, except that no part of human nature should be neglected? If man is made of nothing but reason, let the End of Goods be found in virtue alone. But if he also has a body, then this explanation of nature (that you gave on behalf of the Stoics) will certainly cause us to abandon what we had believed before hearing this explanation. One could even say that living in conformity with nature is the same thing as abandoning nature.

42. "Some philosophers, after establishing the importance of the senses, have then promptly abandoned sense-perception, and moved on to greater and more divinely-inspired human qualities. It is much the same with the Stoic thinkers: after describing the basic human appetites, they gazed on the surpassing beauty of virtue. They quickly tossed aside everything they had ever seen except virtue herself, forgetting that the true nature of desirable things is so broad that it extends from first principles to final ends. They do not grasp that they are weakening the very foundations of these beautiful and admirable things.

XVI. 43. "So as I see it, all those thinkers are mistaken who say that the End of Goods is to live according to moral rectitude. Yet some are more incorrect than others. Pyrrho is certainly the most deluded; under his idea of virtue, there is no place at all for something that is an object of desire. Aristo, who did not dare to exclude desirable things completely, follows right behind him: when explaining what moved the wise man to desire something, he proposed whatever passed through his mind and whatever happened to tickle his fancy. Aristo is better than Pyrrho because he at least acknowledged there were some desirable things, yet worse than the others because he deviated so completely from nature.

"Because the Stoics place the End of Goods in virtue alone, they are similar to these thinkers. Since they are looking for a foundational principle for right conduct, they are better than Pyrrho. Because they do not invent mental fictions, they are superior to Aristo. However, they exclude from the End of Goods the things that they claim are 'in accordance with nature' or that 'should be taken up for their own sakes.' In so doing, they deviate from nature, and in some ways are not too different from Aristo. He was the one who mastered the art of imaginative speculations. The Stoics insist on the importance of the fundamental principles of nature, but exclude them from their Ends or Ultimate Good. They designate them as 'preferred,' so that there is some degree of choice among them. On the surface they appear to be following nature; but because they deny that these things have any connection to a happy life, they are in fact abandoning nature.

44. "Up to this point I have explained why Zeno had no reason for departing from the accepted authority of his predecessors. We will now take up the remaining issues—unless you want to add something here, Cato, or unless we have already spent too much time on this topic."

"Neither one," he replied. "I want you to finish your discussion. Your explanation could never be tedious to me."

"Wonderful," I said with a grin. "What could be more appealing to me than to debate virtue with Cato, that authority on all the virtues! 45. But first consider this: your most crucial idea—the one that supersedes all others—is that moral goodness is the sole good, and that living according to moral rectitude is the End of Goods. This is an idea you will have in common with all those thinkers who place the End of Goods in virtue alone. And your conviction that it is impossible to form an idea of virtue if we consider anything other than moral goodness, is a belief that will be held by the thinkers I named just now.

"As I see it, it would have been more reasonable for Zeno (when he was debating Polemo, and from whom Zeno had taken the concept of nature's fundamental principles) to have begun his analysis with the doctrines they had in common, *and then* to have stated where the difference of opinion first arose. He should not have taken sides with those who rejected the idea that the Supreme Good came from nature—and he ended up using the same arguments and ideas that they used.

XVII. 46. "There is also something else I don't agree with. Once you have demonstrated (as it seems to you) that moral rectitude is the only good, you then say certain pathways that are suitable and appropriate to our nature are placed before us. Virtue is created, you say, from the selection of one of these choices. *But virtue should never be found in an act of selection*; for this would suggest that the Supreme Good itself were trying to obtain something else.[362] Now everything worth adopting, selecting, and desiring ought to be contained in the Supreme Good, so that he who has obtained it does not want anything else. For those whose Ultimate Good lies in pleasure, can you see that it is obvious what must be done, and what must not be done? No one has any doubt about all the duties that they should observe, follow, and avoid. If this doctrine I am now defending is the Supreme Good, then it is clear right away what my obligations and my required actions are. But you Stoics—who have no objective other than moral rectitude and goodness—would be unable to find a formative principle for duty or conduct.

47. "Everyone who is searching for this formative principle will eventually have to return to nature: this applies both to those who say they listen to whatever comes into their minds or attracts their attention, and to you Stoics as well. Nature will correctly remind these people that it is unreasonable to seek the principles of right conduct from nature herself, while at the same time

---

[362] Because by definition, the Ultimate Good cannot need or want anything else.

looking elsewhere for the rules of a happy life. There is one universal rule that governs both the principles of right conduct and the Ultimate Good. Aristo's opinion on this subject—when he said there is no difference between one thing and another, and no difference between anything except the difference between virtues and vices—is no longer accepted as valid. Zeno, therefore, was wrong when he said that 'nothing else except the propensity for virtue or vice makes the slightest difference in reaching the Supreme Good.' It was also incorrect for him to say that 'although other things[363] are irrelevant in determining what makes a happy life, they are in some way relevant to our desires.' As if our desire were somehow irrelevant in reaching the Supreme Good!

48. "What could be less logical than to follow the Stoics' advice, which is *first* to investigate the Ultimate Good and *then later* return to nature in order to uncover the guiding principle of conduct and duty? Regard for conduct or duty does not persuade a man to strive for the things that are in accordance with nature: rather, desire and conduct *are motivated by* the things that are in accordance with nature.

XVIII. "I now come to your brief points which you called 'logical consequences.'[364] I will start with something that could not be shorter: everything good is commendable; everything commendable is morally right; therefore everything good is morally right. O, what a useless dagger this is![365] Who will admit your first premise? And if I do admit the first premise, the second one becomes unnecessary: for if everything good is commendable, then everything good is morally right.

---

[363] I.e., things other than virtue or vice.

[364] *Consectaria*, or something that follows logically from something else.

[365] *O plumbum pugionem!* Literally, "O, leaden dagger!" A *pugio* was a short dagger; one made from lead would of course be entirely worthless.

49. "Who, then, is going to agree with you on this point except Pyrrho, Aristo, and others who have similar views? You don't accept the opinions of these philosophers. Aristotle, Xenocrates, and their entire school will not permit it: they call health, bodily strength, wealth, glory, and many other things *good*, but they do not call them *commendable*. These thinkers do not believe the End of Goods is found in virtue alone, but they place virtue ahead of everything else. But what do you suppose the reaction will be from those who completely separated virtue from the End of Goods: namely, Epicurus, Hieronymus, and those who advocate for Carneades's view of the End of Goods?

50. "Would Callipho or Diodorus be able to concede this point to you? To moral goodness they joined something else that belonged to a different category. Are you satisfied, Cato, with accepting a point you don't agree with, in order to achieve the results you want? Consider this sophistic reasoning, which you think is utterly wrong: 'what is good is to be desirable; what is desirable is to be sought; what is to be sought is commendable.' One could go through the final steps, but I refuse to do so. Just as we noted before, no one will concede that 'what should be sought' is commendable. Your other point is not really a logical consequence; it is truly absurd. Of course, the fault lies with the Stoic thinkers, not you: 'A happy life is truly worth celebrating; and it is impossible for anyone to find a reason to celebrate anything without moral goodness.'

51. "Polemo will grant this point to Zeno. So will his master and the rest of their tribe. So will all those other thinkers who, despite placing virtue far ahead of everything else, still feel the need to attach something additional to it when trying to determine the Ultimate Good. If having virtue should bring someone a sense of pride (as it should), and if virtue is so transcendent that it cannot even be described in words, then Polemo can be happy with virtue alone even while lacking everything else. Yet he refuses to concede that nothing should be regarded as good except virtue. Those who believe in a Supreme Good without virtue will

probably not admit that the happy life has something about it that is rightly commendable—even though these same people sometimes portray certain pleasures as majestic.

XIX. 52. "Thus you are adopting things that have not been conceded. Or, you are accepting things that do not help your argument at all, even if they have been conceded. During the whole time we have experimented with these syllogisms, I certainly would have thought that an objective worthy of philosophy and ourselves (especially since we are seeking the Ultimate Good) would be to correct our lives, plans, and goals, rather than just improve our diction. Who is going to abandon his original opinion after hearing those sharp and well-worded arguments that you say give you so much satisfaction?

"People are ready and waiting to hear why pain is not an evil. The response of the Stoics is to say that, yes, pain is burdensome, troubling, hateful, contrary to nature, and difficult to tolerate; *but despite this* it is not an evil, because it contains no fraud, dishonesty, malice, negligence, or moral corruption. A student hearing this might want to laugh; but he will not leave the classroom any better-equipped to deal with pain than when he first arrived.

53. "But you Stoics deny that anyone can be strong who thinks pain is an evil. Why would anyone be stronger for believing what you yourselves already think, that pain is bitter and hardly bearable? Timidity arises out of life's specific circumstances; it does not spring into existence from words. And you say that if one letter in the edifice is changed, the whole philosophical school will collapse. Does it seem to you that I am changing one letter, or entire pages? Even if it is right for you to praise the Stoics for their maintenance of strict systemic order and precise linkage between concepts (these were the words you used earlier), we are not obligated to follow a line of thought that, despite being internally congruent and undeviating in its purpose, still proceeds from initial premises that are wrong.

A narrow pathway leading to Tusculum

54. "In formulating his basic doctrine, your teacher Zeno abandoned nature's guidelines. He placed the Supreme Good in the superiority of character that we call *virtue*, and said that nothing else was good except moral rectitude. He further proposed that virtue cannot exist if, with regard to the other things, no single thing is better or worse than anything else. He adhered scrupulously to the consequences of these proposals. You speak accurately, and I cannot deny it. But the implications flowing from these propositions are so false that the original ideas spawning them cannot be true.

55. "As you know, the dialecticians teach us that if what follows from an original assumption is false, then the original assumption that birthed it must also be false. Thus the following line of reasoning is not only true, but so transparent that the dialecticians see it as fundamental: if X, then Y; but not Y; therefore not X.[366] So once your conclusions are debunked, your original premises are dealt a mortal blow. What are the ideas that follow from your original assumptions? They are: (1) all who are not wise are equally miserable; (2) all wise men are equally happy; (3) all good deeds are equal, and all misdeeds are equal. While these conclusions may sound grandiose at first hearing, they are less impressive on closer inspection. Each man's own senses, the basic realities of nature, and truth itself all shouted aloud *that a man cannot be coaxed into believing that there is no difference between the things Zeno tried to make equal.*

XX. 56. "Afterwards your little Phoenician friend[367] (of course you know your clients from Citium actually came from

---

[366] Cicero uses pronouns rather than letters: *Si illud, hoc; non autem hoc; igitur ne illud quidem.* Letters are a better choice for conveying the thought in English.
[367] Referring to Zeno, who came from Citium. In the Roman stereotype, the Phoenicians (and Carthaginians, for that matter) were supposed to be especially crafty.

Phoenicia), a quite crafty man, found out that Nature was fighting his ideas. He was unable to make his case, so he began to change his words. First, he conceded that the things we call 'goods' could be labeled as 'valuable' or 'appropriate to nature.' Then he started to admit that for the wise man—that is, the extremely happy man—it would be more suitable for him to have those things that he dares not call 'goods,' but allows to be called 'appropriate to nature.' He denies that Plato (even if he is not wise) is in the same situation as the tyrant Dionysius. Due to his hopeless inability to achieve wisdom, Dionysius's best option would be to die. For Plato, living is best, since he at least has some hope of attaining it. Some misdeeds are tolerable, and others are not under any circumstances. This is because some misdeeds are more offensive, and others are much less offensive, to the performance of one's duties. Some fools are so pathetic that there is no hope of their ever becoming wise, while others might be able to attain wisdom if only they applied themselves rigorously.

57. "He spoke differently from other writers, but the gist of his statements matched what others said. He placed no lesser value on things he denied were good than did those thinkers who said they *were* good. What was he trying to accomplish by changing the terminology? He might at least have taken away some of their importance and valued them a little less than the Peripatetics did, so that it might seem like he was calling attention to some meaningful distinction, instead of just shuffling labels around. What do you think? What thoughts do you have to offer on this 'happy life,' that ultimate objective to which everything points to?

"You will deny that the happy life is the aggregation of all the things nature requires: you will stake everything on virtue alone. Every dispute ultimately hinges on a question of fact or terminology: if someone is ignorant of the facts, or mistaken as to terminology, then one or another type of disagreement results. If neither one of these scenarios exists, then one must take care to use the most familiar and pertinent words: that is, the words that most prominently disclose the facts.

58. "Assuming our predecessors are correct when it comes to the facts, is there any doubt that the words they use are superior? Let us take a look at their opinions. We may return to their words later.

XXI. "They say the following. The mind's desire is aroused when it detects something that appears to be in conformity with nature. Everything that is in accordance with nature has some inherent worth, and that it must be valued according to its relative priority. Some things that are in accordance with nature—namely, things that we consider neither morally good nor praiseworthy—arouse none of that deep desire just mentioned, while other things in accordance with nature stimulate pleasure in every organism, but in man also stimulate reason. Those things that are conducive to human reason are called morally good, beautiful, and praiseworthy. The former things are called 'natural'; and when they are joined with moral goodness, they create and perfect a happy life.

59. "The old philosophers also say this. Of all these benefits—benefits that they who call them goods value no more than does Zeno, who denies they are goods—by far the most outstanding of them is moral goodness and what is praiseworthy. But if two different varieties of moral goodness were proposed, with one version having physical health attached to it and the other version having sickness, there is no doubt as to which of these options nature would direct us. Yet the power of moral goodness is so strong, and surpasses all else so decisively, that neither punishment nor reward can deflect it from what it has judged to be righteous. And everything that presents itself as a difficulty, an adversity, or a handicap can be crushed by those virtues which nature has bestowed on us. Not that this is easy to do, of course, or that such struggles should not be taken seriously (indeed, isn't this the whole purpose of virtue?). The point here is that these

adversities are not the sole factors in determining whether a life is happy or not happy.

60. "This is the important point: those things Zeno said should be adopted, should be highly valued, and are 'adapted to nature' are the same things that the old philosophers called 'goods.' Our predecessors considered a life happy if it contained the greatest number or the most important of these things I just mentioned. According to Zeno, however, the only thing that should be called 'good' was something that had a unique quality of its own that made it worth seeking. The only happy life, he insisted, was a life lived according to virtue.

XXII. "If this debate is to be about reality, Cato, there can be no dispute between the two of us. If we compare the actual substance of our arguments, and make the necessary adjustments for the particular jargons we each use, it is clear that there is no significant difference between your opinions and mine. Zeno was not blind to this truth, but he was intoxicated by the grandeur and majesty of philosophical terminology. If he had truly comprehended the significance of the words that came out of his mouth, would there have been any difference between his teachings and those of Pyrrho or Aristo? And if Zeno did not endorse the ideas of these two men, why did he waste his energy nitpicking with people he agreed with in substance, but differed with in terminology?

61. "Imagine what would happen if Plato's followers, and the followers who came after them, were to reappear now and talk to you in this way: 'We listened to you, Marcus Cato, knowing you are a most learned thinker, an extremely just man, the best of judges, and a most conscientious witness. We have been wondering why you have preferred the Stoics instead of us. The Stoic conception of good and evil is the doctrine Zeno took from Polemo. Zeno used terms that initially seemed invigorating but ultimately elicited scorn once the import of his words was comprehended. If you endorsed these doctrines, why didn't you

keep them within their correct terminology? And if you were influenced by 'authority,' did you really place that impersonal abstraction ahead of all of us, and even ahead of Plato himself?

"The question is pertinent, especially since you want to be an important figure in public affairs. We were the right people to outfit and assist you in protecting the republic under the color of your own prestige. We were the ones who first searched for answers; we outlined the main issues; we made the observations and formulated the precepts. We have written volume after volume on the various species of governments, their dispositions, and the ways they can be changed; we have also discussed their laws, institutions, and societal customs. Eloquence is the public figure's most formidable tool, and we hear you are renowned among orators. How much you might have benefitted from our storehouse of knowledge!' If these old followers of Plato had spoken to you this way, Cato, how would you have answered them?"

62. "I'd ask you," Cato replied, "to speak on my behalf in the same way you composed that speech for them. It would be even better if you gave me a chance to answer these imaginary interlocutors. Yet for the time being I prefer to listen to you. When the time is right, I will be ready to answer them—that is, when I answer you."

XXIII. "Cato, if you wanted to respond with the truth, you should have said something like this. It is not that you reject the views of these old philosophers, as they are men of proven brilliance and authority. You have simply noticed that the Stoics detected things their predecessors overlooked. They discussed the same topics with more sensitivity, and arrived at more profound and subtle judgments. Firstly, they denied that good health was something that should be sought; they said it was 'worth choosing.' They said this not because they thought bodily health was a legitimate good, but because they thought it was not worthless (although those who never doubted it was a good did not really value it any higher).

"The hard truth is you couldn't deal with the fact that these long-whiskered sages (as we like to call our ancestors) taught that a man who lived morally but who also had physical health, wealth, and social stature had a better, more rewarding, and more fulfilling life than someone who, although equally upright, was like Ennius's character Alcmaeon in that he was

Surrounded by disease, exile, and pauperism.

63. "Due to their limited intellectual advancement, our predecessors believed that the former life was the optimal, preferred, and happier one. The Stoics, however, thought that the former life should be no more than *a favored personal choice*. They believed this not because they thought this life was happier, but because they considered it more aligned with nature's teachings. Apparently the Stoics grasped something that had eluded those who came before them: that men stained by criminality and murder are no more miserable than those who, although living honest and moral lives, have not yet achieved the perfected state of wisdom.

64. "And at this point you offered up the standard false equivalencies that the Stoics like to use during arguments. Who doesn't see that, if a group of people are trying to get out of the water, those closest to the surface can't breathe any more easily than those who are more deeply submerged? Because making progress in approaching the water's surface does not save a man from drowning, you Stoics claim that making progress in virtue, and developing one's capacity for it, does nothing to relieve a man's misery until he has actually arrived at the final, perfected state of virtue. And because puppies starting to develop their vision are just as blind as newborns, you say it must be true that

Plato—because he had not yet achieved wisdom—was just as intellectually visionless as the tyrant Phalaris.[368]

XXIV. 65. "Cato, these analogies you give us—where despite making a great deal of progress, a person is still in the same position he wants to escape until he has actually escaped it—are hardly appropriate. A man does not breathe until he has emerged from the water, and puppies are just as blind before they have acquired vision as if they were going to be blind forever. *These* examples are valid analogies: one man's eyes are not working properly, another one has a problem with his health. Once they have undergone treatment, they improve as the days go by. One gets stronger day by day, and the other's vision improves. Similar situations exist with all who are studying virtue: their vices are gradually removed, and their mistakes are gradually corrected.[369] Unless, perhaps, you don't think Tiberius Gracchus the elder[370] was happier than his son, where the elder Gracchus fought hard to maintain the republic, while his son worked to overturn it. Gracchus the father was not exactly a wise man, but then again, how many can claim this title? When, where, or in what circumstances can they claim to be wise? But because he applied himself diligently in the pursuit of renown and honor, he made great progress on the path of virtue.

---

[368] Greek tyrant of the Sicilian city of Akragas from about 570 to 554 B.C. He was legendary for his cruelty, supposedly even constructing a bronze bull in which to roast his political enemies.

[369] *Levantur vitiis, levantur erroribus.*

[370] Tiberius Gracchus the Elder (*maior*) (217? B.C.—154 B.C.) served as consul in 177 B.C. and 163 B.C. He was the father of the two famous agrarian reformers, Tiberius and Caius. His sons attempted to solve the problem of Roman overconcentration of wealth in the hands of a few, and for this were resisted and eventually killed by forces representing the wealthy elites. The younger Tiberius was killed in 133 B.C.; Caius in 121 B.C. Cicero, however, sees the sons not as brave reformers but as dangerous subversives.

66. "Compare your grandfather Drusus[371] with Caius Gracchus, who was politically active at roughly the same time. Drusus repaired the damage that Caius Gracchus had caused to the republic. Nothing makes men quite so miserable as crime and disrespect for tradition (since all reckless fools are obviously miserable), and he who honorably serves his country is not nearly as wretched as he who plots its destruction. Thus, a lessening of personal vice occurs in the lives of those who make significant progress on the road to virtue.

67. "Your Stoic philosophers say that a man can make progress towards virtue, but they also deny that such a man's vices will decrease while he is on this path. There is some value in inspecting the argument used by these subtle teachers to prove their assertions. The argument is the following. With arts that are capable of reaching high levels of refinement, the opposites of these arts can also reach a high level. But nothing can approach the pinnacle occupied by virtue.

Therefore the vices cannot increase either, since they are the opposites of the virtues. So is doubt removed by the obvious, or is the obvious destroyed by doubts? Clearly some vices are worse than others. But there is doubt, however, that what you Stoics call the Supreme Good can be 'increased' in any meaningful sense. Where you Stoics should be illuminating doubts with certainties, you instead work to undercut certainties with doubts.[372]

68. "Thus the same reasoning I used a little while ago would be able to defeat your arguments. If no vice is worse than another because the End of Goods (as you imagine it) cannot be increased, then your understanding of the End of Goods must be changed—

---

[371] Marcus Livius Drusus (?—108 B.C.) served as tribune in 122 B.C., as consul in 112 B.C., and as censor in 109 B.C. He also had a son of the same name.

[372] Another beautifully balanced and poetic sentence: *Vos autem, cum perspicuis dubia debeatis illustrare, dubiis perspicua conamini tollere.*

because it is perfectly clear that human vices are *not* all the same. Let us stick to our rule that when some conclusion is false, the initial proposition on which that conclusion was based cannot be true.

XXV. "So what is the cause of all these difficulties you are having? *It is the narcissistic affectation that so imbues your conception of the Ultimate Good.* If we truly insist that moral goodness is the only good, we permit the neglect of personal health, family responsibilities, the administration of public affairs, the conduct of business affairs, and the duties of life in general. Even moral rectitude itself—which you want to be the cure-all for everything—would in the end have to be abandoned. These were the protests voiced so effectively by Chrysippus against Aristo. From this logical impasse would come the 'corrupt and deceptive speech'[373] referred to by the poet Lucius Attius.

69. "Once the whole concept of responsibilities was taken away, wisdom had nowhere to plant its feet securely. Responsibilities were made meaningless once choice and the ability to make distinctions were removed. Distinctions between things could not be perceived once they were made equal and equivalent by default. And from this chaos came an even more muddled set of doctrines than Aristo's. Nevertheless, his doctrines are simple; yours are full of wily stratagems. If you were to ask Aristo whether he thinks absence of pain, riches, and health are goods, his answer would be *no*. What does this mean? That the opposites of these things are evils? Again, the answer is no. If you were to put the same question to Zeno, his response would be the same as Aristo's. Once we recover from our shock, we might ask these two thinkers how we can live our lives if it makes no difference whether we are healthy or sick, untroubled by pain or tormented by it, or whether we can or cannot keep cold and hunger

---

[373] *Fallaciloquae malitiae.* From a lost work by Attius (*see* II.94).

at bay. Aristo would say: 'You will live nobly and splendidly, and will do whatever seems right to you. You will never experience distress. You will never feel desire. You will never know the meaning of fear.'

70. "And Zeno's response? He says that these ideas are unnatural, and that one cannot live according to such rules. He believes that there is a huge difference between moral goodness and moral turpitude, but that between other things there is not much difference at all.

71. "So far, the same.[374] But listen to what comes after this, and hold back your laughter if you can. Zeno tells us that these 'medium' things, despite not being different from each other, still possess such qualities that some should be chosen, some should be rejected, and others are totally unimportant. In other words, you want some of them, you do not want others, and still others are of no consequence at all. We might say to him: 'But you just said there was no difference between them!' And he would reply: 'Yes, and I am saying the same thing now, but I was talking about there being no difference *with regard to virtues and vices.*

XXVI. 72. "I would certainly like to know who was not aware of that. But let us hear him continue: 'Those things you just listed,' he says, 'that is, health, having money, and freedom from pain, I don't call goods. I will make use of the Greek term *proegmena*, which in Latin means *brought out.*[375] I prefer to use the terms *preferred* or *special,*[376] as these words are more precise and comprehensible. I do not call disease, poverty, and pain evils; one may consider them things that we reject. Thus I do not say these things should be *desired*, but *chosen*; and not *wished for*, but rather *adopted*. And instead of *avoiding* the opposites of these things, we should instead *separate ourselves* from them.'

---

[374] I.e., the same as Aristo's position.

[375] *Producta.*

[376] *Praeposita* and *praecipua*, respectively.

"What do Aristotle and Plato's other students say about this? They consider everything that is in conformity with nature to be good, and everything that is against nature to be bad. Don't you see that your Zeno is consistent with Aristo when it comes to words, yet contradicts him in ideas? And with Aristotle and the rest, that Zeno actually agrees with them in substance, but contradicts them in words? So since we agree in ideas, why aren't we opting to use the customary terminology? How about this: let Zeno prove that I would be more willing to denounce money if I consider it something 'preferred' than if I consider it a good. Or let him prove that I am more courageous in enduring pain if I call it 'rough,' 'difficult to deal with,' or 'against nature,' than if I just call it an evil.

73. "Our good friend Marcus Piso cleverly mocked the Stoics and many others on this issue. 'What are you talking about?' he used to say. 'You deny that wealth is a good, saying instead that it is *preferred*. But what difference does that make? Does that reduce greed? If so, how? If we are examining words, then firstly the word 'preferred' is a longer word than 'good.' The Stoic response might be, 'That is not a problem.' And Piso would answer, 'Possibly, but it is definitely a more serious word. I don't know the etymology of the word 'good,' but I believe 'preferred' means something ranked ahead of something else. To me this indicates something that has superiority.'

Thus Piso is saying that Zeno placed more importance on riches (which he categorized as 'preferred') than Aristotle did, who conceded that wealth was a good. Yet to him it was not a *great good*; and when compared with moral goodness and rectitude, wealth should be looked down on, scorned, and viewed as not much worth chasing. As for all the words that Zeno replaced with his own idiosyncratic neologisms, Piso would say that he coined more favorable terms for the things he denied were good, and less favorable terms for the things he denied were evil, than the terms that we ourselves use. So this was how Piso made

Excavations at Tusculum

his case. He was a great man—and as you know, your very dear friend. Once I have added a few more points to these, let me wrap up my comments. For it would be an arduous task to respond to everything you have said.

XXVII. 74. "From this same deceptive word-play came your kingdoms, empires, and mountains of riches; and these are so immense that you think everything—no matter what it might be— is the wise man's possession. He alone is handsome; he alone is free; and he alone is a good citizen. All men who are the opposite of these things are fools. Besides this, you also paint them as insane. The Stoics call these *paradoxa*; we may call them surprising revelations.[377]

But once we examine them closely, what do we find that is so surprising? I will discuss with you the true meaning of all your terms—there will be no confusion about this. You Stoics say that all misdeeds are equal.[378] I won't get sarcastic now on this issue in the same way I did during the Lucius Murena case, when you were prosecuting and I was handling the defense.[379] My words at that time were addressed to the public, and meant to win the average man's favor.[380] But now I should employ more rigorous logic.

---

[377] See my *Stoic Paradoxes: A New Translation*, Charleston: Fortress of the Mind Publications, 2015. In this short work Cicero describes the six paradoxes.

[378] *Id.* at p. 55 (Paradox III).

[379] Lucius Licinius Murena was prosecuted in 63 B.C. for electoral bribery by Cato the Younger and Servius Sulpicius Rufus. Cicero defended Murena, and his speech to the jury (*Pro Murena*) is one of his most persuasive pieces of oratory. Like many Ciceronian speeches, it is laced with sarcasm and invective. He mocked Cato mercilessly for the classical Stoic position that there were no "degrees" of badness for bad deeds, thus painting him to the jury as a rigid, out-of-touch ideologue. The tactic worked, and the jury acquitted Murena.

[380] *Aliquid coronae datum*, or "somewhat given for the crowd." One of the meanings of *corona* is a circle of bystanders or a crowd.

75. "All wrongdoing is equally bad, the Stoics say. 'But how can this be so?' Because nothing can be more morally good than moral goodness, and nothing more corrupt than moral corruption. 'Go on a bit more, since there is major disagreement on this point. Let us hear your specific arguments as to why all misdeeds are equal.' Imagine, a Stoic would say, that out of a group of string instruments, none of them are strung in a way that they can play harmoniously. All of them are equally out of tune. It is the same way with misdeeds. Since they all deviate from what is right, they are equally deviant. Thus in this sense they are equal to each other. 'But here we are being tricked with an ambiguity. It happens that all the instruments equally[381] are out of tune; but we cannot conclude from this that they are out of tune to the same degree. Thus your analogy does not help you at all. Just because we say all examples of greed are equally greedy, we do not necessarily mean that all examples of greed *are co-equal with each other.*'

76. "Consider another one of these non-analogous analogies. A Stoic says that a ship's captain commits an equal wrong whether he sinks his vessel while carrying either gold or chaff. In the same way, a man is equally at fault whether he beats his parent or his slave unjustly. But imagine not being able to comprehend that the cargo a vessel carries has no connection to the captain's seamanship! Whether a ship carries gold or chaff is irrelevant in evaluating the skipper's competence or negligence; but the distinction between a parent and a slave is one that should and can be acknowledged. For the misdeed in seamanship there is no difference in the natures of the two examples; but for the misdeed in conduct, there is a big difference. Furthermore, if we consider the example of the ship captain, there is a big difference between losing a ship laden with gold and losing one with straw if the cause of the loss was the captain's ineptitude. We would like what is

---

[381] I.e., all the instruments together as a group are out of tune.

commonly called *prudence* to be an essential attribute of all the arts; and everyone who practices in such a field should understand its importance. Thus not all misdeeds are equal, as this example illustrates.

XXVIII. 77. "Yet the Stoics insist on forcing the issue, and refuse to back down at all. They say that since every misdeed is the consequence of weakness and irresolution, and these vices are of equal magnitude in every fool, it must be true that all misdeeds are equal. As if anyone would admit that the level of vice is the same for all idiots, and that Lucius Tubulus was just as foolish and irresolute as Publius Scaevola, who was convicted by his own motion![382] And as if there were no difference in the respective circumstances surrounding the commission of each wrongdoing, so that when the situation is more or less serious, the seriousness of the offense will be correspondingly greater or lesser!

78. "Finally—for now I have to wind up my comments—your Stoics are working under one major delusion, as I see it: they think they can preach two opposing positions at the same time. What could be so contradictory than for the same person to assert *both* that (1) moral goodness is the only good, and (2) a person has a natural appetite for seeking those things fundamental for living life. Because they desperately want to keep the ideas that follow from the former premise, they fall into the same trap as Aristo. When they try to climb out of this pitfall, they end up taking the side of the Peripatetics—while still fanatically clinging to their own special jargon. They refuse to remove this nomenclature from their teachings, preferring instead to take refuge in ever-increasing crudity, harshness, and inflexibility, both in speech and in habits.

79. "Panaetius recoiled from these depressing and severe aspects of the Stoic creed; he did not approve of its thorn-bushes

---

[382] See above, II.54.

of argumentation, nor of the caustic quality of its dogmas. He was more accommodating and intelligible, and the teachings of Plato, Aristotle, Xenocrates, Theophrastus, and Dicearchus[383] were an enduring aspect of his speech—as his writings themselves demonstrate. I especially think these writers deserve your earnest and active study.

80. "But because daylight is fading and I have to return home, I think we should break off at this point. I would very much like it if we could again return to these subjects."

"We absolutely should," he nodded. "For what could be better for us to do? And the first courtesy from you I'd request is that you hear my rebuttal of your discourse. But you should keep this in mind: except for the fact that you like to use different terminology, you basically approve of all our ideas. I, however, do not accept any of your doctrines."

"Well, that sounds like an ominous note[384] to end on," I smiled, "but we will have to see what the future brings." And having said those words, I left.

---

[383] Dicearchus (or Dicaearchus) of Messana (350? B.C.—285? B.C.), a Peripatetic philosopher born in Sicily who studied under Aristotle. He wrote on geographical, mathematical, and political subjects.

[384] *Scrupulum abeunti*. The word *scrupulus* is a source of unease or worry, or a looming problem.

COMMENTARY ON BOOK IV

Cicero's vigorous attack on Stoicism in Book IV demonstrates that his sympathy for the Stoic ethic has not blinded him to its faults. He begins by reviewing some of the views of Plato and Aristotle (IV.4—5), and takes note of the Stoics' lack of interest in politics (IV.7). As a man who had devoted his life to politics, Cicero must have been irritated by this apathy. In logic and physics the Stoic record was a mixed one (IV.9—12); they were content to adopt the views of those who preceded them. Cicero is unwilling to concede the Stoics much originality for their ethics, either: their admonition to "live in accordance" with nature was something that the old philosophers had already counseled (IV.14).

The ancient thinkers knew that self-preservation was our fundamental motive, and were fully aware of the importance of virtue (IV.17—18). Considering how much Zeno adopted from his predecessors, how much did he really innovate? According to Cicero, the Stoics did little but cloak old doctrines in new verbiage (IV.19). The alleged derivative quality of Stoic doctrine is something that Cicero harps on again and again in Book IV. This point has some merit. Yet we may reasonably respond by asking Cicero: *why is this a bad thing*? It is difficult to be original in philosophy without also being mistaken; and sometimes presenting old ideas in new ways is exactly what a new philosophical system calls for. In IV.21, we are reminded yet again of the frustrating Stoic position that there are no "degrees" of virtue.

Cicero chides Cato for the alleged Stoic neglect of bodily goods and external goods, which are certainly worth something (IV.29—32). The Stoic view is too one-dimensional; we must look at the entire organism as a whole, not just at its mind. The Stoic view also forgets the importance of nature's fundamental instincts (IV.40). We cannot, then, make moral goodness the End of Goods (IV.43). Stoic logic is flawed because it represents deductions from inadequate premises (IV.54); and the artificial terminology the Stoics used was little more than a smokescreen to conceal the fact they were not producing any new ideas (IV.60). Zeno should have at least acknowledged, as did the ancient philosophers, that goods of the body could be considered "goods" (IV.58).

Cicero mocks the analogies Cato uses to justify the severe Stoic view that there were no "degrees" of wisdom. If young puppies are as blind as those just born, and if a man drowning far below the water's surface is just as wretched as a man drowning near the surface, then we could just as easily say Plato was as deficient in wisdom as the tyrant Phalaris (IV.64). From a common sense perspective, it is ridiculous to say that there are no degrees of vice or virtue. Nothing could be clearer than that some things *really are* more evil than others; to say otherwise is disingenuous (IV.66, IV.77). The Stoics are guilty of vanity and arrogance in elevating moral goodness as the Supreme Good. Taking this position sounds wonderful, but it causes us to neglect our health, our careers, and our personal affairs (IV.68). Wisdom must be based on something more than just moral rectitude.

Cicero's attacks are razor-sharp. As much as he admired certain aspects of the Stoic creed, he could overlook its imperfections. We cannot say with certainty that Cicero personally believed all the criticisms he levels at Stoicism in Book IV; the statements he writes as coming from his mouth could have been intended as pedagogical devices to provoke readers to analytic thought. Nevertheless, the pungent nature of the critique leaves the clear impression that Cicero regarded the Stoic system as imperfect, despite its many commendable features.

BOOK V

BOOK V

I. 1. You know, Brutus, I was once listening to the philosopher Antiochus speak—as I often did—with Marcus Piso in that institute called the Ptolemaeum.[385] My brother Quintus[386] was

---

[385] Apparently a building or institute named after one of the Greek-speaking Ptolemaic rulers of Egypt.
[386] Quintus Tullius Cicero (102 B.C.—43 B.C.) was Cicero's younger brother and was killed along with him in Mark Antony's proscriptions.

with us, along with Titus Pomponius[387] and Lucius Cicero[388] (whom I loved as a brother, even though he was actually my cousin). We decided to take an afternoon walk in the Academy, mainly because the area would be free of commotions and groups at that time of day. So at the arranged time we all met at Piso's place. Absorbed in conversation on different topics, we made our way about six *stadia* from the Dipylon Gate.[389] When we reached the Academy (which for good reason is considered hallowed ground), we found it as deserted as we had hoped it would be.

2. Piso then broke the silence. "I don't know if it's something that comes from the natural spirit of a place, or if it's just our own perception, but when we actually see a site that history notes as a place where great men of the past went about their work, we are more emotionally moved than if we only hear about their accomplishments or read the things they wrote. I'm definitely moved right now. The image of Plato is filling my mind, the man they say was the first to conduct philosophical discussions here. The gardens close by here not only evoke his memory, but seem also to raise his image before my eyes.

"Speusippus once walked this ground, as did Xenocrates and his student Polemo,[390] whose exact seat was the one we see right here. Even in our own Roman Curia back home (I am talking about the Curia Hostilia,[391] not the new senate-house, which looks

---

[387] Titus Pomponius Atticus (c. 110 B.C.—32 B.C.) is best known as a close friend of Cicero and a frequent recipient of his letters.

[388] Lucius Tullius Cicero was the son of Cicero's uncle Lucius, and was raised with Cicero and his brother Quintus.

[389] The *stadium* was an ancient Greek unit of measurement, probably around 157 m. in length. The Dipylon Gate was the main gate in Athens's city wall, and one of the largest such gates in antiquity.

[390] These philosophers succeeded Plato has heads of the Academy.

[391] The Curia Hostilia was one of the original senate-houses of the republic. It was enlarged by Sulla in 80 B.C., but then burned down in 53 B.C. In its

283

smaller to me now than it was before they expanded it), I used to find myself contemplating the lives of Scipio, Cato, Laelius, and most of all my grandfather.[392] Such are the powers of conjuration retained by these old places."

3. "What you are saying is true, Piso," said Quintus. "While on the way over here, I myself was able to make out that place called Colonus, whose famous resident Sophocles appeared in my mind's eye. You know how much I admire and cherish his legacy. I was struck by an even more profound vision of Oedipus; he was walking right here, and asked us in his so-smooth verses, 'What are these places?'[393] Even if it was just a daydream, the image still made a strong impression on me."

Pomponius then added, "I myself—a man you like to scold as an admirer of Epicurus—spent a good deal of time with Phaedrus[394] (someone very dear to me, as you know) in Epicurus's Gardens. We walked past the site just now. But as the old saying reminds us: *Heed the living.*[395] Yet even if I wanted to, I couldn't forget Epicurus. My fellow Epicureans reproduce his image not only on portrait keepsakes, but also on cups and rings!"

II. 4. "I have a feeling our friend Pomponius is joking with us," I ventured. "And maybe this should be expected. He's adjusted himself so well here in Athens that by now he's practically a native of Attica. It would not surprise me at all if he adopted the cognomen Atticus.[396] But I think you are right, Piso.

---

place was built the Curia Cornelia, and this building in turn was replaced by Julius Caesar's Curia Julia.

[392] The Laelius mentioned here is Caius Laelius (*see above*, II.24). Piso's grandfather is the Lucius Calpurnius Piso noted in II.90.

[393] The opening lines of Sophocles's play *Oedipus at Colonus*.

[394] The same Phaedrus mentioned in I.16.

[395] *Vivorum memini.*

[396] A good-natured joke with Cicero's friend Atticus, who did in fact take on

The intangible spirit that resides in the former haunts of great men evokes their memories with more clarity and resonance. You remember how I once went with you to Metapontum,[397] and refused to go to our lodgings until I had made a detour to see the seat that Pythagoras had actually sat on, and where he had finally left this mortal life. Although there is evidence everywhere in Athens of the past's great men (in the places where they actually lived), right now that conversation-hall[398] over there is what moves me. It was once used by Carneades. I think I can see him now—for everyone knows what he looks like. And I'm guessing that his old seat longs for the sound of his voice, and grieves at the loss of a man of such character."

5. "Well, we all have something, then," Piso added. "What does our friend Lucius have? Does he excitedly frequent the place where Demosthenes and Aeschines used to grapple oratorically with each other?[399] For one is primarily inspired by his own field of study."

His face suddenly flushing with red, Lucius stammered, "Don't ask *me*! I was the one who went down to see the Bay of Phalerum, where they say Demosthenes used to practice orating alone on the beach. By speaking while surrounded by noise, he learned to master his delivery. I also just turned off the road here a little bit on the left to visit Pericles's tomb. It just goes on like this forever in this city: in no matter what direction we go, our steps fall on some distinguished history."

6. Piso then rejoined, "And yet, Cicero, these fields of study are naturally suited to men of ability *if* they encourage us to

---

this surname.

[397] Located in very south of Italy in the province of Matera, very near the modern town of Metaponto. There are varying accounts given of the circumstances of Pythagoras's death. *See* Diog. Laert. VIII.38—39.

[398] *Exedra.*

[399] Two of the most famous Greek orators of the fourth century B.C.

imitate history's great exemplars; but if they serve only to recall the dead memories of the past, they have little more than curiosity value. All of us ask you—as I hope you are already making progress in doing—to prefer to *imitate* these great men, in addition to just learning about them."

"He is already implementing this rule, Piso, as you know," I offered. "But I still appreciate the positive guidance."

As was usually the case, Piso's response was disarmingly friendly. "Well, then, let's all come together to help this young man on his way. Let's encourage him to devote some effort in studying philosophy, either so that he can better imitate the heroes he loves, or so that can better enrich what he is currently studying. But Lucius, is our encouragement useful, or do you already have a natural attraction to philosophy? I get the impression that you are devoting a lot of effort to Antiochus's lectures."

A bit demurely—or perhaps modestly—Lucius answered, "Yes, I am, actually. But have you heard Carneades speak recently? I am somehow drawn to him, but Antiochus still pulls me back. And there is no other lecturer to listen to."

III. 7. "Maybe it will not be so easy to go," said Piso, "while our comrade here (he was referring to me) is around. But I will take a chance and encourage you to leave the New Academy and go to the Old. As you heard Antiochus say, the Old Academy includes not only the philosophers called Academics—Speusippus, Xenocrates, Polemo, Crantor,[400] and the others—but also the original Peripatetics, the most important of whom is Aristotle.[401] With

---

[400] Crantor (?—c. 275 B.C.) of Soli, a moral philosopher of the Old Academy.
[401] Cicero divided the Platonic Academy into two periods, Old and New. In the Old Academy he placed the major names in the following order: Democritus, Anaxagoras, Empedocles, Parmenides, Xenophanes, Socrates, Plato, Speusippus, Xenocrates, Polemo, Crates, and Crantor. In the New Academy he places these names: Arcesilaus, Lacydes, Evander, Hegesinus,

the exception of Plato, I should probably call him the prince of philosophers. I sincerely ask you to go and listen to them. A complete program of liberal[402] education, history, and proper speech can be gleaned from their writings. They also deal with such a variety of natural sciences that no one lacking their tools can aspire to achieve anything of importance. From their ranks have come orators, military commanders, and the republic's best political leaders. When we consider the less prominent lines of work, we see that mathematicians, poets, musicians, and doctors have also been produced by this workshop of all trained experts.

8. It was then my turn to speak. "You know I feel the same way, Piso, but your bringing it up right now is convenient. My Cicero here is anxious to hear both the opinion of the Old Academy that you're talking about, and the views of the Peripatetics, regarding the Ends of Goods. In fact we think you can competently explain these things because you've had Staseas of Naples[403] living with you for many years. We also know you have been probing into this subject under Antiochus for many months now in Athens."

"Well, you asked for it!" Piso said blandly with a grin. "You obviously knew that you wanted me to go first in our debate. Let's put something out there, if we can, for this young man. Our lucky solitude here gives us this chance. If a god himself had told me that I would one day be debating philosophy in the Platonic Academy, I never would have believed it. But I'm a bit concerned that my talking about this might tire out the rest of you."

"You mean me?" I chuckled. "I was the one who asked you to speak!"

Carneades, Clitomachus, and Philo. See *Academica* I.46 and II.16.

[402] In Cicero's day the word "liberal" (*liberalis*), when referring to studies, meant an education befitting a free man or gentleman. *See* Oxford Latin Dict.

[403] Almost nothing is known about this philosopher. According to the Oxford Classical Dictionary, he was the first declared Peripatetic to have settled in Rome, and Piso was one of his students.

Once Quintus and Pomponius said they wanted Piso to give his little summary, he then began. I would ask you, Brutus, to pay close attention to his presentation. Ask yourself whether the Antiochus's ideas have been accurately condensed, since you have often heard the lectures of his brother Aristus. For Antiochus's ideas are the ones I recommend the most.

IV. 9. "You have heard enough from me about the particular details of Peripatetic doctrine. I offered what I could a little while ago in the most concise way possible. This system of thought, like others of its kind, has three parts: one part is concerned with nature, another with speech, and the third with the art of living. The Peripatetics have investigated nature so exhaustively that no sliver of sky, sea, or land—if I may wax poetically—has been overlooked. With regard to the creation of the world and the nature of its component parts, they have accomplished much not only by arguments grounded in probability, but also by the irrefutable conclusions of mathematics. They have used factual data derived from their investigations to enhance our understanding of things that are still shrouded in conjecture.

10. "Aristotle described the origin, sustenance, and forms of all animal life. Theophrastus surveyed the science of botany, and described the fundamental causes and principles underlying the generation of plant life. The exploration of other hidden secrets was made easier by the knowledge gained from their researches. In the field of argumentation, the Peripatetics compiled the basic tenets not only of dialectic, but also of oratory; and the training technique of debating both sides of every question was established by their founder Aristotle. This was nothing like Arcesilaus's method, which was always to try to refute everything; instead, Aristotle would methodically divulge all the points that could be raised on either side of the issue being considered.

The area of the gymnasium at the Platonic Academy

The cistern at the Platonic Academy's gymnasium

11. "The third division of philosophy seeks to formulate the principles of good living. Aristotle's followers sought such rules not only for private life; they were also interested in describing correct behavior for public officials. We have learned from Aristotle the customs, traditions, and teachings—and from Theophrastus the laws—not only of the Greeks, but of nearly all civilized nations. Each of them provided guidance on the leadership traits of a good ruler, and each wrote extensively on what he believed was the best constitution. On this topic Theophrastus wrote more copiously; he examined how and when the evolution of political systems happened, and how these evolutionary forces could be regulated under certain conditions. The mode of living they most endorsed was the tranquil life of contemplation and productive research. Since this ideal was thought to correspond most closely to the life of the gods, it was considered the most suitable life for the wise man. Their eloquence in treating these subjects is both glittering and lucid.

V. 12. "Of their books that deal with the question of the Ultimate Good, there are two general categories. One is written in a more popular style, and is called 'exoteric'; the other is more technical, and is mostly preserved in specialized commentaries. On the surface, these two classes do not always seem to say the same thing on the same subject. Yet in fact there are no contradictions in the essentials of the writings of the philosophers I named above—and neither did they disagree with each other. But the happy life is the main question—that is, it is the one question that philosophy ought to pursue and study. And on this issue there does seem to be some difference of opinion and doubt among them: *does the attainment of the happy life lie within the wise man's complete contol, or can it be undermined or taken away by adverse events?* This difference of opinion can most clearly be seen in Theophrastus's book *On the Happy Life*, in which great significance is placed on the role of Fortune in human affairs.

"Now if Theophrastus's opinion is true, then wisdom alone is no assurance of a happy life. If I may speak frankly, this theory to me is too enfeebling and mushy-headed to be worthy of virtue's intrinsic power and importance. For this reason we must look to Aristotle and his son Nicomachus, whose detailed books on ethics[404] are said to have been written by Aristotle himself; yet I see no reason why the son could not have followed in his father's literary footsteps. We may still consult Theophrastus on many issues, as long as we acknowledge that there is more strength and inherent soundness in virtue than he was aware.

13. "But let us be content with the resources we have. In my view, the successors of these philosophers are better than the thinkers of the other schools, but they fall so short of the standard set by their predecessors that they almost seem to have been produced spontaneously.[405] For example, Strato, one of Theophrastus's students, wanted to devote himself to the natural sciences. Although he distinguishes himself admirably in this occupation, he is still basically going his own way; and he pays almost no attention to ethics. After him comes Lyco, who is abundant in speech but sterile in content. Lyco's successor Aristo has an elegant and sumptuous literary presence, but he does not have the kind of gravitas needed in a great philosopher. While his output is prodigious and smooth, there is a certain lack of authority in his prose that is hard to describe.

14. "I am neglecting to mention many philosophers, including Hieronymus, who is both scholarly and pleasant to read. But I do not know why he is considered a Peripatetic. For him the greatest good was freedom from pain; and he who expounds a view of the

---

[404] Referring to Aristotle's *Nicomachean Ethics*. Its authorship is attributed to Aristotle, not his son.

[405] *Sed ita degenerant ut ipsi ex se nati esse videantur*, with the sense that they seem almost to have learned nothing from their predecessors.

Ultimate Good that differs from another's view of it is contradicting that person's philosophical system. Critolaus wanted to emulate the classical philosophers; his gravitas is comparable to theirs, and his literary style is finely-tuned. And yet even he diverges from the principles laid down by his forefathers. His student Diodorus adds on 'absence of pain' to moral goodness. He is another one of these thinkers who is in his own category; and because he dissents from the Peripatetic conception of the Ultimate Good, he cannot be considered one of them. I believe that our guide Antiochus followed the doctrines of the ancient philosophers most faithfully, and he taught that these doctrines were the same as those espoused by Aristotle and Polemo.

VI. 15. "So our fellow-traveler Lucius is being very smart by wanting to learn as much as possible about the Ultimate Good. For when something has been arranged properly in philosophy, it has been resolved universally.[406] In other areas of philosophy, overlooking or ignoring some point causes only as much damage as the relative significance of the neglected point allows. But if our knowledge of the Ultimate Good is riddled with confusion, we are necessarily groping in the dark for the very rules of life; and the resulting ignorance is of such consequence that a philosophical traveler will have no way of knowing at which port he should dock his ship. Once we have understood the nature of Moral Ends—and we have grasped the significance of the Ends of Goods and Evils—a roadmap for life and the proper configuration of all the duties are revealed to us, something that serves as the standard to which all else is referred.

16. "From this, one can discover and compose a rule for the happy life that everyone seeks. But because there is a great divergence of opinion as to what the Ultimate Good really is, we must follow the categorization system of Carneades, a system that

---

[406] *Hoc enim constituto in philosophia, constituta sunt omnia.*

our guide Antiochus preferred. Carneades treated not only the views of all the philosophers regarding the Ultimate Good, but he also considered all possible views that could be held in general. He refuted the idea that any art could originate from itself; it is instead always conceived by some knowledge outside of itself. There is no need to provide tedious examples of this, for a cursory inspection shows that no art is entirely self-contained. The purpose of the art is something separate from the art itself. Therefore, just as medicine is the art of health and ship pilotage is the art of sailing, *so must it be that prudence—which is the art of living—was constructed from, and birthed by, something outside of itself.*

17. "It is generally accepted that prudence's subject matter and desired objective is something that should be suitable and fitted to human nature; it should entice and arouse the soul's deepest craving, or what the Greeks call *horme*. But there is no accepted answer to the question of *what causes* this instinct of desire in our nature from the moment of our inception. It is from this point that all the arguing begins among the philosophers who study the question of the Ultimate Good. When we consider the entire question of the Ends of Goods and Evils—and specifically which of them is ultimate and final—we must remember that the roots of the issue lie in nature's first inducements.[407] Once these are identified, the original source, or the wellspring, of the dispute over the nature of the Ultimate Good and Ultimate Evil will then be revealed.

VII. 18. "One group believes that our original, primary desire is for pleasure and our original antipathy is to pain. Another group, however, holds that the absence of pain is the first impulse embraced, and pain the first impulse shunned. Still others begin their analyses with what they call the 'first things in accordance

---

[407] *Prima invitamenta naturae.*

with nature'; within this term they include the safety and preservation of every part of the body, sound health, the integrity of the senses, the absence of pain, physical strength, beauty, and other similar things. Among such similar things are the first instincts of the human mind, which function somewhat as the sparks or seeds of the virtues.

"Our nature is moved to feel desire or revulsion by the operation of one of these three categories. The explanation cannot be found outside these three possibilities. It must be true that every duty to avoid something or to seek something relates back to one of these three categories. Prudence—which we have identified as the art of life—is shaped, molded, and arises from one of these three: *and from there begins the launching point for all of life.*

19. "Prudence will thus resolve how human nature is first aroused. A theory of moral rectitude and goodness would then begin to take shape, a theory that would be consistent with one or another of the three categories mentioned above. Thus moral goodness may be defined as doing everything for the sake of pleasure, even if this goal is never reached; or it may lie in not feeling any pain, even if one cannot attain this state; or it may lie in seeking those things that are in accordance with nature, even if the search proves to be fruitless. So there is a dispute about nature's first principles that perceptively corresponds to the different views on the Ends of Goods and Evils. Other philosophers, making use of the same first principles, will judge the rightness of every deed by asking whether it brings pleasure, freedom from pain, or the obtainment of those primary things that are in accordance with nature.

20. "Having now presented the six views of the Supreme Good, we can state that these philosophers are the major advocates for the last three views just listed: Aristippus (of pleasure); Hieronymus (of freedom from pain); Carneades (of the enjoyment of those things we have identified as the primary things in conformity with nature). We should note that Carneades was

Ruins of the gymnasium at the Academy

not the architect of this viewpoint, but he certainly defended it for the sake of argument.

The three former viewpoints were possible views of the Supreme Good, but only one of them has been advocated—and most strenuously at that. No one ever said we should do everything for the sake of pleasure; and no one ever said that we should persist in this same course of action for its own sake even if we fail to get pleasure, and believe this path to be the only good and righteous one. Nor does anyone think that avoiding pain is in itself something desirable, in the situation where one cannot actually avoid it. In contrast, however, the Stoics teach that what is morally good is *doing everything possible to attain the things that are in accordance with nature, and that even if this quest is unsuccessful, it remains the only objective worth pursuing and the only true good.*

VIII. 21. "So these are the six basic positions on the Ultimate Goods and Evils. Two of them have no proponent, but four have actually been advocated. There are three views of the Ultimate Good that are twofold or synthesized; and if you examine the matter closely, you will see that there cannot be more than this. We have the joining of pleasure to moral goodness, as advocated by Callipho and Dinomachus; or the joining of 'freedom from pain' to moral goodness, as proposed by Diodorus; or the joining of the 'first principles of nature' to moral goodness, as proposed by the ancient philosophers (as we call both the Academics and the Peripatetics). Not all of these positions can be described at one time. For now it is enough for us to note that *pleasure must be set aside*, since we have come into this world for greater things, as will become apparent shortly. The same criticisms made about pleasure could just as easily be made about 'freedom from pain.'

22. "Nor do we have to look for other flaws in Carneades's opinions to use against him. Any conception of the Ultimate Good that lacks the element of moral goodness simply cannot be consistent with right duties, the virtues, or friendship. Linking

moral goodness to pleasure or to freedom from pain brings about the precise moral corruption that such linkage is intended to prevent. To try to use two parallel standards of conduct—one of which says that the absence of evil is the Ultimate Good, while the other remains focused on the shallowest part of human nature—is to tarnish, or perhaps even desecrate, all the splendor of moral rectitude.

"We are left with the Stoics, who imported all their ideas from the Peripatetics and Academics, pursuing the same objectives while using their own special terminology. It would be a better plan to discuss each of these views separately, but for now we must stay focused on what we are doing. We may deal with them later as we wish.

23. "The mental security of Democritus, which is the tranquility of soul he called *euthumia*, has had to be omitted from our debate. The reason is that this tranquility of soul is the same happy life we are talking about: *and we are not trying to discover what the happy life is, but where it comes from.* The discredited and abandoned opinions of Pyrrho, Aristo and Erillus cannot be included in the circle we have drawn, and so they have not been reviewed at all. This entire investigation into the Ends (or rather the 'ending points') of Goods and Evils begins from a point we said was (1) both suitable and fitted to nature, and (2) was also the first thing desired for its own sake. This entire interpretation is destroyed by those who oppose the idea that, among those things that contain no trace of moral goodness or moral corruption, any one thing should be valued over another: they do not see any difference between such things. And if Erillus really believed that nothing was good except 'knowledge,' then he has dismantled the basis for sound decision-making and the realization of our proper responsibilities.

"We have thus disposed of the views of the rest of the philosophers. As no other opinions are possible, the view of the ancient philosophers must alone be valid. We will now take up the tradition of the ancients, a tradition that the Stoics also drew from.

IX. 24. "Every animal cherishes itself and, from the moment of its inception, acts to protect its own life. The first instinct given it by nature for its sustained preservation is the drive for self-preservation, and the impulse to support itself as best it can according to its own nature. At first this all-embracing rule is hazy and uncongealed, so that it just tries to stay alive no matter what its nature may be: it does not really understand itself, what it can do, or what its true nature may be. As the years gradually go by, and it realizes the extent to which various things affect it, it begins to gain a deeper appreciation of these matters. It begins to learn more about itself, and comprehends the reason why it has the basic impulse we mentioned just now; it starts to seek the things it feels are suitable to its nature, and to reject the things that are contrary to this. Therefore, the object of each organism's appetite is to be found in what most matches its nature. The End of Goods originates from this principle: *to live in accordance with nature, and to live in the circumstances most suitable to nature that one possibly can.*

25. "Because every organism has its own nature, it necessarily follows that the End for each organism is that which completes its nature.[408] Nothing prevents certain things from being held in common by the beasts, and by the beasts and humans, since they are all possessed of a common nature. But these final and ultimate goods we are seeking must be separated and apportioned among the different species of organisms; each kind of animal must have its own individual and specialized goods that match what its inner nature desires.

26. "Thus when we say that the End of all animals is to live in accordance with nature, it must be understood that we are in no way saying that there is one identical End for all animals. But just as it can be correctly said that all the arts have in common the fact that they deal with some field of learning—with each art having its own area of knowledge—so is living in accordance with nature

---

[408] I.e., that which satisfies its nature.

Ruins located in other areas of the Platonic Academy grounds

a common shared goal for all organisms. Yet their individual natures are disparate: so a horse has one nature, a bull another, and a man yet another. The Ultimate End, however, is held in common by all of them; and this is true not only for animals, but also for every living thing that nature sustains, fosters, and protects. By way of illustration, we see that plants can themselves perform many tasks required for their own sustenance and propagation; and by such techniques do they reach their End.

"Thus one may say, with an all-embracing comprehension that unquestionably applies to every living thing, that all nature is a Protectress of itself;[409] and its purpose—that is, its end and objective—is to preserve itself in the best condition possible in the customary habit of each species. It follows that all things animated with life by nature have a similar End, but not the same one. From this it ought to be understood that for man the Ultimate Good is to live in accordance with nature; and we may interpret this to mean *living in conformity to our human nature, a nature that is entirely perfected and in need of nothing.*

27. "These are the kinds of things that we need to explain. So you will forgive me if I need to elaborate on what has already been said. Since it is possibly the first time Lucius has heard these ideas, we should press on for the young man's benefit."

"I very much agree," I interjected. "Although the things you have said so far have been suitable for a listener of any age."

X. "Now that we have marked off the boundaries and scope of desired things," he said, "we must next explain why this issue is as I have described. Let us begin from the place I first proposed—the place that is first in reality—and recognize that *every organism cherishes itself.* This statement is beyond dispute; it is a reality embedded in nature, and can be readily comprehended by each person's senses. Anyone trying to say otherwise would be

---

[409] *Omnem naturam esse servatricem sui.*

ignored. Nevertheless, in order not to omit anything, I think reasons should be presented that show why this axiom is true.

28. "But honestly, who can imagine or picture an animal that hates itself? The images run contrary to each other. Its soul's desire would begin deliberately to draw something to itself that hurts it, due to the fact that it is its own enemy. Since it is doing this for its own sake, it would then hate and cherish itself at the same time—which obviously cannot happen. And it must also be true that if a man is his own enemy, he will think that good is bad and bad is good; he will avoid what should be sought, and seek out what should be shunned. Without doubt this is the inversion of life itself. We find some who want to bring about their own deaths with a noose or some other manner. And indeed one of Terence's dramatic characters announced (as the playwright tells us) he had 'decided that the more he made himself miserable, the more he would diminish the injury he caused to his son.'[410] But neither of these examples should be cited as people who are enemies of themselves.

29. "Some are moved by sorrow, and others by greed; many are animated by blind rage, and slide knowingly into a life of evil while under the impression that their choice was the very best one. So they speak like this, without any shred of self-doubt:

I've found my own way; whatever you need to do, do it.[411]

Men who have truly declared war against themselves would want to be crucified by day and tortured by night. They would not blame themselves and say that they had poorly thought through their own affairs; for regrets like these are expressed by those who value and care about themselves. Hence whenever it is said that a

---

[410] Terence, *The Self-Tormentor* 147.
[411] *Id.* at 80.

man abuses himself, acts as his own enemy and foe, or seeks an escape from life itself, we must remember that there is some underlying reason—even in this type of situation—confirming the truth that every man cherishes himself.

30. "It is inadequate to argue that there is no man who hates himself; it must also be understood that there is no man whose personal situation holds no interest for him. If we believe the very things that affect us really make no difference at all, then the soul's desire would be negated. There are some things that do not concern us, and our disposition towards them is neutral.

XI. "It would be ridiculous if anyone tried to say that, even if a person loves himself, that love really is focused on some external thing and not on the person doing the self-loving. When this is said about friendship, duties, or the virtues—whether rightly said or not—the statement still makes rational sense; but when it comes to ourselves it makes no sense to argue that we love ourselves for the sake of some external object (e.g., pleasure). It is for our own sake, and not for pleasure's sake, that we love ourselves.

31. "Indeed what is more obvious than that every man not only cherishes himself, but passionately cherishes himself? For when the hour of death draws near, what person—or persons—will there be whose

Blood does not surrender to apprehension, and face goes white with terror.[412]

---

[412] A line from Ennius's play *Alcmaeon* (also quoted in IV.62).

Certainly it is a vice to tremble so fearfully at the prospect of the end of our physical form—and the same cravenness is just as reprehensible when one is facing bodily pain. But because nearly everyone is influenced by these sentiments, our point is adequately made that human nature is averse to physical extinction. The more people so shamefully allow themselves to behave this way (as indeed they do), the more we should appreciate the fact that these kinds of excessive displays of apprehension would never happen if the human fear of annihilation were not a natural mental impulse. I am not talking about those people who fear death because they think death will deprive them of life's good things, or those who think they will face certain terrors after death, or those who worry that their dying will be accompanied by physical agonies. Very often young children—who never obsess about these things at all—become terrified if we jokingly threaten to drop them from some high place. As Pacuvius tells us, even

> Wild beasts devoid of the ability to sense peril become terrified
> When the fear of death enfolds them in its iron grip.[413]

32. "Who really thinks that the wise man, when he has decided that his life must end, will not be emotionally moved by saying goodbye to his family, and by leaving behind the flame of life? The power of our nature is quite clearly apparent in this predictable result, since many men will tolerate destitute beggary in order to continue living; some men advanced in age are distressed by the realization of their impending death, and suffer what we witness Philoctetes suffering in Accius's play. Despite being tormented by physical agonies that could not be alleviated, he prolonged his life by taking up the sport of bird-catching:

---

[413] A line from an unknown play by Pacuvius.

He was slow, but brought down the speedy with arrows;
And standing, he brought down the swift in flight.[414]

Accius also tells us that by weaving together feathers, Philoctetes constructed a functional article of clothing.

33. "But why should I talk about humans and animals, when the nature of trees and other plant life is practically the same? Whether some higher or more divine authority has instilled this power in them from birth (as the most well-informed experts believe), or whether it has simply come about by accident, we can see that plants are maintained in health by their bark and roots; and these are analogous to the distribution of the senses and the structure of the limbs in animals. Indeed on this point I agree with those who believe that all these things are controlled by nature; for if nature were to ignore them, nature herself would not be possible. Nevertheless I am willing to concede that those who dissent on this issue may think as they wish. Let them understand that when I speak of the 'nature of man,' I also mean 'man': there is no distinction between the two terms.

"A person cannot lose his instinct to acquire the things that are beneficial to him any more than he can discard his own essence. Thus the greatest philosophers have rightly sought the Ultimate Good in nature, and have correctly believed that our desire for things suitable to our nature is an instinct fundamental to all of us—a result of that natural, preservative affection with which humans love themselves.

XII. 34. "Since we have sufficiently explained that self-love arises from nature, we should next discuss the nature of man. This is the information we are trying to discover. Now it is clear that man is composed of body and mind; the mind's role is primary,

---

[414] A line from Accius's play *Philoctetes*. See also the reference in II.94, above.

and that of the body is secondary. We may also see that the fabric of the human body is superior to that of other organisms. Man's mind is configured with senses, and supports a powerful mental capacity that compels his nature to submit to it; this capacity includes the wondrous powers of reason, of productive thought, of knowledge, and of all the virtues. The body's parts are not equal in importance to the components of the mind, and are less difficult to understand. Let start, then, from here.

35. "In form, appearance, and disposition, the various parts of our body are clearly well-suited to our nature. Neither is there any doubt that the utility to man of the face, eyes, ears, and other bodily parts can be readily comprehended. But it is certainly a requirement that these bodily parts be healthy, well-conditioned, and capable of their natural movements and functions, to the extent that no vital component should be missing, unsound or incapacitated. Nature indeed wishes it to be so. There is, moreover, an expected kind of activity which holds the motions and physical positions of the body in congruence with nature. If a man were to violate these requirements through some distortion, deviation, or deformity of movement or physical bearing—for example, if he were to walk on his hands, or walk backwards instead of forwards—then he would look as if he were running away from himself, discarding his humanity, and despising his own nature. For this reason certain ways of sitting, various hunched-over postures, and physically weak movements (of the type habitually done by the impudent or the unmanly) are contrary to nature; and although such behavior arises from a mental deficiency, it nevertheless appears as if man's nature is being bodily degraded.

36. "Conversely, a posture that communicates sobriety, steadiness, a sound mental disposition, and a purposeful use of the body is considered to be in conformity with nature. As for the mind, it should not just passively exist, but should have a specific quality; every part of the mind should be unimpaired, and none of

the virtues should be missing. Each of the senses has its own virtue, whose purpose is to ensure that nothing hinders the senses in the discharge of their duties in quickly and efficiently perceiving what is within the range of their capabilities.

XIII. "But the mind, and that foremost part of the mind we call intellect, have many virtues. Of these we find two general categories. One is composed of those virtues embedded by their own nature, and are called involuntary. The other category is grounded in voluntariness, and is a more suitable bearer of the term 'virtue'; for its excellence in advancing the mind's glory is unmatched. Learning ability and memory are found in the former category. Almost all the virtues of this category are given the name 'aptitudes,'[415] and those who have these virtues are called 'apt.' The other category consists of those great and pure virtues we consider voluntary, such as prudence, temperance, courage, justice, and others of the same type.

37. "These are some of the things that briefly needed to be said about the body and the mind: they allow us to form an idea about what man's nature requires. From all this it can be seen that, because we love ourselves and want everything in our minds and bodies to be perfect, these attributes are precious to us for their own sakes, and are of the utmost significance in leading a happy life. If a man's objective is to preserve himself, he will certainly hold his constituent parts to be most dear. The more perfect they are, and the more praiseworthy they become in their own category, the more dear they will be held. We seek a life that should be permeated with the virtues of body and mind: *and this life must constitute the Supreme Good, since it exists as the Ultimate End of all desirable things.* Once this is clearly understood, we cannot doubt that, since men cherish themselves

---

[415] The word used is *ingenium*, meaning an innate quality or natural disposition.

Ruins in various parts of the Platonic Academy grounds

for their own sakes and of their own free will, the parts of the body and mind and the respective capabilities of each that are in motion or at rest are cultivated for their own special value, and desired for their own sakes.

38. "We may conclude from these observations that the capabilities most desired by us are those that display the greatest excellence; *so that the virtue we should most seek, the virtue that is desirable for its own sake, is the virtue derived from the best part of our being.* It is thus inevitable that the mind's virtue will come before the body's virtue, and the mind's voluntary virtues will be superior to the involuntary ones. The voluntary virtues are indeed preeminent and truly deserving of the name, because they arise from reason, the quality in man that is the most divinely inspired. The Supreme Good for all insentient or nearly insentient organisms created and guided by nature resides in their physical bodies. Along these lines, I believe it has been accurately said about the pig that its mind was given to it by nature to act as salt, so that its body would not spoil.

XIV. "However, there are some beasts in which we find something similar to virtue, such as lions, dogs, and horses. We detect in them not only movements of the body, as in pigs, but also some measure of cognition. But in man the greatest significance lies in the mind and in the mind's powers of reason: this is the seat of his virtue. Virtue is defined as the *consummation of reason*, a point they believe should be stated again and again.

39. "The raising and rearing of plant life is not much different from that of the animals. Thus we say that a vine 'lives' and 'dies,' that a tree is 'young' or 'old,' or that it is thriving or growing old. So it would not be wrong to think that certain things are in accordance with, or foreign to, their nature. There is a faithful attendant who takes care of raising and protecting them, and this is the science and art of agriculture. She clips, prunes, raises, lifts, and supports vines until they can reach the destination that nature intends. The vines themselves, if they possessed the power of

speech, would admit that this is how they should be managed and watched over. What actually protects the vine, if I may use this particular example, is something external to it. If no agricultural aid is brought in to help it, the vine by itself does not have the requisite power to reach its full natural potential.

40. "But if the vine were to acquire physical sensation, so that it might have articulable desires and the ability to move itself, what do you think it would do? Would it not strive on its own to acquire the same benefits it previously received from its attentive horticulturist? Do you see that its developing priority would be to safeguard its physical senses and all their appetites, and any organs connected to them? Thus the vine adds these later-acquired characteristics to those that it always possessed. It will not have the same End that its cultivator had; it will prefer to live in accordance with the nature it obtained later. Its End will be similar to the one it possessed before, yet not the same; it would not seek the Good of a plant, but that of an animal.

"What if our plant were given not just physical sensation, but also a human intellect? Isn't it inevitable that, while the plant would still take care of its original characteristics, its added qualities would be valued even more, with the best part of the mind considered the most precious of all? Does its Ultimate Good consist in this final perfection of its nature, since mind and reason are superior by far to all other attributes? Thus we find the outer limit of all appetition. Starting from nature's first sentiments, we progress many steps to arrive at our final destination, *a condition that is the fusion of bodily integrity and the perfection of our mental power of reason.*

XV. 41. "I have laid out the general scheme of our nature. As I said at the beginning, if someone from the moment of birth could know himself and comprehend the power of his entire nature and its individual parts, he would immediately see what we are searching for: the Highest and Ultimate objective of all the things we desire. And he would not be able to make any kind of mistake.

*Views of the remains of Aristotle's Lyceum (Lykeion) in Athens,
the home of the Peripatetics*

Yet from the beginning, our nature is remarkably hidden, and we are unable to observe or comprehend it; with the progression of years, however, we are gradually—or lately—able to understand who we are. Thus the first sense of endearment that nature has implanted in us towards ourselves is uncertain and enigmatic; the first desire that occupies our minds is directed towards our safety and self-preservation. When we begin to look around, however, and sense what we are and how we differ from other animals, we then begin to seek out those things for which we have been created.

42. "We see a similar pattern in the case of animals. They do not initially leave the place where they were born; they are eventually stirred to action by their internal desires. Young snakes prospectively slither; newly-hatched chicks take to the water; and blackbirds flutter about. We see oxen testing their horns, and scorpions their stingers; each is led by its own nature in the conduct of its life. An analogous process is observed in the case of humanity. Newly-born infants at first lie prostrate, as if they were without an intellect; when their limbs gain a bit more firmity, and their senses and minds are activated, they then struggle to stand upright. They use their hands, and recognize those who rear them.

"Eventually they delight in being with their peers; they willingly join them in groups, engage them in games, and participate in story-telling. They seek to share with others the overflowing vitality contained in themselves, and show great curiosity with regard to the happenings that take place at home. They begin to take note of things and to learn, and they do not like being unfamiliar with the names of people they see. If they excel in contests with their peers, they are carried away with joy; when defeated, they are broken and cast down in spirits. None of these scenarios should be thought to happen without a good reason.

43. "Man's powers are so created by nature that they seem to have been configured for him to acquire every virtue. So children are moved by the likenesses of the virtues without needing to be

taught, since they carry the seeds of virtue within themselves; these are the primary elements of human nature that, once they have germinated, will grow into fully-developed virtue. For we have been designed from birth to hold within ourselves the principles of creative action, love, kindness, and gratitude; we also possess intellects well-adapted for knowledge, prudence, and courage. The opposites of these qualities are alien to us.

"It makes perfect sense that we detect in children those sparks of virtue I have just noted; the flame of the philosopher's reason should be kindled from these divine sparks, so that a mature man, following reason as a divine light, may attain nature's ultimate purpose. As I have often said, the capabilities of our nature are understood through a fog of uncertainty in our early years, since our minds remain feeble; yet with the progress of years, the intellect is fortified, and apprehends the power of human nature. It learns that this nature can make further progress: by itself, its power remains inchoate.

XVI. 44. "One must, therefore, probe into the heart of things, and see with unobscured clarity what the features of this inner nature truly are. For if it were any other way, we would not be able to know ourselves. Because this precept was considered too elevated to have come from a man, it was attributed to a god. Thus the Pythian Apollo[416] admonishes us to 'know ourselves.' Yet the only way to gain this knowledge is to understand the power of the body and the mind, and to live the kind of life that permits the full development of their capabilities.

"Our original mental desire was to acquire the things I mentioned earlier in their most perfect state. When this desire has been satisfied, we must recognize that our nature basically 'plants its feet' here: and this is the Ultimate Good. Without doubt this End must, as a whole, be desired in itself and for itself, since we

---

[416] The high priestess of the temple of Apollo at Delphi was known as the Pythia. The maxim "know thyself" was a famous Delphic admonition, repeated by many of the Greek philosophers.

demonstrated earlier that each constituent part must be separately desired.

45. "If anyone believes I have overlooked pleasure in our inventory of the body's benefits, my response is that this issue will be addressed in due course. It is irrelevant to our discussion whether pleasure is or is not among those things we have called 'first principles in accordance with nature.' If pleasure does not, as it seems to me, contribute to the totality of nature's goods, then it has justifiably been passed over; but if it truly has the attributes some would like it to have, then our understanding of the Supreme Good is not hindered at all. If pleasure were added to the list of things we have identified as the first principles of nature, this would only add one more bodily benefit. The character of the Supreme Good as we have expounded it would remain unchanged.

XVII. 46. "The path we have traced thus far has relied entirely on the primary affinities of nature. Let us now, however, turn to another kind of argument, one that does not depend solely on the fact that we love ourselves. Because each part of our nature—both mental and physical—has its own inherent potential, it follows that the activity of these components is entirely voluntary. Let me begin with the body. Do you notice that people will conceal a limb that is deformed, dysfunctional, or impaired, and that they make great efforts to hide, if possible, this physical impairment, or at least minimize its visibility?

"They will endure much pain to rehabilitate their bodies, even if the condition of their limbs will not only *not* improve, but will even get worse. All men inherently believe themselves to be desirable as a whole—not because of some external reason, but because of themselves. Thus it must follow that when an entire thing is desired for its own sake, the parts of that thing must also be desired for their own sakes.

47. "What do you think? Is there nothing in the body's movement or position that nature herself believes should be noticed? However someone walks or sits, or whatever the appearance and expression of his face—is there nothing in these things that we consider suitable or unsuitable for a free man? Don't we think that

313

Additional views the remains of Aristotle's Lyceum

many people who apparently violate some law or rule of nature through their bodily actions or postures are deserving of scorn? And because these undesirable habits are often eliminated, is it not right that beauty should be desired for its own sake?

"For if we believe that bodily debilitation and impairment should be avoided for their own sakes, why shouldn't we also—perhaps even more intensely—seek excellence of form? And if we shun degeneracy in bodily posture and movement, shouldn't we also strive for beauty? We should likewise seek health, bodily vigor, and the absence of pain for their own sakes, not just for their usefulness. Because our nature wants to satisfy the purpose of all its components, it seeks for its own sake that bodily condition which is most in alignment with that nature. Nature is utterly at a loss when confronted with situations of bodily debilitation, pain, or loss of vigor.

XVIII. 48. "Let us now turn to the parts of the mind, which are more eminent. The more elevated they are, the more they provide us with indisputable indications of nature's guiding hand. This love of knowledge and science is so innate in us that no one can doubt we are drawn towards these enticements even without the prospect of any material reward. Do we see how children, even when faced with physical punishment, are not scared away from analyzing and investigating their surroundings? How when we push them away, they soon return? How they experience joy in acquiring knowledge? How they passionately desire to share their learning with others? How they are captivated by parties, games, and these kinds of spectacles, and will endure hunger and thirst in order to participate in them?

"Do you see my point? Do we not see how someone devoted to the studies and arts of a free-born person[417] will neglect his

---

[417] Meaning the liberal or gentlemanly arts (*ingenuus*).

health and domestic affairs, will endure anything when imbued with the passion for knowledge and understanding, and will accept the greatest pains and labors as a fair price for the pure pleasure he receives from learning?[418]

49. "It seems to me that the poet Homer had something like this in mind when he imagined the songs of the Sirens.[419] For it appears that it was neither the seductiveness of their voices, nor the uniqueness and variety of their singing, that used to divert unwary mariners; rather, it was because they claimed to have *a storehouse of special knowledge*. It was man's lust for learning that caused him to become ensnared by the Sirens' fateful rocks. This is how they called out to Ulysses (I have translated these relevant verses below, as well as others):

O Ulysses, great man of Argos, will you turn your ship
And your ears, so that you can learn our sacred songs?
For no one has ever passed through this blue-watered causeway
Who could not first linger, held in rapture by our sweet voices,
And having then satisfied his eager soul with all kinds of special music,
Sail away much wiser back to his homeland's shores.
We know well the dark truth of conflict and the devastation of war

---

[418] A majestic sentence, deserving to be quoted in full: *Qui ingenuis studiis atque artibus delectantur, nonne videmus eos nec valetudinis nec rei familiaris habere rationem omniaque perpeti ipsa cognitione et scientia captos et cum maximis curis et laboribus compensare eam quam ex discendo capiant voluptatem?*

[419] The Sirens were mythical creatures who, through the hypnotic beauty of their singing, lured to their deaths mariners passing by their island. *See* Odyssey XII.180—200. Cicero's conjecture on the reason for the seductiveness of their songs is an interesting one.

That the Greeks brought to Troy by divine command,
And the secrets of all things manifested on this earth.[420]

"Evidently Homer saw that if a man could be mortally ensnared by some middling song, his fable would not be accepted.[421] The Sirens are promising knowledge; and it is no wonder that this would be more precious to a lover of wisdom than his own country. To wish to know everything under the sun, with no regard for boundaries, is to wish to be counted among the meddlesome; but to be guided by the contemplation of great ideas to a genuine love of knowledge must be recognized as a mark of the greatest of men.

XIX. 50. "What devotion to study do you think existed in the scientist Archimedes, who was so attentive to the figures he had sketched in the sand that he did not realize his city had been taken![422] What incredible intellectual ability do we see exerted by Aristoxenus[423] in his work on music! What energy did Aristophanes pour into literary activities during his lifetime! What can I even say about Pythagoras, Plato, or Democritus? We know that they traveled to the ends of the earth on account of their devotion to knowledge. Those who do not see this have never loved anything truly great and worthy of devoted study. In this regard, those who think these studies I mentioned are cultivated only for mental pleasure miss the point that, because the mind finds joy in them even without the expectation of practical utility, such studies

---

[420] *Odyssey* XII.184 *et seq.*

[421] I.e., accepted by his audience as plausible.

[422] According to legend, when Archimedes's city of Syracuse was captured by the Romans in 212 B.C., the scientist was found contemplating mathematical figures he had drawn in the sand. When he warned a Roman soldier not to step on them, the enraged soldier slew him.

[423] Aristoxenus of Tarentum (c. 375 B.C.--?), an Aristotelian philosopher who wrote on ethics and music.

should be pursued solely for the knowledge they provide. The mind rejoices in knowledge itself, even if it may prove to be troublesome.

51. "Is there a need for continued discussion of matters so clear? We wish to know why we are motivated to discover the motions of the stars, to contemplate the nature of heavenly bodies, and to divine the secrets of all things shrouded by nature in obscurity. We ask why the study of history, which we like to examine in the minutest detail, so captivates us; we go back to the subjects we have passed over, and take pains to finish what we have started. I am well aware, of course, that there is practical advantage to be gained from the study of history, as well as enjoyment.

52. "But what about creative fiction,[424] a form of writing which offers nothing in the way of real practicality? What about the fact that we want to know the names of those who have achieved something great, as well as their lineage, place of origin, and many other less important bits of information? What about men of the lowest social class—even common laborers who have no hope of attaining any position of authority—who are yet fascinated by history? We may observe that those who most like to read and hear about current events are those who, due to their elderly condition, have no opportunity to participate in such matters. We must conclude, therefore, *that there are intrinsic inducements in the things we learn and discover that stimulate us to the activities of learning and discovery.*

53. "Certainly the ancient philosophers imagine what the life of the wise would be on the Islands of the Fortunate. They speculate that, freed from every worldly care and requiring none of life's essential contrivances or accoutrements, such people will do nothing except spend every waking hour investigating and

---

[424] *Fictas fabulas*, or literally "invented stories."

studying the subtle workings of the universe. We, however, consider this not only the healthy diversion of a happy life, but also the consolation for our suffering. Thus many who have found themselves under the control of enemies or tyrants, or who have been confined to prison or punished with exile, have solaced their bereavements by devoting themselves to learning.

54. "Demetrius of Phalerum, a former ruler of Athens, made his way to King Ptolemy in Alexandria after he had been wrongly expelled from his own city. He was a student of Theophrastus, and a man who excelled in the very same philosophical system we are now advocating.[425] He wrote many first-rate books during his calamitous leisure. These were not for his own use, since he had been forbidden to participate in politics; rather, the process of nurturing and focusing the mind was a way for him to sustain his humanity.

"Indeed I often heard the learned praetor Cnaeus Aufidius[426] say, after he had lost the use of his eyes, that he was more affected by the lack of light than by the inability to see. And what about sleep? Were it not for the fact that sleep brings us bodily refreshment and acts as a tonic for our labors, we might consider it an unnatural imposition, for it steals away our senses and denies us all capacity for action. If nature did not insist on bodily rest, or if it could be achieved by some other method, we would easily be satisfied; for we are already accustomed to tolerating sleeplessness for the sake of work and study, nearly to the point of offending nature.

XX. 55. "There are, however, very clear, transparent, and nearly irrefutable indications from nature (mostly in humans but

---

[425] Demetrius of Phalerum (c. 350 B.C.—c. 280 B.C.) was a student of Theophrastus and one of the first Peripatetics. He ruled Athens for ten years from 317 to 307 B.C., when he was forced into exile.

[426] Praetor about 107 B.C. Cicero says elsewhere (*Tusc. Disp.* V.38) that he composed a history of Rome after becoming blind.

Two views of the Dipylon Gate (or Thriasian Gates) in Athens, mentioned in the text at V.1. It was one of the largest such gates in antiquity, containing four towers and a courtyard, and was built at the time of the Themistoclean walls in 478 B.C.

also in other animals) that the mind always looks for something to do, and is unable to tolerate perpetual quietude under any condition. This fact is easily observed during the formative years of young children. Here I am afraid I might be seen as pressing this idea too much; but it is clear that all the old philosophers (those of my own school especially) look to man's period of infancy. For it is when they study childhood that they are most readily able to discern nature's purposes.

"Indeed, we see that infants are unable to remain continuously at rest. When they advance a bit in age, they love to participate in strenuous games, to the point that not even corporal punishment can dampen their enthusiasm for them. This love of physical action grows stronger with each passing year. We would never wish to experience the sleep of Endymion,[427] even if we could revel in the most engrossing dreams; for if this happened, we would consider it the slumber of the tomb.

56. "We see that even the most inactive types of men—the ones addicted to sloth—will retain a continuous vigor of body and mind; when they are not preoccupied with life's necessities, they demand game-boards, seek out some sporting events, or busy themselves with conversation. Since they are incapable of the noble pleasures derived from learning, they instead seek out any available social group or circle. The animals that we confine in zoos for our own amusement do not readily accept being caged, even though they may be better nourished than when they were in the wild; they miss the prerogative of unfettered movement given to them by nature.

57. "Thus he who is most endowed with natural aptitude and accomplishments would never want to live a life in which he was

---

[427] According to myth, Selene, the Titan goddess of the moon, fell passionately in love with Endymion. Especially loving how he looked in sleep, she asked Zeus to keep Endymion in eternal slumber. *See, e.g.,* Apollonius of Rhodes, *Argonautica* IV.57—60.

stripped of his ability to act, even if he were able to indulge in the most seductive pleasures. Such men prefer to focus on their personal affairs; if they happen to have a more elevated spirit, they may seize the opportunity for a position of civil or military command; or, instead, they may dedicate their energies to intellectual study. Physical pleasure is so far from being their goal that they will accept stress, burdens, and sleeplessness in the service of the best part of man's nature, which in us must be considered divine.

"They delight in the acuteness of their minds and characters, requiring neither physical pleasure nor respite from their labors. They never fail to extend their admiration for the achievements of the ancients, or their enthusiasm for new mental pursuits. Their hunger for study is never satisfied; they blot out all distractions from their work, never permitting debased thoughts to occupy their attentions. So transfixing for them is the power of these studies that even those who claim to follow other Ends of Goods (ends based on advantageousness or pleasure) may be observed devoting their lives to investigating and explaining the workings of nature.

XXI. 58. "So it is evident that we have been created for the purpose of taking action. The different varieties of activity are many, and those of greater importance overshadow those of lesser significance. It seems to me—and to those whose philosophical system we are now analyzing—that the most important activities are (1) the study and investigation of the heavenly bodies and of those things hidden and concealed by nature that reason can evaluate; (2) knowledge of the administration and management of public affairs; and (3) the understanding of prudence, temperance, strength, and justice, along with the other virtues and the actions congruent with their meaning (all of which we may include under the one phrase 'moral goodness'). As we advance in years, we are led towards a proper understanding and use of these virtues by the positive reinforcement of nature herself.

"All things have small beginnings, but become progressively larger through natural growth. And this happens for good reason. From the first moment of birth, an organism possesses a certain softness and vulnerability that inhibit it from understanding and doing what is in its own best interest. The light of virtue and happiness—the two things we should seek the most—only comes to us later in life; later still do we actually comprehend the nature of these things. As Plato rightly said, 'Happy is the man who, even though he has reached a great age, is still able to find wisdom and form correct opinions.'[428] Since enough has been said about nature's primary goods, we may now evaluate the more important issues that follow as logical consequences.

59. "Nature created and shaped the human body so that some parts were perfected at the time of the body's inception, and other parts were contrived with the progress of time. Neither external nor accidental assistance was much used in this process. To the same degree as the body, nature also perfected the mind with its surviving attributes. She provided the mind with senses capable of performing their duties of perception, so that they needed little or no help in consolidating their powers. But when it came to the greatest and most surpassing aspect of man's character, nature stayed her hand. She provided us with a mind good enough to accept every virtue; without formal instruction, she instilled in us at birth little reminders of the noblest concepts. She ordained to instruct us; and along with her other gifts, she introduced what we might call the basic elements of virtue. But she only sowed virtue's most primitive seeds; nothing more was done in the way of cultivation.

60. "It is, therefore, our responsibility (and when I say 'our responsibility,' I mean the responsibility of our acquired knowledge) to seek the consequences that flow from these fundamental principles

---

[428] *Laws* 653A.

Part of the cemetery at Kerameikos.
A tortoise is in the foreground at center right.

Near the Dipylon Gate are the remains of the Pompeion, a building that
served as a staging area for the Panathenaia festival.

provided to us by nature until we have achieved our desired goals. Indeed, this is much more critical and worth pursuing than either the senses or the attributes of the body we described above; for the overpowering excellence of the mind takes precedence over these things to a degree that can scarcely be comprehended.

"Thus every reward, veneration, and devotion relates back to virtue and to those things consistent with virtue: and all such things that are either in the mind, or managed by the mind, may fall under the single name of 'moral goodness.' We will soon examine the implications of these ideas, the significance of the terminology used to explain them, and their relative importance and characters.

XXII. 61. "For the moment, we will state that this moral goodness I am talking about is something that must be sought not only because we hold ourselves dear, but also because moral goodness has its own inherent value. This can be seen with children, in whose experience nature is reflected with mirror-like fidelity. With what ferocity do they tussle with each other! How intense their competitions! What joy they display when winning, and how ashamed they become in defeat! How they hate to be accused of anything! How they love being praised! What labors will they exert so they can stand toe-to-toe with their peers! What a strong memory they have for those who have treated them kindly, and how eager are they to return the favor! These qualities are most readily observable in those with the best innate character, those children in whom these positive moral qualities, as we understand them, have already been sketched out by nature.

62. "But this is how things are with children. Their traits and characteristics, however, are fully determined once they leave the childhood phase. Is there anyone so inhuman that he is not aroused to indignation by moral corruption, and moved to satisfaction by moral goodness? Who is not disgusted by seeing someone's youth squandered in lustful, reckless frivolity? On the contrary: who would not prefer to see young people—even if he did not know them personally—embrace the virtues of modesty and diligence?

"Who does not loathe the traitor Pullus Numitorius,[429] even though he was useful to our country? Who does not generously praise Codrus, the protector of this city, or Erechtheus's daughters?[430] Who does not hate the name Tubulus, or cherish the memory of the deceased Aristides?[431] Or do we forget how much we are inspired by reading or hearing about some act of piety, friendship, or greatness of soul?

63. "And what do I say of ourselves, we who have been born, raised, and conditioned for glory and distinction? What a roar of approval flares up from the common, ignorant crowd in the theater when these words are spoken from the stage:

I am Orestes,[432]

and also when the response comes:

---

[429] According to Cicero (*De Inventione* II.34) the city of Fregellae was betrayed by one Quintus Numitorius Pullus to the Romans during a revolt in 125 B.C. Neither Livy (LX) nor Velleius Paterculus (II.6) mention this incident (nor does any other historian) although this may be due to its minor importance.

[430] King Codrus was supposedly the last of the mythical kings of Athens. He is said to have sacrificed his life during the Dorian invasion of Greece around 1068 B.C. A Delphic prophecy stated that the invasion would succeed if Codrus did not die; on hearing this, the king allowed himself to be slain by the enemy. Erechtheus was another mythical Athenian king; he sacrificed his youngest daughter to thwart an invasion, an event which caused her sisters to commit suicide.

[431] For Tubulus, *see* II.54 above. Aristides (530 B.C.—468 B.C.) was an Athenian statesman famous for his leadership during the war against the Persians.

[432] Another reference to the play *Orestes* by Pacuvius (*see above*, II.79). The quotes refer to the scene in which Orestes and Pylades choose to die together rather than betray each other.

No, absolutely not! I am telling you that *I am* Orestes!

Then after the king, in his dismay and bewilderment, is offered a solution by each one of them:

Then we beg you to execute both of us together.

No matter how many times we see this scene, doesn't it still merit our greatest admiration? It is therefore clear that every man endorses and praises the mental attitude that not only refuses to seek its own advantage, *but maintains its integrity even when doing so is a detriment to its own advantage.*

64. "Such examples are found not only in works of fiction, but also in the pages of historical works—especially in the annals of Roman history. Indeed, we chose our best man to accept the sacred images from Mount Ida;[433] we sent guardians to kings;[434] and our generals sacrificed their lives for the sake of their country. Our consuls warned a king who was their arch-enemy to beware of being poisoned when he was close to our city walls.[435] In our republic was a young woman who cleansed the shame of the sexual violation she had suffered by choosing a self-inflicted death.[436] Roman to the core also was the anguished father who

---

[433] When the worship of the goddess Cybele was established in Rome, Publius Cornelius Scipio Nasica was selected in 204 B.C. to receive the image of the goddess Cybele from Mount Ida.

[434] Probably a reference to Marcus Aemilius Lepidus, sent to Egypt as a "guardian" to the immature king Ptolemy V.

[435] Two consuls warned their enemy King Pyrrhus of Epirus in 278 B.C. that his doctor had approached the Romans with an offer to poison him.

[436] The legend of Lucretia, who committed suicide around 510 B.C. after her rape by the Etruscan king's son Sextus Tarquinius, thereby preserving her honor. *See* Livy I.58.

slew his own daughter to save her from dishonor.[437] Who is incapable of understanding that all these actions (and many others like them) were done by men fired by the majesty of moral rectitude, that they were not motivated by what was advantageous to themselves personally, and that we praise them for no other reason than for their raw moral power?

XXIII. "This explanation has been a brief one. Because the topic was not really one subject to dispute, I have not spoken as much as I might otherwise have. We must conclude from these examples, then, that all the virtues, and the moral rectitude that emerges from them and exists within them, should be sought for their own sakes.

65. "Yet in the realm of moral goodness that we are discussing, nothing is more brilliant or so expansive as the genuine fellowship of men with one another. This solidarity and fraternity of interests, this genuine human sentiment felt for someone else, manifests itself at the moment of our birth, due to the fact that infants are loved by their parents and the entire household is connected by the bonds of marriage and consanguinity. It gradually seeps outside the home, first through extended familial relations and then through the links of marriage; it extends wider through friendships and the ties of local communities, progressing to other citizens and then to political friends and associates, and ultimately ending with the inclusion of all humanity.

"This human inclination—that of granting each person what is his due and preserving, through generosity and equity, those social and fraternal bonds I speak of—is called justice. Linked to it are social responsibility, integrity, generosity, benevolence, kindness, and other related qualities. These attributes are specific features of justice, but are commonly held by the other virtues as well.

---

[437] The story of Verginia (or Virginia) is found in Livy III.44. Lucius Verginius killed his daughter Virginia in 449 B.C. in the belief that it was the only way he could prevent the loss of her freedom and honor.

Tomb of the Lacedaemonians at the Kerameikos cemetery

View from the Tomb of the Lacedaemonians

66. "For human nature is so designed that is possesses an inherent civil and communitarian quality, something the Greeks call *politikon*. Whatever each virtue does, it will be consistent with the fellowship, common sentiment, and solidarity I discussed earlier; and justice, just as it percolates through the other virtues, will have a corresponding need for them in turn. For justice can be served only by a man who is both strong and wise.[438] This collaboration and harmony of the virtues that I am talking about has the same quality as that of moral goodness; for moral goodness is either virtue itself, or action that is considered virtuous. A life consistent with these doctrines, and one responsive to the virtues, may be judged upright, morally good, steadfast, and congruent with the laws of nature.

67. "This admixture and intermingling of the virtues may, as a matter of conjecture, be untangled by philosophers. For although the virtues are so comingled and interconnected that each one influences all the others, and no one virtue can be isolated from another, each one nevertheless has its own specific purpose. So valor is proven through experience with labors and dangers, temperance in the abstinence from physical pleasures, prudence in the correct selection of goods and evils, justice in the granting to each that which is rightfully his.

"There is in every virtue a certain quality that gazes outward from itself, a characteristic that seeks out and embraces others; from this we must conclude that our friends, brothers, family members, relatives, fellow citizens, and finally all men (since we hold that all mankind constitutes one society) are desirable for their own sakes. None of these relations, however, merits being considered part of the End and Supreme Good.

68. "Thus we discover that there are two categories of things that are desirable for their own sakes. One category includes the things that make up the Supreme Good (i.e., the goods of the mind or body); the other category includes external[439] goods, meaning

---

[438] *Servari enim iustitia nisi a forti viro, nisi a sapiente non potest.*

[439] *Extrinsecus*, meaning external, extraneous, or extrinsic.

goods that are found neither in the mind or the body, such as friends, parents, children, extended family, and homeland. We consider these inherently valuable, but they do not belong to the former category I just mentioned. No one would ever be able to reach the Ultimate Good if all those goods that are external, yet still desirable, were included in the Ultimate Good.

XXIV. 69. "You may ask, then, how it can be true that all things relate back to the Supreme Good, if friendships, personal relations, and the other external goods are not contained within the Supreme Good? The unambiguous answer is this: we safeguard these external goods by carrying out the duties that arise from the specific class of virtue associated with each. The act of supporting friends and parents is an advantage to the person who performs the duty, because performing the duty is a morally right action—and morally right actions arise from the virtues.

"The wise, following nature's lead, strive for moral goodness in their actions; yet some men, flawed but still gifted with exceptional character, are often actuated by a desire for glory, which has the pretense and facade of moral rectitude. But if they could truly comprehend moral goodness in its all-embracing perfection and immaculacy—this one thing that surpasses everything else in brilliance and merit—how intoxicated with joy would they be, considering how much they revere its mere shadow and outline!

70. "What person addicted to pleasures, what man burning with unquenchable lusts, do we think feels as much joy in acquiring his deepest desire as Scipio Africanus the Elder did in crushing Hannibal, or Africanus the Younger did upon causing the downfall of Carthage? What person ever derived as much pleasure from a descent of the Tiber on festival day as did Lucius

View of Kerameikos towards the Acropolis

*View of the Kerameikos Cemetery in the direction of the Dipylon Gate.
Note the Acropolis in the background.*

Paulus when he made his famous riverine journey with the captured King Perses?[440]

71. "Act now, my brother Lucius, to raise this majestic edifice of the virtues in your consciousness; you will never doubt that the men who have mastered the virtues, living under the guidance of an incomparable mind so constructed, are always happy. Men so guided will know that all disturbances of fortune, all changes of external conditions at whatever time, will be trivial and insignificant once they are confronted with the might of virtue. The things we count as bodily goods do indeed have a role in a happy life; but a happy life can exist without these things. For just as the stars in the sky are overwhelmed by the brilliance of the sun, so do these ancillary goods appear trifling and insignificant when compared to the incandescent splendor of the virtues.[441]

72. "While it is true to say that these benefits of the body are of minor importance in living a happy life, to assert that they mean nothing at all is too strong a statement. It seems to me that those who take this position have lost sight of those basic principles of nature that they themselves created. Some allowance must be made for bodily goods once one decides what that legitimate allowance should be. The philosopher who sincerely seeks the truth instead of applause should assign at least *some value* to the things these famous advocates themselves say are in accordance with nature.

---

[440] King Perses (Perseus) of Macedon (c. 212 B.C.—166 B.C.) was crushed by the Romans in the Third Macedonian War (171 B.C.—168 B.C.). He surrendered to Lucius Aemilius Paullus after the Battle of Pydna and was paraded in triumph in Rome during a festival day along the Tiber in 167 B.C. According to Plutarch (*Aemilius Paullus* 37), Perses either starved himself to death in prison or was killed through sleep deprivation.

[441] A luminous sentence: *Ita enim parvae et exiguae sunt istae accessiones bonorum ut, quemadmodum stellae in radiis solis, sic istae in virtutum splendore ne cernantur quidem.*

333

"At the same time he will appreciate that virtue has such power, and moral goodness has such authority, that by comparison the other goods, while not rendered entirely worthless, are so deficient in value as to appear to be worthless. This is not the utterance of someone who disregards everything except virtue; it is the statement of one who wishes to exalt virtue by describing its incomparable merits. And this, finally, is the complete and comprehensive explanation of the Supreme Good. Other philosophers have tried to poach bits and pieces of this edifice, each one wanting to be seen as offering his own original idea.

XXV. 73. "Learning for its own sake was often praised by Theophrastus and Aristotle to a remarkable degree; Erillus, entranced by this notion, proposed that 'knowledge' was the Supreme Good and that nothing else but this was worth seeking for its own sake. The ancient philosophers said a great deal about looking down on, and feeling contempt for, mundane human affairs. Aristo clung to this idea; he held that nothing should be avoided or sought except vice or virtue. We[442] counted the 'absence of pain' among those things that are in accordance with nature; but Hieronymus claimed it was the Supreme Good. Neither Callipho nor Diodorus after him could renounce moral goodness (the thing our school praised above everything else), even when the former became infatuated with physical pleasure and the latter with freedom from pain.

74. "Even these pleasure-seekers look for ways to cover their tracks. 'Virtue' comes out of their mouths constantly, and they claim that pleasure should only be a priority at first. Eventually, through force of habit, a kind of 'second nature' is created that is a major stimulant in generating action unrelated to pleasure-seeking. Then we have the Stoics.

"They have taken not some random thing or another from us: they have appropriated our entire philosophical system. It is a

---

[442] Meaning "our school," i.e., the view of the Academy under Antiochus.

common practice among thieves to tamper with the marks of ownership on the goods they steal; and in order to present our doctrines as their own, the Stoics altered our terminology—which are the identifying marks of ideas. Our teachings, therefore, occupy a special place as the only system worthy of the student of liberal arts, worthy of the learned, worthy of great men, worthy of true leaders, and worthy of kings."[443]

75. After he finished this sentence, he was briefly silent, and then resumed. "What do you think? Were my comments useful enough to have made your listening to me worthwhile?"

"Today and at other times, Piso," I said, "you seem to know these subjects so well that, if we had the chance to interact with you more often, I don't think we would even need the help of the Greeks. I approved of what you said even more because I recall that your teacher Staseas of Naples—a Peripatetic of real distinction—used to offer a slightly different version of your doctrine. He agreed with those who thought that considerable importance should be attached to favorable or unfavorable fortune, and to goods or evils of the body."

"You are right about that," he replied. "But our comrade Antiochus explains these ideas with much more clarity and power than Staseas ever could. But I'm not trying to know how much *you* favor my system. It's the opinion of our young friend Cicero[444] I'm thinking about, since I'd like very much to entice your student away from you!"

XXVI. 76. "Your points have persuaded me, and my cousin seems convinced as well," Lucius here interjected.

---

[443] A sentence making wonderful use of emphasis and repetition: *Ita relinquitur sola haec disciplina digna studiosis ingenuarum artium, digna eruditis, digna claris viris, digna principibus, digna regibus.*
[444] I.e., Lucius.

"Well, what then?" said Piso. "Does the young man have your permission to be instructed? Or would you rather he study a system that will give him no knowledge at all, even when he has completely learned it?"

"I certainly allow him to go," I responded. "But don't you remember that it's up to me whether I can approve of what you've said? Who can resist endorsing things that to them seem likely?"

"But can anyone approve of something that he has no perception, comprehension, or understanding of?" he asked.

"There is no dispute on this point, Piso," I told him. "The only thing that might make me deny the likelihood of perception is the way the Stoics define 'perception.' They don't think anything can be 'perceived' unless it has such inherent truth that it cannot be false. So I have a disagreement with the Stoics here, but no problem with the Peripatetics. But let us pass over these issues, since they will unavoidably draw us into a long and acrimonious dispute.

77. "It seems to me that you have made a certain claim a bit too hastily: namely, the idea that all wise men are happy. I am not sure how your presentation flew by this point. Unless this claim is proved, I will have to say that Theophrastus was right when he decided that fortune, suffering, and bodily torment could in no way be reconciled with a happy life. For it is an offensive incongruity to say a man is happy when he is being crushed by a variety of evils. I honestly have no idea how these two opposites can be harmonized."

"Which proposition do you have a problem with?" he asked. "That virtue has such power that it needs nothing except itself for a happy life? Or, if you agree with this, do you deny it is possible for those who have mastered virtue to be happy when they are being affected by evils?"

"I have no doubt that the power of virtue is unmatched. We should set aside, for the moment, the question of exactly *how great* its power is. For now it is enough to ask this: would virtue's power be so great if anything outside of virtue were considered a good?"

78. "But if you accept the Stoic position that the possession of virtue alone is enough to make a happy life, you also grant this to the Peripatetics. The things that the Stoics do not dare call evils—yet concede are bitter, harmful, despised, and foreign to nature—*we* say are evils, even though they may be small and almost trivial evils. Thus, if a man who is neck-deep in bitter and detestable circumstances can still manage to be happy, he can likewise be happy when steeped in trivial evils."

"Piso," I said bluntly, "if anyone is perceptive enough to know what is important in a discussion like this one, it certainly is you. So I would ask you to listen to me. Perhaps it is my fault, but I can see that you don't yet understand what I'm asking."

"I'm ready to listen," he answered. "And I hope you'll respond to what I was asking."

XXVII. 79. "I will respond by saying," I said firmly, "that my purpose right now is not to discover what virtue can accomplish. Rather, I want to know what we can reliably say about virtue, and what internal contradictions virtue may have."

"What are you trying to say?" Piso asked me.

"Zeno himself," I replied, "laid down the law with oracular certitude that 'Virtue needs only itself for a happy life.' And when someone asks why this is so, he answers, 'Because there is no other good except what is morally good.' I'm not trying to discover right now if this is true. I am only pointing out that what Zeno says is lucid and coherent.

80. "Epicurus might say the same thing—I mean, that the wise man is always happy. I say this because he's in the habit of rattling on about it sometimes. And of course if the wise man were ever afflicted with the most terrible agonies, Epicurus would say: 'How delightful this is! This does not bother me at all!' I have no fight with Epicurus as to why he wanders so far away from the true nature of the Good; but *I do* firmly believe that he fails to grasp the consequence of his dictum that 'pain is the greatest evil.' I'm making the same point right now to rebut you. You're saying all

The Temple of the Olympian Zeus (Olympieion),
with the Athenian Acropolis in the background.

the same things right now about goods and evils that every person says who has 'never even seen a philosopher in a picture' (as the saying goes). So health, strength, posture, physical beauty, and bodily integrity down to every last toe-nail are things you consider 'goods.' Unattractiveness, disease, and weakness are things you consider 'evils.'

81. "You certainly allocate external goods sparingly. But since these things are goods of the body, you will certainly count as goods the things that produce such goods (for example, friends, children, relatives, wealth, honors, and resources). Understand that I'm *not* saying anything against this. What I *am* saying is this: if these occurrences that can happen to a wise man are indeed evils, then being wise is not enough to produce a happy life."

"Well, it's more accurate to say that wisdom alone may not provide enough for the *happiest* life, but it does provide enough to make life *happy*," Piso corrected.

"I noticed that you phrased the issue this way a little while ago," I rejoined. "And I know this statement was one that our teacher Antiochus liked to make. But what could be more unacceptable than to label someone 'happy,' but not 'happy enough'? When something is added to what is already enough, it makes it too much: and no one is *too happy*. Thus no one can be happier than happy."[445]

82. "Then what is your view," Piso shot back, "of Quintus Metellus,[446] who lived to see three sons made consuls (one of whom was also a censor who received a triumph), a fourth son made praetor, and who left his sons alive and well[447] and his three daughters married? Metellus himself had served as consul, censor,

---

[445] *Igitur nemo beato beatior.*

[446] Quintus Caecilius Metellus Macedonicus (c. 210 B.C.—c. 115 B.C.), a successful Roman general and statesman.

[447] I.e., they did not die in battle or otherwise during his lifetime.

and augur, and was also awarded a triumph. If he was a wise man, don't you consider him happier than Regulus,[448] who died in enemy captivity after being subjected to starvation and lack of sleep, assuming Regulus was also a wise man?

XXVIII. 83. "Why are you asking *me* this?" I demanded. "Ask the Stoics that question."

"And how do you think they would respond to such a question?" he pressed.

"They would say that Metellus was no happier than Regulus."

"Well then," he said, "one must begin from this point."

"But we are drifting away from our original purpose here," I objected. "I am not trying to find out what is true, but what each philosophical school should be saying. I only wish they could say that one is happier than another! Then you might see some ideas fall apart. Since the Good is found only in virtue and in moral goodness, and since neither virtue nor moral goodness (as they[449] claim) may grow incrementally,[450] and since the only thing that can be called 'good' is that which necessarily makes its owner happy (when that which alone creates happiness cannot be increased by degrees), how can anyone be happier than anyone else? Do you see how these ideas concur with each other?

"By Hercules! Here I have to admit my true feelings: their ideas are perfectly fitted together and form a marvelous philosophical architecture. Their conclusions follow from their initial propositions, and the middle points harmonize with both the initial propositions and the conclusions. Every part coheres with every other part. They know what follows from something,

---

[448] The fate of Marcus Atilius Regulus in the hands of the Carthaginians is noted above in II.65.

[449] I.e., the Stoics.

[450] Meaning that neither virtue nor moral rectitude can increase by degrees. As noted earlier, this was the traditional Stoic position. One was either virtuous, or one was not.

and what is not compatible with something. It is just like how it is in geometry: if you concede the initial propositions, you must concede everything that follows from that.

Concede that nothing is truly good except moral rectitude, and one must inevitably concede that the happy life can only be found in virtue. Or look at it backwards: if you concede that the happy life can only be found in virtue, you must concede that nothing is truly good except moral rectitude.[451]

84. "But your school's arguments are not so tightly constructed. You talk about 'three categories of goods': and your presentation moves forward with no problem. But then your presentation reaches the end, and it gets entangled in difficulties. It wants to say that the wise man lacks nothing necessary for a happy life: this is the argument based on moral goodness, the argument of Socrates and Plato. 'I dare to say it!' he says.[452] No, you can't do that, unless you rephrase what you said before. If poverty is an evil, then no beggar can be happy, no matter how wise he might be. But Zeno had the temerity to say that a pauper was not only happy, but wealthy. To endure pain is evil: thus someone who is being crucified cannot be happy. Children are a good; so childlessness is misery. A homeland is a good thing; so exile is misery. Health is a good; so sickness is misery. Bodily integrity is a good; so bodily impairment is misery. Sharp vision is a good; so blindness is misery.

"Although an act of consolation might ease one of these burdens, how would someone ever be able to cope with them all together? Imagine a man who is blind, debilitated, seriously sick, living in exile, childless, poor, and enduring torture on the rack. *What are you going to call him now, Zeno?* 'I call him happy,'

---

[451] The translation makes clear what is a very short sequence: *Vide rursus retro. Dato hoc, dandum est illud.*

[452] "He" meaning the follower of Socrates and Plato (the adherents of the Academic school).

View of Athens from the Acropolis

Remains of the Roman Agora in Athens, near the Acropolis

Zeno says. Would you call him an extremely happy man, Zeno? 'Certainly,' he would say, 'because I have demonstrated that there are no degrees of happiness, just as there are no degrees of virtue—and happiness itself is found in virtue.'

85. "To you it is inconceivable that he could be happy. Why? Are your views any more believable? If you were to call me to testify before an average jury, you would never convince them that a man carrying so many burdens is happy. If you pled your case before more knowledgeable people, they might be in doubt about one of the issues: namely, whether virtue has such power that someone roasting in Phalaris's bull[453] can still be happy. They will not have any doubt about the other issue: namely, that the Stoic creed is internally consistent, and that your ideas are at odds with themselves."

"So do you endorse the views of Theophrastus expressed in his book *On Happiness*?" Piso queried.

"We are getting away from ourselves here," I suggested. "But to cut to the chase, yes, I do endorse what Theophrastus said, if these things you're talking about really are evils."

86. "Don't they look like evils to you?" he asked.

"You are asking a question where no matter how I respond, you will be caught on the horns of a dilemma," I rejoined.

"In what way?" he demanded.

"Because if they are evils, the person who has to deal with them will not be happy. But if they are not evils, the whole reasoning system of the Peripatetics comes crashing down."

"I see what you are doing here," he said with a laugh. "You're afraid I'm going to take your student away from you!"

---

[453] See IV.64 above. The hollow bronze bull of Phalaris (tyrant of Akragas in Sicily from c. 570 B.C.—554 B.C.) was a torture device supposedly activated by lighting a fire under it when a victim was placed inside.

"You're welcome to take him away if he wants to go," I shrugged. "For even if he happens to be with you, he will be with me."[454]

XXIX. "Listen to me, Lucius," said Piso. "For my arguments should be directed to you. The entire value of philosophy, as Theophrastus reminds us, lies in its ability to provide the tools needed for a happy life. All of us are animated by a passion to live happily. 87. Your cousin and I both concur on this point. But what remains to be seen is whether philosophical reasoning can show us the way to the happy life. It certainly claims that it can. If philosophy could not do so, then why did Plato scour Egypt to glean the secrets of mathematics and astronomy from foreign priests? Why did he seek out Archytas at Tarentum? Why did he bother to visit at Locri[455] the remaining Pythagoreans—Echecrates, Timaeus, and Arion[456]—in order to add Pythagorean ideas to the doctrines Socrates had taught, and to gain additional knowledge that Socrates had rejected? Why did Pythagoras himself roam through Egypt, and speak with the Magi of the Persians? Why did he traverse so many barbarian regions on foot, or sail through so many seas? Why did Democritus do the same thing?

"It is said—and we need not ask if the story is true or spurious—that Democritus deliberately robbed himself of his vision so that his intellect would be diverted as little as possible from philosophical ruminations. He neglected his inherited estate,

---

[454] *Erit enim mecum si tecum erit.*

[455] The Pythagorean community was located in southern Italy (*Magna Graecia*). Locri (or Locris) is located in the province of Reggio Calabria, Italy.

[456] Echecrates of Phlius appears in Plato's *Phaedo* (57a—59c); he is also mentioned by Diogenes Laertius (VIII.46) as one of the last Pythagoreans. Timaeus of Locri was a 5th century Pythagorean philosopher, identified by Plato in his dialogue *Timaeus*. Arion was a Pythagorean of the 5th or 4th century.

and abandoned his uncultivated fields. What else except the happy life was he seeking? Even if he believed the happy life consisted in knowledge, he still wished to conduct his researches into nature's secrets in order to raise his spirits. This for him was the Supreme Good. He calls it *euthumia*; the term *athambia* he also uses often, which means 'freedom from mental terror.'

88. "But although these insights were brilliant, they were not developed or refined beyond the rudimentary stage; Democritus said very little on the subject of virtue, and what he did say was insufficiently explained. Later these questions first began to be investigated by Socrates in this city,[457] and eventually such philosophical discussion was brought to the place where we are now standing. No one doubted that hope should be placed in virtue for discovering the nature of goodness and a way of living happily. Zeno cobbled together these ideas from our school and then offered them 'on the same matter in a different way,'[458] as the language in a courtroom pleading is normally written. You are now giving your endorsement to what he did. Of course he can evade the accusation of inconsistency by altering his words, but we ourselves have no such dodges available! He states that Metellus's life was not happier than that of Regulus, but says it should be 'preferred.' It says it was not more desirable, but should be 'adopted.' Furthermore, if one is presented with a choice between the two, he should pick Metellus's life and reject the life of Regulus. The life he says is 'preferable' and 'worthy of adoption,' I myself call happier—but I don't give this life one bit more importance than the Stoics give it.

---

[457] I.e., Athens.

[458] The words are: *de eadem re fecit alio modo*. This seems to have been language inserted into a legal petition or pleading to (1) offer alternative arguments in the event a judge dismissed one or more of its counts, or (2) preserve the litigant's right to seek relief in the event that one or more counts in a petition were ruled *res judicata*.

89. "Except for the fact that I call well-known things by recognizable names while they hunt for new words to describe the very same concepts, what really is the difference? Just as in the senate there is always someone who asks for an interpreter, so these Stoics have to listen to us with an interpreter. Whatever is in accordance with nature, I call that good; what is against nature, I call that bad. And I'm not the only one. You, Chrysippus, do the same in public and in the privacy of your home; yet when it comes to the classroom, you forget this rule. How do you explain this? Do you think the public should speak one way, and the philosopher should speak differently? In their relative appraisals of things, the educated and the uneducated may differ. When the educated have reached a consensus about what something is worth, they should, if they are normal human beings, conform their speech to accepted verbal usage. As long as the significance is the same, let them create new words as they see fit.

XXX. 90. "But let me address the accusation of inconsistency, so that you don't say I'm prone to lose my focus on the topic at hand. While you think inconsistency is found in the words that one uses, I think it should be based on one's stance on some issue. If there is one thing that must clearly be understood—and here we have the Stoics as our sturdiest proponents—it is that virtue has such power that everything else placed beside it becomes barely noticeable. Consider everything that the Stoics say is favorable and should be adopted, chosen, and preferred (which they define as having significant value). I try to proceed. But these things are given so many different names by the Stoics! Some of them are new and creative (like the terms 'promoted' and 'reduced'), and some of them have the same meaning. For what is the difference between 'seeking' something and 'choosing' it? Something that has been 'chosen,' something to which a special affection has attached, sounds to me more elegant.

"But when I call all these things good, everything hinges on *how good I say they are*. When I say they are desirable, what matters is how desirable they are. But if, however, I don't consider them any more desirable than you consider them 'selectable,' and if I who call them good don't consider them any more valuable than you who call them 'promoted,' then all these things must be blotted out and made invisible by the brilliant luminescence of virtue, whose rays emanate with heliacal power.

91. "But here your objection may be: 'A life that has some element of evil cannot be happy.' According to that logic, a field crop cannot be called a rich and fruitful harvest if you see a single tuft of wild grass in it somewhere; neither can a business be called successful if amid fantastic profits there are some unremunerative transactions. Is there one standard valid for every situation, but a different standard when it comes to life? Won't you judge an entire life by evaluating most of it, rather than just a part? Is there any doubt that virtue is the central actor in the majority of human activities, to the extent that it overshadows all other variables? Therefore I will go out on a limb, and call the other things that are in accordance with nature 'goods.' I refuse to strip them of their old names and pin some new label on them; but I *will* place the weight of virtue on the other plate of the balance scale.

92. "Believe me, that scale's plate will outweigh land and sea. The nature of an entire thing is known by that which forms its largest part, and is most extensively distributed within it. Suppose we say that someone enjoys a pleasant life: if at some point he is stricken with sadness, has his entire pleasant life slipped away from him? This was not the situation with Marcus Crassus, a man whom Lucilius said laughed only once in his entire life. This was certainly no obstacle, Lucilius says, to Crassus's being called 'The Glum.'[459] People gave Polycrates of Samos the moniker 'The Happy.' Nothing adverse ever happened to him except that he threw his cherished ring into the sea.[460]

---

[459] The Greek word used is Ἀγέλαστος, or "having no smile."

[460] A reference to an anecdote of Herodotus (III.40 *et. seq.*). Polycrates was

"Did his life become unhappy through this one vexation, and then happy again when the ring was found in a fish's stomach? If he was unwise—which he, being a tyrant, certainly was—then he was never happy; and if he was wise, then he was never miserable, even when he was enduring crucifixion at the hands of Oroetes, one of the governors of the Persian king Darius. Here you might object, 'But he was stricken by many evils!' My response is, 'Who's denying it? *Yet those evils were far outweighed by the preponderancy of his virtue.*'

XXXI. 93. "Won't you allow the Peripatetics to say that the life of all good men—that is, of all those who are wise and endowed with all the virtues—always has, in every part, more good than evil? Who says this? The Stoics, of course. No, certainly not. But don't those who judge everything according to pleasure and pain insist that the wise man always has more of what he wants than what he doesn't want?

"When those who place so much importance in virtue admit that they will not lift a hand for virtue's sake unless it gives them 'pleasure,' what should we do? We, who say that the smallest amount of intellectual greatness outweighs all bodily goods, such that they become utterly eclipsed? Who would dare to say that it is appropriate for a wise man to reject virtue permanently (if he could even do this) in order to be free of all pain? What thinker from our school—which is not afraid to call evils what the Stoics call 'adversities'—ever said that it was better to do something pleasurable and morally corrupt, than to do something painful and morally good?

---

advised that his unbroken streak of good luck might provoke some ruinous counterbalancing event by an offended Fortune. So he threw his favorite ring in the sea; it was, however, later returned to him by a fisherman. The point of the tale was to show that a man could not escape his destiny, for Polycrates was eventually deposed and executed.

94. "In our view, Dionysius of Heraclea disgracefully abandoned the Stoic school on account of his eye disease.[461] As if he ever learned from Zeno that when he was in agony, he was not really feeling pain! Although he never absorbed the point, what he had actually been taught was this: pain is not an evil because it is not a moral corruption, and that it is something that should be endured like a man. If Dionysius had been an adherent of the Peripatetic school, I believe he would have retained his beliefs. They say that pain is an evil; but with regard to enduring its effects with bravery, their view is the same as that of the Stoics. As for your comrade Arcesilaus, he was one of our own, since he studied under Polemo—even though he was too intolerant in debates. Once when he was enduring the pain of gout, his close friend Charmides (the Epicurean philosopher) paid him a visit. When Charmides left feeling dejected, Arcesilaus said, 'Please stay, brother Charmides. Nothing from *that part* has come to *this part*.' As he said this, he pointed to his feet and then to his heart. He would, however, have preferred not to endure any physical suffering.

XXXII. 95. "This, then, is our doctrine. To you it seems contradictory. Yet the divinity and transcendence of virtue is so great that despair and distress can never flourish wherever virtue, and the great deeds and glorious acts done in its name, are found. And even though toil may yet exist, and hardship may yet exist, one must say with all confidence that every wise man is always happy—but it may be that one is happier than another."

---

[461] Dionysius of Heraclea (c. 330 B.C.—250 B.C.), a Stoic philosopher and student of Zeno. Diogenes Laertius (VII.166) says that he was afflicted with ophthalmia, and that his physical suffering caused him to lose faith in the Stoic doctrine that pain should be endured without complaint. He abandoned Stoicism and adopted the overt pleasure-seeking ideas of Aristippus of Cyrene. For this ignominious defection he was nicknamed "Dionysius the Renegade."

"Piso," I said, "this statement is one that will need a considerable amount of justification. But if you can support it, you may just win over not only my cousin Cicero, but me as well."

96. Quintus here interjected, "As far as I'm concerned, I believe he's made his case. And I'm gratified that this system of philosophy features lineaments I cherish more than the distinctive features of all the other systems. For me it was rich enough to provide whatever I truly wanted in our studies; and I'm grateful to have discovered it to be profounder than the other schools. Some people said that it fell short in this regard."

"Well, it is certainly not as refined as our system," laughed Pomponius. "But by Hercules! Your explanation was full of insight, and I had not believed it possible for someone to articulate in Latin the concepts that you explained. Using just the right words, you communicated these ideas no less clearly than the Greeks would have. But our time has come to an end, if I may say so. Let us go directly to my place."

When he said this, the consensus was that there had been enough debate. We all departed for the town to Pomponius's house.

COMMENTARY ON BOOK V

The fifth and final book presents the eclectic Platonism of Antiochus of Ascalon. As we noted in the Introduction, he was an important Academic figure in that he tried to reconcile the positions of the Stoics and Peripatetics with that of the Platonists. The dialogue in Book V is set at a much earlier date (79 B.C.) than the dates of the other dialogues. Cicero himself studied philosophy in Greece around this time; the opening passages of Book V (V.1—7) have a personal and nostalgic feel that set them apart from the rest of *On Moral Ends*. They no doubt evoke the pleasant memories of Cicero's student days.

When Cicero studied in Athens in 79 B.C., the city's glory days were long gone. Yet the grandeur remained. Cicero notes that one could hardly take a step in Athens without encountering reminders of the great men of the past. The city had aged nicely; it had the character of what we might today call a venerable university town. V.1 sets the scene of the dialogue on the grounds of the Academy itself, and the chief speaker is Marcus Pupius Piso Calpurnianus. It will be his task to present the views of Antiochus.

Piso begins by commenting on various aspects of the Peripatetic system (V.9—12). An appropriate End of Goods must take into account human nature and our fundamental instincts (V.15). He explores various possible theories of the End of Goods (V.18—19), but concludes by noting that virtue must play a critical part in any such theory (V.21—22). The first three sentences of V.22 are very important, for I believe they state a vital feature of Cicero's conception of moral goodness: moral goodness should never be linked to, or adulterated with, things like pleasure or freedom from pain. It does not need their assistance; it can stand and shine on its own merits. Anyone who tries to do so desecrates the beauty of moral rectitude.

The best theory of the End of Goods, he suggests, is one based on a life lived in accordance with human nature and developed to its fullest extent (V.26). Self-love and self-preservation are universal; moral goodness represents the highest component of our nature. Our Chief Good should be to perfect our nature to its greatest extent (V.44).

The virtues spring from reason, and are desirable for their own sakes (V.60). Piso shows himself an Academic philosopher by naming justice as the highest virtue (V.65). Virtue itself is enough to provide a happy life, but we cannot say that the goods of the body are negligible (V.71—72). One of the main points Piso emphasizes is that his system has been appropriated, to one degree or another, by the other philosophical schools; the Stoic are primarily guilty of this, and have simply attached new names to old concepts. Cicero and Piso tussle over whether virtue alone is enough to provide a happy life (V.78—79); Piso believes it is, but Cicero has his doubts. Some of the most moving and eloquent passages in Book V are found in the closing sections (V.90—96), where the transcendence of virtue is discussed. Evils do abound in life, but when the scales are actually weighed, we will find that virtue is more important than anything else (V.92). We are ultimately left with the impression that Cicero preferred a philosophy that was grounded in the importance of wisdom and virtue, but was not so doctrinally inflexible as to be unable to cope with life's changing practical difficulties. This passage from V.95 seems to encapsulate his personal views as well as any: "Yet the divinity and transcendence of virtue is so great that despair and distress can never flourish wherever virtue, and the great deeds and glorious acts done in its name, are found. And even though toil may yet exist, and hardship may yet exist, one must say with all confidence that every wise man is always happy—but it may be that one is happier than another." And with this the dialogue ends, and the speakers depart.

INDEX

Democritus, 7, 29, 53, 55, 56, 61,
90, 160, 239, 286, 297, 317,
344, 345
Demosthenes, 285
desires, 8, 30, 34, 55, 73, 77, 78,
80, 83, 84, 85, 110, 111, 113,
114, 118, 134, 137, 167, 171,
190, 192, 200, 224, 234, 241,
242, 259, 298, 309, 311
Dicearchus, 278
Dio Cassius, 224
Diodorus, 9, 108, 119, 163, 260,
292, 296, 334
Diodorus Siculus, 163
Diodotus, 26
Diogenes, 29, 32, 47, 98, 99, 109,
110, 112, 140, 197, 207, 211,
344, 349
Diogenes Laertius, 29, 32, 98, 99,
109, 110, 140, 344, 349
Dionysius, 15, 147, 264, 349
Dionysius of Syracuse, 147
Dipylon Gate, 5, 20, 283, 320,
324
dishonesty, 78, 261
duschrestemata, 220
dynamic pleasure, 100, 101, 105,
116, 118, 144, 145

E

Echecrates, 344
Efficientia, 211
eidola, 56
Electra, 46, 86
Empedocles, 286
Ennius, 46, 47, 48, 122, 163, 268,
302
ennoia, 189
Epaminondas, 10, 136, 139, 157,
172
ephippia, 186

Epicureanism, 7, 8, 16, 19, 24, 28,
29, 30, 31, 33, 38, 39, 60, 64,
90, 140, 172, 173, 227
Epicurus, 7, 8, 9, 10, 15, 28, 29,
30, 31, 48, 51, 52, 55, 56, 60,
61, 62, 67, 69, 71, 73, 80, 83,
84, 85, 86, 87, 88, 89, 90, 91,
96, 97, 98, 99, 101, 102, 104,
107, 108, 109, 110, 111, 112,
114, 115, 116, 117, 119, 120,
124, 127, 128, 129, 132, 133,
135, 137, 139, 140, 141, 142,
147, 148, 149, 152, 153, 154,
155, 156, 157, 158, 159, 160,
161, 162, 164, 171, 172, 173,
177, 237, 239, 248, 260, 284,
337
epigennematikon, 196
equity, 9, 77, 134, 149, 221, 328
Erechtheus, 326
Erillus, 12, 119, 123, 252, 255,
297, 334
euchrestemata, 220
eudoxia, 211
eukairia, 205
Euphrates, 224
Euripides, 46, 86, 122, 162
euthumia, 297, 345

F

First Punic War, 138, 169
fortitude, 74
Fortune, 84, 153, 224, 290, 348
Frascati, 20, 180, 183, 191
friendship, 8, 10, 85, 86, 87, 88,
91, 146, 147, 148, 149, 150,
159, 172, 173, 181, 220, 222,
234, 246, 296, 302, 326

A pathway leading to Tusculum.

THANK YOU, PATIENT READER.

QVINTVS CVRTIVS

FORTRESS OF THE MIND

www.ingramcontent.com/pod-product-compliance
Lightning Source LLC
Chambersburg PA
CBHW051846090426
42811CB00034B/2231/J

* 9 7 8 0 5 7 8 4 0 9 6 7 2 *